PRAISE FOR

THE ECCLESIOLOGICAL RENOVATION
OF VATICAN II

From the Book Presentation of the Greek Edition,
June 18, 2015, in Thessaloniki, Greece

Fr. Peter Heers' book, *The Ecclesiological Renovation of Vatican II*, is remarkable in every way. . . . I want to congratulate the author, for he labored on his subject with objectivity and sobriety and has presented us with an important work which assists us all, especially when, due to our lack of time and many responsibilities, we are unable to have access to the sources. The book is written in an academic manner, that is, objectively, as the tradition of the Fathers of the Church designates.

Father Peter worked methodically, examining both the theological currents which preceded the Second Vatican Council and the context within which the council itself labored. Moreover, he studied in depth the texts of the council and the analyses of various theologians that followed the council.

Having read this as a dissertation many times and as closely as possible, I have come to understand how papal theology became estranged from Orthodox patristic theology and tradition; how the views of papal theologians with regard to baptism and ecclesiology developed from Blessed Augustine, Thomas Aquinas, and subsequent theologians; and how this line of thinking evolved through a variety of decisions and finally arrived at the Second Vatican Council, which then produced a new ecclesiology.

The book which we present today is very important and must be read both by theologians and the wider public. However, most especially it must be read by Bishops, and in particular those who are involved with theological and inter-Christian issues and with the theological and inter-Christian dialogues.

— *Metropolitan Hierotheos (Vlachos) of Nafpaktos and Agios Vlassios*

The Ecclesiological Renovation of Vatican II is one of the most significant works of Orthodox sacramentology to appear since Fr. George Metallinos' *I Confess One Baptism*. Fr. Peter's work is a fulfillment of Fr. Georges Florovsky's plea that Orthodox theologians "re-experience" the dialectical twists and turns of Western theology, the goal being the clearing away of any unnecessary occlusions that stand between the non-Orthodox and the Church of Christ. Only through such a neopatristic approach as Fr. Heers' are we able to sympathize with the "existential" situation of the non-Orthodox while at the same time preserving and proclaiming the Orthodox faith.

— *James L. Kelley, author of* A Realism of Glory: Lectures On Christology in the Works of Protopresbyter John Romanides

We are very grateful to Fr. Peter Heers for this invaluable contribution! In his book he clearly defines the boundaries of the Church, which is so necessary today for our seminarians who will need to teach and defend this Dogma of the Church. We anxiously await the appearance of his book in our bookstore!

The Very Rev. Archimandrite Luke (Murianka), Abbot of Holy Trinity Monastery and Rector of Holy Trinity Seminary

The Ecclesiological Renovation of Vatican II is a book of great importance for our contemporary ecclesiastical life. In it we learn not only of the origins and development of "baptismal theology," unknown to all but a small circle of experts, but also of the consequences this new theory has for the Church today. Highly recommended!

Hieromonk Luke of the Holy Monastery of Grigoriou, Mt. Athos, Greece

THE ECCLESIOLOGICAL RENOVATION OF VATICAN II

The Baptism of Christ by St. John the Forerunner

The Ecclesiological Renovation of Vatican II

An Orthodox Examination of Rome's Ecumenical Theology Regarding Baptism and the Church

Protopresbyter Peter Heers

THE ECCLESIOLOGICAL RENOVATION OF VATICAN II
AN ORTHODOX EXAMINATION OF ROME'S ECUMENICAL THEOLOGY
REGARDING BAPTISM AND THE CHURCH

First Printing November 2015

© 2015 by Protopresbyter Peter Heers

Copy Editor: Xenia Sheehan
Assistant Editors: Vincent DeWeese and Patrick Barnes
Index by T. L. Ryan
Cover Design by George Weis (think-cap.com)
Interior Design by Mygdonia Graphic Artists (ekdoseismygdonia.gr)

All Scriptural quotations are taken from the King James Version
of the Holy Bible.

This book is also available as an e-book from uncutmountainpress.com.

Uncut Mountain Press – US Division
903 Willow Branch Drive
Simpsonville, SC 29680

ISBN: 978-618-81583-1-3

Originally published in Greek as Ἡ ἐκκλησιολογικὴ ἀναθεώρηση τῆς Βʹ Βατικανῆς Συνόδου μία Ὀρθόδοξη διερεύνηση τοῦ Βαπτίσματος καὶ τῆς Ἐκκλησίας κατὰ τὸ Διάταγμα περὶ Οἰκουμενισμοῦ *by Uncut Mountain Press, 2014.*

To
Presbytera Kyriaki

Is Christ divided?

– *1 Corinthians 1:13*

There is one body, and one Spirit, even as ye are called in one hope of your calling; One Lord, one faith, one baptism, One God and Father of all, who is above all, and through all, and in you all.

– *Ephesians 4: 4-6*

CONTENTS

III

A Summary and Conclusion

FOREWORD
to the Greek Edition

A basic presupposition for a serious theological dialogue between the Orthodox Church and the heterodox West is a thorough knowledge of Western theology. This knowledge is especially dependable when it arises from an exhaustive investigation of primary research material. Indeed, when it happens that this source material is not only important for academic research but also is the latest official text of its kind, as is the case with the Decree on Ecumenism *(Unitatis Redintegratio)* of the Second Vatican Council (1962–1965), then the academic and ecclesiastical interest is piqued.

As is well known, from the middle of the twentieth century, we have been engaged in an important theological dialogue with the Christian West. In particular, beginning in 1980, the Joint Theological Dialogue between the Orthodox Church and Roman Catholicism commenced its work. This dialogue, from the perspective of the West, has focused especially upon the Second Vatican Council and, in particular, upon the Decree on Ecumenism. Scholarly recognition of this point decisively aids in understanding the character of this joint dialogue.

The book which you hold in your hands by my beloved student and doctor of theology, Fr. Peter Heers, presents, in an unprecedented way, the new Roman Catholic ecclesiology from an Orthodox critical perspective. The study is academically both objective and convincing. For the first time the historical process by which Baptism was separated from the other mysteries and came to serve as a basis for the "broadening" and "extension" of the Church is exhaustively examined.

In support of his academic findings, Fr. Heers provides lengthy excerpts from the conciliar decrees and documentation, as well as from the leading theologians who drafted and interpreted the documents. With a precise theological critique of the new ecclesiology the author also presents to the reader the main points of Orthodox ecclesiology, achieving a therapeutic result. Such spiritual healing of the discord engendered by the new ecclesiology is the ultimate goal of this present study.

In addition, the author introduces forgotten contributions of Orthodox theologians, which can serve as a corrective to the views of certain contemporary Orthodox theologians and open new horizons for the Joint Theological Dialogue of Orthodox and Roman Catholics. This book thus deserves to be read both by the representatives of the Local Orthodox Churches and by those Roman Catholic theologians who participate in the theological dialogue. In this way, then, our hope (as it pertains to scholarship) for a return of Western Christianity to the patristic vision of the Church increases.

In conclusion, I would like to state that this work by Fr. Peter Heers constitutes, not simply an academic contribution to a very serious theological matter, but rather a study of an ecclesiological nature which offers a great deal to the Church today, for it opens up new horizons for every good-willed reader, whether Roman Catholic or Orthodox. At the same time it contributes dynamically to the existing theological dialogue.

Demetrios Tselingides
Professor of Dogmatics at the Theological School
of the Aristotle University of Thessaloniki
October 7, 2014

FOREWORD
to the English Edition

I consider it an exceptional honor that my beloved brother in Christ, the Protopresbyter Father Peter Heers, has asked me to write this foreword to the English edition of his book. My acceptance was not so much dependent on our personal friendship as upon the importance of his work and its contribution to the contemporary inter-Christian dialogue.

Ecumenism, both political and religious, is the foremost problem of our age, an age that has rightly been characterized as a "new age," for it has witnessed not only the structural change of the world but a process of globalization, in which the mutual acceptance of all religions (πανθρησκεία) has played an essential part. It has become clear that religious dialogue, both inter-Christian and inter-religious, moves in the same direction and serves the same ends as global political objectives. This is why ecumenism, on each and every level, poses such a great challenge and temptation for Orthodoxy, because for decades now it has continued to take consciences hostage, luring them into grievous errors against our blameless Faith, causing many "of the elect" to fall as Lucifer once did.

Today the Mystery of Baptism is found to be at the center of theological reflection on account of its being the foundation of the unity of the Church, both in its local and universal aspects. Thus, as a basic element of ecclesiology and ecclesiastical identity, it was only to be expected that it would attract the attention of the inter-Christian unity dialogue, for the sake of which "baptismal theology" was created.

Fr. Heers' book explores the issues surrounding baptism on the basis of the foundational decree on ecumenism of the Second Vatican Council (1962–1965), *Unitatis Redintegratio.* His study fills a gap in the related bibliography and identifies the deeper aims of this key decision of the council, which reordered the relations of Roman Catholicism with the remaining Christian world.

The author, as he makes clear in his work, possesses all the necessary qualifications to examine such a subtle and sensitive subject. He sheds light both on the presuppositions and aims of the Decree, hidden beneath its adeptly crafted façade, and on their relation to the actual objectives of the dialogue itself. The study, moreover, is the only one of its kind, penetrating into the core of both the Roman Catholic and Orthodox teachings on the Mysteries. The central element in the author's navigation of the subject is his clarification, in the most unambiguous manner, of the entirely different presuppositions concerning baptism held by Roman Catholicism and Orthodoxy. With Fr. Heers' study, many issues are clarified, older positions are overturned, and new research perspectives are opened up for an objective and dispassionate evaluation of the dialogue and its real prospects.

Especially noteworthy is the author's finding that, with the Decree on Ecumenism, the Second Vatican Council added a "new dogma," an essential departure from the consensus patrum, such that Rome, with its "new reformation," is brought closer to Protestantism. Quite correctly, the historic path is traced, with the departures of Western theology being indicated, such that today the convergence of Orthodoxy and Roman Catholicism (as it pertains to this issue, as well) is essentially made impossible, for the reality is that there exist two different understandings. A characteristic example of this is the centuries-in-the-making separation within the Latin Church of the Mysteries of Baptism-Chrismation from the Divine Eucharist, with all the necessary consequences. This finding, as it pertains to baptism, justifies those who hold the view that the "dialogue of truth/faith" should not have succeeded the "dialogue of love" so quickly, since with regard to many issues the former is shown to be, humanly speaking, entirely impossible. A methodical transcending of the problems is not possible by skirting them and tacitly affirming the deviation (as happens now) for the sake of paving the way for the sought-after end within a context of the mutual acceptance of all religions (πανθρησκεία).

The author effectively calls attention to missing pieces of the historical and ecclesiological puzzle, which he then fills in with the unfailing guide of the ancient Christian Tradition, which remains whole and intact within the historical continuity of patristic Orthodoxy. The successive maneuverings for the sake of achieving the aims of Vatican II and facilitating the dialogue are critiqued soberly and objectively. The author's precision in his critical analysis is successful on account of his rich knowledge of the Orthodox Patristic Tradition and the medieval and contemporary West. His critique consistently remains within the limits of frankness and yearning for an honest dialogue aimed at realization of true unity according to the words of Christ (Jn. 17, 21, 24). He rightly poses the question as to the path of Roman Catholic theology –"*Ressourcement* (return to the sources) or renovation?"– a question that arises from the continual Roman Catholic theological and dogmatic reassessments with respect to baptism.

In my humble estimation, this book is an essential contribution to today's ecumenical relations and will be considered carefully. Traditional, patristic-oriented Orthodox will be pleased reading it. However, the reaction, whether positive or negative, of the "unionist" ecumenists among us is also anticipated. Appearing at a most critical juncture in the dialogue, the book fulfills the aim of its composition: to present "a critical examination of the place and understanding of Baptism in the development of the ecclesiology of the Second Vatican Council." It goes further, however, in its closing thoughts, injecting a direct and categorical intimation: "It is ironic and tragic that precisely when the dead end of Scholasticism and Tridentine Catholicism came into sight and a beginning of a return to the Fathers was made, those Orthodox who were sought out for counsel did not guide them to the consensus patrum but were, in part, a source for further innovation."

With respect to this last point, we are obliged to note something, which the author will, with additional experience and time, come to recognize. His point is correct, of course, that the Roman Catholic side, in seeking the assistance of its Orthodox interlocutors, was probably seeking to test the other side in order to determine the ease or difficulty of the future path of the dialogue; whereas the Orthodox, continuing the practice of the unionists of a Byzantium in decline, were ready to accept the Latin ecclesiological views without contest. (It is, of course, understood that such matters cannot be the object of a doctoral dissertation.) In the final analysis, as the author points out, the new ecclesiology of Roman Catholicism (of Congar, Bea, et al.) has clearly influenced the Orthodox side of the dialogue, as also with regard to other issues of the dialogue. It is enough for one to call to mind the Balamand agreement (1993) and all that was expressed therein.

Fr. Heers' ecclesiological study constitutes not only a contribution to academic theology and the bibliography of the ecumenical dialogue, but also an essential critical check on the supporting discoveries of our ecumenists, such as the "baptismal" and "post-patristic" theologies. However, we would like to believe that a few of the enlightened spirits of Roman Catholic theology–fortunately such do exist–will also welcome the book and recognize its contribution.

It goes without saying, of course, that as it pertains to the Orthodoxy and completeness of the work, my elect colleague, the renowned dogmatician and supervising professor Demetrios Tselingides, is the guarantor.

Protopresbyter George Metallinos
Emeritus Professor of the University of Athens
September 19, 2014

FOREWORD
by Bishop Basil of Wichita

"Do not remove age-old boundaries, erected by your fathers."

Proverbs 22:28

We will not remove the age-old landmarks which our fathers have set, but we keep the tradition we have received. For if we begin to erode the foundations of the Church even a little, in no time at all the whole edifice will fall to the ground."

St. John of Damascus

I n this present work the author, Father Peter Alban Heers, presents in clear and concise language an in-depth critique of two important documents of the Second Vatican Council, formally known by its Latin title "Concilium Oecumenicum Vaticanum Secundum": *Unitatis Redintegratio* (Decree on Ecumenism) and the council's chief ecclesiological document, *Lumen Gentium* (Constitution on the Church). Reading these documents in light of patristic texts and works of past and contemporary Eastern Orthodox and Roman Catholic theologians, Father Peter explains how the council came to conclusions which redefined who and what constitutes the Church as the Body of Christ.

We are indebted to Father Peter for helping us navigate our way through these documents and for his clarion call to vigilance as we evaluate what the council considered to be a return to the sources (*ressourcement*). In doing so, it would be

beneficial for us to consider what St. John of Damascus coun-
seled when he wrote, "Therefore my brethren, let us stand on
the rock of faith in the Tradition of the Church, not remov-
ing the landmarks set by our holy fathers; not giving room to
those who wish to introduce novelties and destroy the edifice
of God's holy, catholic and apostolic Church."

Dear Reader, as you wend your way through the following
pages make your own the following profession of St. Maximus
the Confessor: "In no way will I say anything of my own, but
what I have learned from the Fathers, altering nothing of their
teaching."

†Basil
Bishop of Wichita and Mid-America
Antiochian Orthodox Christian Archdiocese of North America

PREFACE

At the center of theological speculation within the ecumenical movement today stands the mystery of Baptism. Baptism as the basis for Christian unity has been touted and painstakingly explored by both Roman Catholic scholars, especially since the Second Vatican Council in 1962, and Protestant scholars, within the World Council of Churches. Orthodox theologians have also taken part in this discussion, but largely from the outside looking in. This is because, while Roman Catholics and Protestants share a common history and many common ecclesiological assumptions, the Orthodox approach the question from an entirely different historical experience and set of theological presuppositions. They have an historical memory that retains the patristic consensus of the first four centuries as the starting point and heart of the matter even today.

The potential of Baptism to be the key that will open the door to unity was not fully acknowledged until the Second Vatican Council. With this council's recognition of both the validity and efficacy of non–Roman Catholic Baptism and an already existing ecclesiastical unity, all eyes were set on Baptism.

In spite of the extensive ecumenical literature on the subject, scholars have neglected to examine important inconsistencies, historical and ecclesiological, contained in the conciliar document of the council on the subject, *Unitatis Redintegratio* (Decree on Ecumenism), as well the historical and theological road that led to its drafting. As a result, premature theological conclusions have been reached and even celebrated without due consideration of the patristic and Orthodox outlook.

The Ecclesiological Renovation of Vatican II seeks to rectify this neglect by presenting a critical examination of the place and understanding of Baptism in the unity of the Church as expounded in the Decree on Ecumenism. The critique offered here likewise contributes to a fuller understanding of the Orthodox view of the place of Baptism in the unity of the Church.

In this study, our principal aim is to present systematically the main points of the dogmatic teaching on Baptism and the Church in the Decree on Ecumenism, with important references to the council's chief ecclesiological text, *Lumen Gentium*. In order better to understand the historical and theological context of the Decree, we review key aspects of the historical and theological development of the new ecclesiology it expounds. As our examination is from the perspective of the Orthodox Church, we concentrate on those points that are at odds with Orthodox dogma.

As a secondary goal of our study, we examine the claim put forward by the authors and defenders of the council's new ecclesiology that it represents *ressourcement*, a return to the sources, and that the council, far from being a departure from the Tradition or an innovation, was a new actualization of Tradition. We answer the question: Were the theologians of Vatican II successful in returning Catholicism back to the ecclesiology of the Church of the first millennium, or did they, despite their stated intentions, fail in this regard?

Our study is divided into three parts. In part 1 we present key aspects of the historical development of Roman Catholic teaching on Baptism and the Church. In part 2, we examine the teaching of the council on Baptism and the Church, as it is set forth in the two encyclicals that expressed the will of the council, and we examine the *communio* ecclesiology as the guiding concept of the council's teaching. In part 3 we offer a summary of our critical examination followed by our conclusion regarding the Orthodox response to the theological challenge before us.

I would like to express my heartfelt thanks first of all to Dr. Demetrios Tselingidis, professor of Dogmatic Theology at the Theological School of the University of Thessaloniki, for his invaluable guidance, patience, and instructive assistance throughout the writing of this book. Likewise, sincere thanks are due to His Grace Basil, Bishop of Wichita and Mid-America, for his initial encouragement and continued prayers, and to the Abbot of the Holy Monastery of Xeropotamou on Mount Athos, Archimandrite Joseph, for his unwavering support of this undertaking. Finally, I am indebted to the ever-memorable Metropolitan of Ierissou and Mount Athos, Nikodemos, for his gracious blessing to be absent from my duties in order to do research in the libraries of Oxford and Cambridge. Most of all, however, I thank my long-suffering family for their unflagging encouragement and patient endurance throughout.

Petrokerasa, Greece,
December 12, 2014,
St. Spyridon the Wonderworker

ABBREVIATIONS

De Baptismo	*De Baptismo Contra Donatistas Libri Septem*, PL 43.107–244, NPNF 4.
LG	*Lumen Gentium, Pastoral Constitution on the Church in the Modern World*, Second Vatican Council, Dec. 7, 1965, ed. Austin Flannery (Northport, NY: Costello Publishing, 1966)
Mansi	*Sacrorum Conciliorum Nova et Amplissima Collectio* (Graz: J. D. Mansi, 1960–61)
NPNF	*The Nicene and Post-Nicene Fathers*, ed. Philip Schaff (Peabody, MA: Hendrickson, 1994)
PG	*Patrologiae cursus completus series graeca* (Paris: Migne 1857–66; Turnhout, Belgium: Brepols, 1960)
PL	*Patrologiae cursus completus, series latina* (Paris: Éditions Garnier Frères, 1958)
UR	*Unitatis Redintegratio*, Decree on Ecumenism of the Second Vatican Council
UUS	*Ut Unum Sint*, Papal encyclical, 1995

THE ECCLESIOLOGICAL RENOVATION
OF VATICAN II

The Second Vatican Council

INTRODUCTION

THE HISTORICAL AND THEOLOGICAL CONTEXT OF THE COUNCIL

T he Second Vatican Council, the Twenty-first Ecumenical Council according to the Roman Catholic Church, was announced by Pope John XXIII on January 25, 1959, and held 178 meetings in the autumn of four successive years. The first gathering was on October 11, 1962, and the last on December 8, 1965.

The world in which Vatican II was convened and carried out was a world undergoing radical change, "marked by the end of colonialism, the rapid spread of industrialization and major advances in communication."[1] Industrialization in formerly agricultural countries such as Italy, Spain, and Mexico, helped create a new, "more dynamic, often restless" mentality, "more open to innovation, as linked to an industrial economy."[2] This state of things on the eve of the Council meant that the Church

1. Raymond F. Bulman, "Vatican Council II (1962–1965)," in *Encyclopedia of the Vatican and Papacy*, ed. Frank J. Coppa (Westport, Conn.: Greenwood Press, 1999), 429.

2. Giacomo Martina, "The Historical Context in Which the Idea of a New Ecumenical Council Was Born," in *Vatican II: Assessment and Perspectives*, ed. René Latourelle (New York: Paulist Press, 1988–89), 10, 13; quoted in Raymond F. Bulman, "Introduction: The Historical Context," in *From Trent to Vatican II: Historical and Theological Investigations*, ed. Raymond Bulman and Frederick J. Parrella (Oxford, UK: Oxford University Press, 2006), 9.

found itself "on the defensive, immobile, in the face of a rapidly changing world."[3] It was in the midst of this situation, and in response to it, that the Second Vatican Council was convoked.

The council drew more than 2,000 bishops from 134 countries, including many from Africa, Asia, and Central and South America. It also included approximately 80 non–Roman Catholic observers from the major Christian denominations, 480 *periti* (theological advisors), and 1,000 members of the world press.[4]

The council's deliberations produced four constitutions, nine decrees, and three declarations. The Decree on Ecumenism, *Unitatis Redintegratio*,[5] approved by the council on November, 21, 1964, and formally promulgated by Paul VI on the same day, was the fifth of the sixteen council decisions to be accepted.

Unitatis Redintegratio, at once both the result of a long effort for reorientation and a fairly abrupt and surprising reversal of stance, together with the Constitution on the Church, *Lumen Gentium*,[6] stand out among the conciliar decrees for their novel ecclesiological formulations. The authors and signers of *Unitatis Redintegratio* were intent on much more than a simple restatement of older papal encyclicals or regurgitation of worn-out Tridentine slogans. They were striving for a complete reorientation of the mindset of Roman Catholics in regard to their fellow Christians; and, for the most part, they were quite

3. Ibid.

4. Michael J. Walsh, "The History of the Council," in *Modern Catholicism: Vatican II and After*, ed. Adrian Hastings (New York: Oxford University Press, 1991), 36.

5. Hereafter the Decree on Ecumenism, *Unitatis Redintegratio*, is abbreviated UR in the notes.

6. In this book the Constitution on the Church, *Lumen Gentium*, will be referred to in notes using the abbreviation LG.

successful. The depiction of the Church and its unity as set out in *Unitatis Redintegratio* enabled statements from the Roman Catholic Magisterium that were previously unthinkable.[7]

It would not be an overstatement to say that this new ecclesiological perspective, consciously, even painstakingly, sensitive to ecumenical concerns,[8] is the "key" to unlocking the meaning of the Second Vatican Council. Indeed, the ecumenical perspective underlies all the teachings proper to the council.[9] The primacy of ecumenism in key conciliar documents is seen not only in the texts themselves but also in their origins. Besides *Unitatis Redintegratio* itself, the most novel and controversial texts produced by the Second Vatican Council, *Nostra Aetate* and *Dignitatis Humanae*, began as chapters four and five of the

7. Johannes Feiner, "Commentary on the Decree," in *Commentary on the Documents of Vatican II* (London: Burns and Oates Limited, 1968), 2:69. As our examination shows, the image of the Church as set forth in article 3 of chapter 1 set the stage for the remarkable statements regarding non–Roman Catholics in article 4 and further on.

8. In his opening address to the second session of the council on September 29, 1963, Paul VI declared: "What attitude will the Council adopt towards the vast number of brethren separated from us . . . what will it do? The question is clear. This Council itself was also called for this reason" (cf. *Vaticanum Secundum* 2:69). W. Visser't Hooft, head of the World Council of Churches at the time of the council, in his report to the Central Committee of the WCC, says similarly that "the existence of the ecumenical movement was one of the reasons for the holding of the Council." *Die Zeichen der Zeit* 20 [1966], 197.

9. Referring to Pope Paul VI's declaration at the start of the second session of the council that ecumenical rapprochement was one of the purposes for which the council was called, Cardinal Walter Kasper stated that, "If due consideration is given to this declaration, all the texts of the Council should be read in an ecumenical perspective." See Cardinal Walter Kasper, "The Fortieth Anniversary of the Vatican Council II Decree *Unitatis Redintegratio*." Information Service of the Pontifical Council for Promoting Unity, No. 115 (Vatican City, 2004), 19.

original conciliar draft document, *De Oecumenismo*, which later became *Unitatis Redintegratio*.[10] Even the landmark Constitution on the Church (*Lumen Gentium*) contains binding affirmations that are either summed up or developed in the first chapter of *Unitatis Redintegratio*.[11] Clearly, *Unitatis Redintegratio* holds a central place among the council's decrees in terms of "setting the tone" and expressing the "spirit of Vatican II."

That the Roman Catholic Church underwent an ecclesiological renovation is admitted even by the council's staunchest supporters.[12] Without doubt there was a new attitude; but, more important, there was a new understanding of the Church.[13] In spite of claims by Cardinal Walter Kasper of continuity with Roman Catholic theology of the nineteenth and early twentieth centuries—as in theologians Möhler and Newman, and in

10. Walter M. Abbot, S.J. (General Editor), *The Documents of Vatican II* (New York/Cleveland: Corpus Books, 1966), 660, 672.

11. Kasper, Walter, Cardinal. "Communio: The Guiding Concept of Catholic Ecumenical Theology." In *That They May All Be One: The Call to Unity Today*. London/New York: Burns and Oates, 2004.9.

12. Karl Rahner said that "Vatican II was a council which concentrated upon ecclesiology as no other Council had. It proposed a new image of the Church. . . ." ("The New Image of the Church," trans. David Bourke [London: Darton, Longman, and Todd, 1973], 10:4). Yves Congar said that "the Second Vatican Council was a council of reform . . . . One could also say very rightly that it marked the end of the Counter-Reformation. . . . It was open to ecumenism and to a pluralist world." ("Martin Luther sa foi, sa reforme: Études de théologie historique," *Cogitatio Fidei* 119 [Paris: Cerf, 1983], 79.) See also Walter Kasper, "The Decree on Ecumenism—Read Anew after Forty Years," Pontifical Council for Promoting Christian Unity, Conference on the 40th Anniversary of the Promulgation of the Conciliar Decree *Unitatis Redintegratio*," Rocca di Papa, Mondo Migliore, November 11, 12, and 13, 2004.

13. Kasper, *That They May All Be One*, 9; see also his "Decree on Ecumenism."

Popes Leo XIII, Benedict XV, Pius XI, and Pius XII[14]—*Unitatis Redintegratio* is elsewhere admitted by the same Cardinal to be a clear break with both Leo XIII's *Satis Cognitum* and Pius XI's *Mortalium Animos*.[15] In fact, *Unitatis Redintegratio* represents a break not only with the recent past of Roman Catholic theology, but even with a thinker so important to Latin theology as Blessed Augustine of Hippo.

A detailed look at how this reorientation came about is beyond the scope of our purposes here; but we can say that the new ecclesiology was neither simply a benign development of doctrinal formulation nor a blatant overthrowing of doctrine. Rather, it was, paradoxically, a revolutionary development from within, which then unexpectedly came to be advanced from above.[16]

Cardinal Kasper forthrightly concedes that *Unitatis Redintegratio* "overturned the narrow post-Tridentine Counter-Reformation outlook of the church," but he maintains that it was not "modernism" but a return to "the Biblical, patristic and early-medieval tradition."[17] According to Cardinal Kasper, *Unitatis Redintegratio* even "refers to the confession of the faith of the Church and to the earliest Councils."[18]

14. Kasper, ibid.

15. See Reflections by Cardinal Walter Kasper on the "Nature and Purpose of Ecumenical Dialogue," http://www.vatican.va/roman_curia/pontifical_councils/chrstuni/sub-index/index_card-kasper.htm.

16. Paul Lakeland, in his introduction to the writings of Yves Congar, bluntly describes the changes brought about at Vatican II as a "theological revolution" that swept away "the ultramontane, neo-scholastic, and plainly world-hating mien of nineteenth century Rome." *Yves Congar: Essential Writings* (Maryknoll, NY: Orbis, 2010), 13.

17. Kasper, "The Decree on Ecumenism."

18. Walter Kasper, "The Fortieth Anniversary of the Vatican Council II Decree *Unitatis Redintegratio*." Information Service of the Pontifical

In the decades leading up to the Second Vatican Council, two parallel but essentially opposing currents of thought flowed within Roman Catholicism vis-à-vis ecclesiology and the movement for the unification of Christians. On the one hand, for the first half of the twentieth century, with rare and only superficial exceptions, the leadership in the Vatican maintained an uncompromising, polemical stance against the ecumenical movement, always deeply suspicious of theologians who actively engaged it.[19] This was the "official" position, which had as its

Council for Promoting Unity, No. 115 (Vatican City, 2004), 21. These are weighty claims that stand out for an Orthodox observer—claims that this study examines and critiques.

19. Yves Congar is perhaps the most notable example of those "under suspicion." He was ordained a priest in the Dominican order in 1930 and from the outset had ecumenical sensitivities and goals. In 1937 he published a trailblazing book on principles for a Catholic ecumenism, *Divided Christendom: A Catholic Study of the Problem of Reunion*. The book immediately brought him under Vatican suspicion for having argued that separated Christian communions had preserved elements of Christianity more vitally than the Catholic Church had, so that a possible reunion would bring qualitative as well as quantitative enhancement to the church. Remarkably, this idea was later incorporated into UR (4) and is now a widely accepted idea among Roman Catholics. See the papal encyclical *Ut Unum Sint* of Pope John Paul II (UUS, 14, 28, 57). In section 14, Pope John Paul II writes: "The elements of this already-given Church exist, found in their fullness in the Catholic Church and, without this fullness, in the other Communities, *where certain features of the Christian mystery have at times been more effectively emphasized*" (emphasis mine; see also Kasper, "The Decree on Ecumenism," 2.5). In 1950 Congar wrote another ecumenically significant work, *Vraie et fausse réforme dans l'Église*. A response to calls for renovation arising from the creative postwar years in Catholic France, the book set out the conditions and criteria for reform without schism. This book, too, brought him under suspicion, and translations of it were forbidden. In February 1954, Fr. Congar was forbidden to teach, and along with fellow colleagues Fr. Marie-Dominique Chenu (whose book *A School of Theology: Le Saulchoir*

reference point Scholastic[20] and Counter-Reformation theology, and which used phrases like the "true church" and "a return of the dissidents." This stance found expression in the encyclical *Mortalium Animos* of Pius XI in 1928, which condemned the ecclesiological assumptions prevalent in the ecumenical movement and forbade any involvement of Roman Catholics. Pius XI made it very clear that Christian unity was a matter of return and not mutual reconciliation, of bringing back to the fold lost sheep instead of trying to realize an existing but incomplete communion: "The unity of Christians can be achieved only through a return to the One True Church of Christ of those who are separated from it."[21]

Doubtless this was the established Roman stance; and it continued through the decades of the forties and fifties, when Catholic observers were forbidden to participate in the assemblies of the World Council of Churches held in Amsterdam in 1948 and Evanston in 1954. Only with the instruction *Ecclesia Catholica* in 1949 did this posture relax slightly, allowing for limited and supervised ecumenical engagement.

was condemned and placed on the Index of Forbidden Books in 1942), Fr. Henri-Marie Feret, and Fr. Pierre Boisselot, was expelled from Le Saulchoir and sent into exile. All his writings were subsequently subjected to prior censorship—see Gabriel Flynn, *Yves Congar's Vision of the Church in a World of Unbelief* (Burlington, VT: Ashgate, 2004), 10. However, in June 1960 everything changed for Congar when he was unexpectedly appointed a consultant to the theological commission that was to prepare doctrinal texts for the council. His contribution to the council would end up being enormous and crucial, especially for effecting a reversal vis-à-vis ecumenism.

20. Pope Pius X, in his encyclical *Pascendi*, held that Scholasticism, and in particular Thomas Aquinas, was the remedy for modernism.

21. Pius XI, *Mortalium Animos*, January 7, 1928.

Beneath this official veneer of intransigence, however, there was, from the 1920s onward, a growing movement of dissatisfaction and a desire for a new approach. A new development in France heralded the widespread portrayal of the church as a "theandric union" of all Christians with Christ. Although this initial effort at reform did not entail an overthrow of the juridical model of the church developed in Scholasticism and afterwards, "by the end of the 1930s a new militancy had emerged in favor of the spread of what has been described as 'vitalism.'"[22] The theologians of this French effort were convinced that "the only way to attract non-catholics into the Church was through its presentation in terms of the vital and organic."[23] Out of this arose a new movement that came to be known as the *nouvelle théologie*.[24]

Nouvelle théologie was a dynamic movement of theologians —mainly in France, Belgium, and Germany—who were decidedly "ecumenical" in outlook and who worked for reform by way of *ressourcement*, that is, a return to the sources. *Ressourcement*, as defined by one of the movement's leading figures, the French Dominican theologian Yves Congar, was "a new examination [reinterrogation] of the permanent sources of theology: the Bible, the liturgy, the Fathers. . . ."[25] There were many aims of this new movement: to recover that which had been forgot-

22. Gabriel Flynn, *Yves Congar's Vision of the Church in a World of Unbelief* (Burlington, VT: Ashgate, 2004), 33–34.

23. Ibid., 34.

24. The phrase *nouvelle théologie* is a standard representing a diversity of visions, which, however, share the same goal of restoring the connection between theology and experience and thus with the sources of the faith. Theologians of the movement preferred to describe their efforts as *ressourcement*, a French term meaning a return to the sources.

25. Yves Congar, *La Foi et la Théologie dogmatique* (Tournai: Desclée, 1962), 1:271, quoted in Gabriel, *Yves Congar's Vision*, 28.

ten or neglected in the course of history; to enact a theological renewal; to move beyond Scholasticism; to establish closer links with modernity; to return to the Fathers; and to clarify the link between nature and grace.[26]

These new theologians rejected the domination of Thomism as a system, seeking instead a "return to the Thomas Aquinas of the thirteenth century, to the patristic period, and via the Church Fathers to the Bible and the liturgy."[27] Alongside this movement, and influenced by it, was what R. Guardini called an "awakening of the Church in the soul,"[28] which, translated to the theological level, included a movement for the renovation of ecclesiology. This new perspective was the "unofficial," "underground" voice of Roman Catholicism, which came to be accepted as mainstream during and after Vatican II.[29]

The leading figures of this movement were the theologians Maurice Blondel (1861–1949), Pierre Teilhard de Chardin (1881–1955), Marie-Dominique Chenu (1895–1990), Father Henri de Lubac (1896–1991), Yves Congar (1904–1995), Karl Rahner (1904–1984), Hans Urs von Balthasar (1905–1998), Jean Daniélou (1905–1974), Louis Bouyer (1913–2004), Ed-

---

26. Flynn, *Yves Congar's Vision*, 34.

27. Jürgen Mettepenningen, *Nouvelle Théologie, New Theology: Inheritor of Modernism, Precursor of Vatican II* (New York: T and T Clark International, 2010), 142.

28. R. Guardini, *Vom Sinn der Kirche* (1922), in *Commentary on the Documents of Vatican II*, p. 1.

29. Mettepenningen, in *Nouvelle Théologie*, also states: "The Thomistic *ressourcement* was followed by a theological *ressourcement*, and the French-speaking implantation of the *nouvelle théologie* was followed by a period of internationalization that contributed to a broader support base for the assimilation of the central points of the *nouvelle théologie* during Vatican II" (143).

ward Schillebeeckx (1914–2009), Hans Kung (1928–), Jean
Mouroux (1901–1973) and Joseph Ratzinger (1927–).[30]

The great break for these theologians came when most of
them were invited by Pope John XXIII and the bishops to
serve as *periti* (theological experts advising the Bishops) at the
Second Vatican Council. Thanks to their influence, "the Roman Catholic tradition of reform attained its fullest expression
at the Second Vatican Council."[31] It is widely recognized that
the theologians "were the engineers of the massive reforms
that were initiated at Vatican II."[32] Their contribution "was
remarkable. . . . The bishops of Vatican II were aware of the
importance of the theologians."[33] The Council extended official
acceptance to their decades of work for the renovation of theology, and in particular, of ecclesiology.[34]

30. Although sharing much in common, the theologians of the *nouvelle théologie* school held a diversity of opinions on just how far the
renovation of the church should extend. This divergence became most
apparent after the Second Vatican Council when two separate international theological journals were formed: *Concilium* and *Communio*. *Concilium* was begun in 1965 by Marie-Dominique Chenu, Yves Congar,
Karl Rahner, Edward Schillebeeckx, and Hans Kung, among others.
Communio was begun in 1972 by Hans Urs von Balthasar, Herni de
Lubac, Joseph Ratzinger, Walter Kasper, Louis Bouyer, and others. Of
the two, *Concilium* is recognized as more "liberal" in its approach to
theology.

31. Flynn, *Yves Congar's Vision*, 61. See René Latourelle, *Vatican II:
Assessment and Perspectives*, 1:xv–xix.

32. Leonard Swidler, "The Context: Breaking Reform by Breaking
Theologians and Religious," in *The Church in Anguish: Has the Vatican
Betrayed Vatican II?*, ed. Hans Kung and Swidler (San Francisco: Harper
and Row, 1987), 189, as quoted in Flynn, *Yves Congar's Vision*, 57.

33. Yves Congar, *Le Theologien dans l'Église aujourd'hui*, 12, as quoted
in Flynn, *Yves Congar's Vision*, 57.

34. See Mettepenningen, *Nouvelle Théologie*. "[T]heir influence, as we
can see from the *acta* of the Council and different Council diaries, turned

For those opposed to this new departure from traditional (Post-Tridentine) Latin theology, the mark these theologians left on the council's decrees amounted to heresy.[35] They asserted that the new ecclesiology that Vatican II had adopted, and especially its approach to ecumenism, stood in direct contradiction to the universal teaching of the Roman Catholic Church.[36] In particular, they pointed out that the new view enshrined in *Unitatis Redintegratio* and developed by such theologians as Yves Congar—the view that unity is no longer a matter of return to the one true Church but of mutual reconciliation—is directly opposed to the teaching of *Mortalium Animos* of Pius XI. The council's stance "is not ecumenical as an echo of the constant and universal teaching of the Church, but because it has established as the basis of its theories a clearly ecumenical will that lacks any foundation and that the entire prior Magisterium condemns."[37]

Cardinal Walter Kasper, representing defenders of Vatican II, responded that, "It would be . . . erroneous to interpret the Second Vatican Council, and especially the Decree on Ecumen-

out to be quite considerable" (6). See also Thomas G. Guarino, *Foundations of Systematic Theology* (New York: T and T Clark, 2005), 288: "The names associated with this movement . . . were ultimately to give impetus to some of the great theological themes of Vatican II."

35. For an extensive critique of Vatican II from this perspective, see Romano Amerio, *Iota Unum: A Study of the Changes in the Catholic Church in the Twentieth Century* (Kansas City: Sarto House, 1996).

36. Lanterius, "The Dogma of Ecumenism," in *Si Si, No No*, June 2005, Vol. XXVIII, No. 6, trans. Fr. Du Chalard (Kansas City, MO: Angelus Press).

37. Fr. de La Rocque, "Le présuppose oecumenique de *Lumen Gentium*," in *Penser Vatican II quarante ans après: Actes du VI Congres Theologique de si si no no* (Rome: Publications Courrier de Rome, 2004), 307–308.

ism as a break with tradition. Actually, one of the most important reasons for this council was a *ressourcement*, a return to the
sources; the council dealt with a new actualization of Tradition,
and in this sense, with its *aggiornamento* . . ."[38]

Kasper's description reveals just how deep the imprint of
the *nouvelle théologie* on the council was. Supporters and critics
of Vatican II agree on one thing: "the theological objectives ...
of [the] reforming theologians were realized at Vatican II."[39]
From an Orthodox point of view, however, important questions
arise, such as: To which sources did they return? How did they
interpret these sources and on what basis or experience? How
can ancient Church Tradition, from which the Post-Tridentine,
Counter-Reformation interval had separated Roman Catholicism for centuries, be "actualized anew" when the very meaning of tradition is to hand down from one generation to the
next, especially by word of mouth?

Indeed, the degree to which the tables had been turned at
Vatican II is remarkable and revealing: the very men who had
such an influence on the council were, in the years leading up
to it, on the Vatican's "black list." Karl Rahner, John Courtney
Murray,[40] Yves Congar, Edward Schillebeeckx, Henri de Lubac,

---

38. See Kasper, *The Fortieth Anniversary,* 21.

39. Flynn, *Yves Congar's Vision,* 53.

40. John Courtney Murray (1904–1967) edited the magazine *America*
and the journal *Theological Studies*. In 1954, after a decade of publishing on church-state issues and religious freedom, he was ordered to
cease writing on these topics by the Vatican because the Roman Curia
had objected that his views were unorthodox. Ten years later, however,
with the Pontificate of John XXIII, he was invited to serve at the Second Vatican Council as an expert on religious freedom. He was largely
responsible for drafting the "Declaration on Religious Freedom," considered one of the most important documents by supporters and most
unacceptable by detractors of the council.

Hans Urs von Balthasar, and Joseph Ratzinger had all been singled out at one time or another as being "under suspicion" of heresy.[41] But, now, at Vatican II, they rose to become highly regarded consultants to the bishops, instrumental in shaping the theology of the council and Catholicism for generations to come.

It is significant that forty years later Cardinal Joseph Ratzinger, who would later become Pope Benedict XVI, referred to the four decades leading up to the council (1920–1960) as a period "full of ferment and hope," leading to the adoption of the new "theological currents and tendencies" as "part of the patrimony of the whole church."[42] During those same four decades, however, the Vatican leadership saw in these very currents and tendencies not signs of hope for the future but signs of "the heresy of modernism."[43]

There is no doubt, then, that Vatican II was an epoch-making event for Roman Catholicism. At its heart was the *nouvelle théologie*, both as a movement—with its chief representatives

41. See *Informations Catholiques Internationales* 336 (May 15, 1969), 9. See also Mettepenningen, *Nouvelle Théologie*, where he discusses the measures taken by the Vatican against these theologians during the decades leading up to Vatican II.

42. Joseph Ratzinger, *The Ecclesiology of Vatican II*.

43. Pope Pius XII, in his encyclical *Humani Generis, Concerning Some False Opinions Threatening to Undermine the Foundations of Catholic Doctrine* (sections 29, 30, 32, and 34), issued on August 12, 1950, condemned some theological opinions and doctrines held by these theologians as expressing "neo-modernism." The charge against this movement or school of theology is that it departed from Thomism using relativistic historical analysis and employing modern philosophical axioms, such as positivism or existentialism, and that many of these scholars expressed dogma with concepts of modern philosophy (existentialism, immanentism, idealism, or other systems).

present as theological experts—and as a new spirit and out-look[44] decidedly ecumenical in its expression and directly op-posed to earlier papal decrees. It left its mark on all conciliar documents, but in particular on *Unitatis Redintegratio,* which demarcated a great divide with Catholicism's theological past. For with *Unitatis Redintegratio,* together with *Lumen Gentium,* a new theological vision of the Church had arrived.

44. John W. O'Malley says that, of the three categories that the coun-cil wrestled with (*aggiornamento,* development, *ressourcement*), "*ressource-ment* was the most traditional yet potentially the most radical. It was also the most pervasive at the council." John W. O'Malley, *What Hap-pened at Vatican II* (Cambridge, MA: Harvard University Press, 2008), 301.

I

Key Aspects of the Historical Development
of the Roman Catholic Teaching
on Baptism and the Church

Blessed Augustine

Thomas Aquinas

Yves Congar

Augustin Bea

From the outset our Lord Jesus Christ placed Baptism at the foundation of man's salvation (John 3:3, 3:7; Matt. 28:19) and at the forefront of the evangelical preaching and mission of the Church. Baptism was everywhere and always understood as the portal both to salvation (1 Pet. 3:21) and to the Church, for salvation was given in and by the Church to the world (Acts 2:38–42). The mystery of salvation, the mystery of the Church, and the mysteries of the Church were understood to be indissolubly bound together. All men were understood to be baptized by "one Spirit . . . into one body" (1 Cor. 12:13), for there is only "one body, and one Spirit . . . one Lord, one faith, one Baptism, one God and Father of all" (Eph. 4:5–6).

The newly illumined one became not only a Christian believer but a Spirit-bearer (1 Cor. 3:16), one who had put on Christ (Gal. 3:27). Acceptance of the preaching was but a prerequisite of Baptism unto salvation, not salvation itself (Acts 2:41). Baptism was considered, moreover, not merely a washing away of sins but an initiation into the new state of being that is experienced in the life of the Church.

The Lord commanded the Apostles to make disciples, baptize, and teach (Matt. 28:19). They made disciples by way of the kerygma, the preaching of the Gospel calling all to repentance and entry into the Church, which came by Baptism. After Baptism there was a second teaching, in order that the regenerated might retain the salvation given in Baptism by observing "all things whatsoever" Christ had commanded (Matt. 28:19). Baptism was the indissoluble link between the preaching of the Gospel and the living out of the Gospel; after Baptism one was exhorted to continue in His word, in the faith and in the doctrine (John 8:31, Col. 1:23, 1 Tim. 4:16).

According to the Orthodox understanding, the entirety of salvation is given in Baptism. The whole man is submerged in the waters, body and soul, emerging a new creature (2 Cor. 5:17, Gal. 6:15), having put on Christ (Gal. 3:27, 1 Thess. 5:23). He who has been "buried with Him through baptism unto death" (Rom. 6:4–11), who has been clothed in Christ, can he be said to be lacking in anything as it pertains to salvation? "Of His fullness have we all received, and grace for grace," says the Apostle John the Theologian (John 1:16). As Clement of Alexandria wrote, "Straightway, on our regeneration, we attained that perfection after which we aspired."[1]

Yet, the context in which this fullness is received is the Eucharistic assembly, in which the baptized one becomes a member of the Church by partaking of the Body and Blood of Christ. Man is called by God increasingly to make Christ "all in all" in his own person (1 Cor. 15:28, Eph. 1:23). Even as Christ Himself is our salvation and the kingdom of God (Rev. 12:10), and there is no end to His kingdom, so our salvation is no static reality, obtained and then simply preserved once and forever, to be buried in the ground until the day of reckoning (Matt. 25:25). Man is regenerated in and through the mysteries of the Church in the timeless life of Christ, initiated through Baptism, Chrismation, and the Holy Eucharist into the one mystery of Christ, receiving grace upon grace, God giving the increase (1 Cor. 3:7; 2 Cor. 9:10).

This is so because all the mysteries of the Church are but one mystery, the mystery of Salvation flowing from the mys-

---

1. Paedagogus, 1.6.25.1, PG 8.280: "ἀναγεννηθέντες γοῦν εὐθέως τὸ τέλειον ἀπειλήφαμεν, οὗν ἕνεκεν ἐσπεύδομεν."

tery of the Church, the same Holy Spirit always present and working (Phil. 2:12–13). There is only "one Lord, one faith, one Baptism" (Eph. 4:5), one life in Christ. The unity of the mysteries flows from the unity of the Head with His Body. There can be no participation in the Mystery of the Church outside this unity. That is because the Church is the locus of all Christian life and is known only from within, experientially, in the living out of a life of grace, in the entirety of the doctrine of the faith. One cannot enter into this life in a piecemeal way, partially, selectively. One can only be immersed within it, overwhelmed by it, receiving it entirely, unconditionally.

As is apparent in the epistles of Saint Paul, especially Ephesians 4:5, there was no doubt as to boundaries of the Church and the identity of the Christians vis-à-vis schismatics and heretics. As Archbishop Peter Huillier wrote, "It is obviously inconceivable that the Baptism conferred by the heretics mentioned in the Pastorals might have been equated with that performed in the Church."[2] Even if some in the Church in the West would later suffer an identity crisis and lose this clarity of vision and self-understanding, nevertheless, the simple truth of "one Lord, one faith, one Baptism" (Eph. 4:5) remained self-evident to the Church, for which Christ is the same "yesterday, and today, and forever" (Heb. 13:8).

What was inconceivable for the Apostle Paul with regard to the heretics of his day has nevertheless been clearly conceived in *Unitatis Redintegratio* with regard to the schismatics and heretics of the late twentieth century. The authors of *Unitatis Redintegratio*, following the councils of Florence and Trent, considered any Baptism canonically performed by anyone with

2. Archbishop Peter Huillier, "Believing in One Church: An Insight into Patristic Tradition," *St. Vladimir's Theological Quarterly* 48:1 (2004), 21.

the proper disposition to be the one Baptism of the Church—
regardless of their state of schism or heresy. But they went further than previous Latin councils in establishing a new theory
of Church unity based upon this conception.

1

BAPTISM AS THE BASIS
FOR A NEW ECCLESIOLOGY

That all men are in one sense brothers, all being sons and daughters of Adam and Eve, is a universally accepted truism. However, this is not the sense meant in *Unitatis Redintegratio*. In virtue of Baptism, so it is held, all who have been baptized in Christ with the Trinitarian formula become subjects and members of the One Church[3] and thus "are correctly accepted as brothers by the children of the Catholic Church" (UR 3)—brothers in Christ.

Pope John Paul II, in his 1995 encyclical *Ut Unum Sint* (On Commitment to Ecumenism), restates the essential teaching first formulated in *Unitatis Redintegratio* concerning the status of non–Roman Catholic Christians following their baptism in the Name of the Trinity:

> [A]cknowledging our brotherhood is not the consequence of a large-hearted philanthropy or a vague family spirit. It is rooted in recognition of the oneness of Baptism and the subsequent duty to glorify God in his work. The Di-

---

3. UR 3. Jerome-Michael Vereb puts the teaching this way: "In virtue of Baptism, all are subjects and members of the Church, who have been baptized in Christ with the Trinitarian formula. The effect is not removed by either heresy or schism." *"Because He Was a German": Cardinal Bea and the Origins of Roman Catholic Engagement in the Ecumenical Movement* (Grand Rapids, MI: Eerdmans, 2006), 291.

rectory for the Application of Principles and Norms on Ecumenism expresses the hope that Baptisms will be mutually and officially recognized. This is something much more than an act of ecumenical courtesy; it constitutes *a basic ecclesiological statement*.[4]

It is this basic ecclesiological statement, stemming as it does from the oneness of Baptism, that is of interest to us. That there is a new-found brotherhood means also that there is a new ecclesiological stance or vision of the Church, made possible by a new recognition of the implications of Baptism. These three changes in understanding are interrelated, the latter calculated to bring about the former.

It would not be an exaggeration to say that, in its Decree on Ecumenism, the Second Vatican Council presented "a new and irreversible image of the Church Universal."[5] Integral to this vision, even the "key" that enabled Catholicism to open up and embrace this new image of the Church, is a new view of the mysteries of those outside Catholicism, especially the mystery of Baptism. With a new understanding of the mysteries of those "churches and ecclesial communities" not in communion with the pope, there came a new understanding of the nature of the Roman Communion itself.[6]

---

4. Pope John Paul II, *Ut Unum Sint* (On Commitment to Ecumenism), May 25, 1995 (http://www.vatican.va/ holy_father/john_paul_ii/ encyclicals/documents/hf_jp-ii_enc_25051995_ut-unum-sint_en.html) (emphasis added).

5. Vereb, *"Because He Was a German,"* 290. Vereb is here describing the vision of Cardinal Bea presented on the eve of Vatican II, the same vision soon thereafter adopted by the council in UR.

6. The Mysteries and the Church are inseparable and mutually related. As Prof. Vlassios Phidas puts it: "[The] inner relationship between Ecclesiology and Sacraments is an indissoluble one, because, according

Whereas Baptism was once thought to avail for the forgiveness of sins only within the unity of the Church,[7] today the sacrament itself, performed by those formally separated from the Church, is thought "to produce all its fruits and is a source of grace."[8] Once schismatics and heretics enjoyed only a suspended state of grace by virtue of their Baptism—a grace retained in spite of their state of schism or heresy—which became active only upon entry into the communion of the Catholic Church.[9] These "separated brethren" are now, however, believed to enjoy a "life of grace" (UR 3b) and "access to the community of salvation" (UR 3c), and the dissident bodies as such[10] are considered "means of salvation" (UR 3d). The formulation of the Second Vatican Council's new ecclesiology was made possible by an earlier shift among Roman Catholic theologians from considering the status of schismatic or heretical individuals vis-à-vis the Church to considering the status

to the Patristic tradition, the sacraments manifest and indicate the whole ecclesial body. Hence, any differentiation whatsoever in Ecclesiology is fully expressed in the specific sacramental praxis of the Church, which, in its turn, expresses the corresponding awareness of the Church's limits." Vlassios Phidas, "The Limits of the Church in an Orthodox Perspective," *The Greek Orthodox Theological Review* 43:1–4 (1998), 525.

7. St. Augustine, *On Baptism*, NPNF 3.17.22.

8. Fr. Jorge A. Scampini, O.P.,*"We acknowledge one Baptism for the forgiveness of sins,"* a paper delivered at the Faith and Order Plenary Commission in Kuala, Malaysia, July 28–Aug. 6, 2004. PDF available online. See also UR 3b.

9. St. Augustine, *On Baptism*, NPNF 4.21.29.

10. UR 3d. Cf. *Commentary on the Documents of Vatican II* (London: Burns and Oates Ltd., 1968), 2:75–76; Francis A. Sullivan, S.J., "The Significance of the Vatican II Declaration that the Church of Christ 'Subsists in' the Roman Catholic Church," in René Latourelle, *Vatican II: Assessment and Perspectives, Twenty-five Years After (1962–1987)* (New York: Paulist Press, 1989), 2:281–82; Scampini, *"We acknowledge one Baptism."*

of schismatic or heretical bodies per se.[11] Several prominent theologians contributed significantly to this reorientation, so fundamental to the entry of Roman Catholicism into the ecumenical movement. Theologians such as Karl Rahner, Edward Schillebeeckx, Henri de Lubac, and Gregory Baum exercised considerable influence. However, the French Dominican Yves Congar claimed, and is upheld by many, to be the trailblazer.

In Congar's important and ground-breaking book *Divided Christendom, A Catholic Study of the Problem of Reunion*, first published in 1939,[12] "he affirmed that ecumenism begins when we start to consider the Christianity not just of schismatic Christian individuals, but of schismatic ecclesiastical bodies as such."[13] He claimed that reflection on such groups brought one to the conclusion that the hitherto accepted view of schismatic persons "being united to the single, visible Catholic Church through a *votum*, an 'implicit desire,' was inadequate. For how could such a 'dissident Christianity"—that is, a group—have such a desire *as a group?* Thus he was led to put forward his own version of the concept that the schismatic communities retained *elements* of the Una Sancta in their schismatic situation."[14] According to Congar, if these elements, chiefly the

11. The related passage of UR, to which we will return further on, is the fourth paragraph of section three.

12. M. J. Congar, *Divided Christendom, A Catholic Study of the Problem of Reunion*, trans. M. A. Bousfield (London: Geoffrey Bles: The Centenary Press, 1939).

13. Aidan Nichols, *Yves Congar* (London: Morehouse-Barlow, 1989), 102.

14. Ibid. (emphasis in original). Avery Dulles, S.J., in his article "The Church, The Churches, The Catholic Church," in *Theological Studies* 33:2 (1972), 199–234, provides background information on Congar's important "elements" theory: "It asserts that although the Church of Christ exists fully or perfectly in one communion alone, it is found imperfectly

holy mysteries, first of which is Baptism, preserve "through good faith" "the essential[s] of [their] efficacy," they bring about in the soul of the dissident "a spiritual incorporation (voto) in the Church," making the dissident a member of the Church, tending toward "an entire and practical incorporation in the ecclesiastical Catholic body."[15] This new theory will prove extremely important for the formulation of the Second Vatican Council's new ecclesiology.

In spite of Congar's new theory gaining recognition, the accepted, traditional view that Congar advocated overturning was restated only a few years later in the most official manner. Pope Pius XII, in his encyclical of 1943, *Mystici Corporis Christi*, distinguished between those who are really (in re) incorporated into the Church as members and those joined to it only in intention (in voto). In this he was doing little more than repeating the traditional Roman Catholic teaching on the status of good-willed dissidents, whether schismatics or heretics. After Vatican II, the Pope's words concerning the status of

or by participation in others, inasmuch as they too possess certain gifts or endowments that belong by right to the one true Church. This nuanced position derives from the doctrine of *vestigia ecclesiae*, which has been traced back as far as John Calvin (John Calvin, *Institutes of the Christian Religion* 4 [1559 ed.], chap. 2, nos. 11–12). After being revived in the twentieth-century ecumenical movement, this doctrine was taken into Roman Catholic theology by Yves Congar and others. Since about 1950, however, it has been customary to speak not so much of 'vestiges' of the Church as of 'elements,' 'gifts,' 'endowments,' etc.—expressions which seem more irenic and positive. . . . [T]he idea that there are 'elements' of the true Church outside of Roman Catholicism has given rise to theories that other Christian communions may be 'imperfect realizations' of the Church of Christ or even, in an analogous sense, 'Churches.'"

15. Congar, *Divided Christendom*, 234–35.

good-willed non-Catholics became, for the council's opponents, the most often quoted official statement in contradiction to the new ecclesiology:

> Even though by an unconscious desire and longing [in-scio quodam desiderio ac voto] they have a certain rela-tionship with the Mystical Body of the Redeemer, they still remain deprived of those many heavenly gifts and helps which can only be enjoyed in the Catholic Church. Therefore may they enter into Catholic unity and, joined with Us in the one, organic Body of Jesus Christ, may they together with us run on to the one Head in the So-ciety of glorious love.[16]

This teaching was restated again only six years later, in 1949, in a more systematic manner in the letter known as *Suprema haec sacra* by the Supreme Sacred Congregation of the Holy Office, with the same Pope's approval. In this letter the *maxim extra ecclesiam nullus salus* was being explained, includ-ing the positive potential for one who is blamelessly ignorant to be united to the Church without becoming a member by sacramental initiation:

> [I]n order that one may obtain eternal salvation, it is not always required that he be incorporated into the Church actually as a member, but it is required that at least he be united to it by intention and desire. However, this de-sire need not always be explicit, as it is in catechumens; but, when a person is involved in invincible ignorance, God accepts also an implicit intention (votum) which is

---

16. Pope Pius XII, *Mystici Corporis Christi,* On the Mystical Body of Christ, June 29, 1943, no. 103.

so called because it is included in that good disposition of the soul whereby a person wishes his will to be conformed to the will of God.[17]

The possibility of salvation without visible membership in the Body of Christ is accepted. Even so, this consideration of the dissidents' relationship to the Church will be challenged by Congar and others and will, moreover, prove far too limited for the demands of ecumenical engagement. For, if, as Congar saw early on, the official teaching would be understood to limit participation of dissidents in the life of Christ and the Church to a good intention and that on a personal level, Roman Catholic participation in the ecumenical movement would have remained an impossibility.[18] On the strength of a valid Baptism the dissidents' participation must be seen to be much more extensive and considered as an essential, even if partial, communion, and a real, albeit impaired, membership.

These official pronouncements came only four and ten years after Congar's *Divided Christendom* and just over a decade before the Second Vatican Council. This fact makes all the more clear the internal struggle being waged at that time within Ca-

17. Supreme Sacred Congregation of the Holy Office, Letter of August 8, 1949, to the Archbishop of Boston, Richard J. Cushing, published by the Archdiocese of Boston on September 4, 1952, as Protocol *Suprema haec sacra*, in *AER* 127:4 (Oct. 1952), 307–15.

18. The abandonment of the teaching on the connection of the dissidents to the Church is evident both in the introduction to *Unitatis Redintegratio* and in chapter one, article three. The commentators agreed with Congar that this change was essential: "Without this positive evaluation of non-Catholic communities it would not be possible to speak of ecumenism in the modern sense, for the object of ecumenical dialogue is not individual believers, but Christian communities as such." Johannes Feiner, *Commentary on the Decree*, in *Commentary on the Documents of Vatican II* (London: Burns and Oates Ltd., 1968), 2:61.

tholicism and the unexpected and tremendous victory won by
the reformers at Vatican II.

The new ecclesiology of Vatican II was anticipated by Congar's ecumenical concerns nearly twenty-five years in advance.
Already present in *Chrétiens désunis* were key elements of the
new ecclesiology: "recognition of Protestants as 'frères séparés,'
the identification of 'éléments d'Église' within them, the expression of degrees of communion, and acknowledgement of the
salvific presence of the Holy Spirit among other Christians."[19]

Congar's reflections on the status of "the dissidents," although viewed as unorthodox by the Vatican at the time, were
soon taken up for further consideration by his peers in theology. Dom Jean Gribomont,[20] Christophe Dumont,[21] and later J.
Maritain,[22] among others, were all inspired by Congar's speculations to examine the question of the Church and the "separated brethren" in earnest.

19. Dennis M. Doyle, "Journet, Congar, and the Roots of Communion
Ecclesiology," *Theological Studies* 58 (1997), 471.

20. Nichols, 102. Gribomont went further than Congar and spoke of
"imperfect realizations" of the single sacrament of the Church in non-Catholic bodies. He claimed that "the Church is so ordered that each
element in her reality implies, objectively, all the rest: one cannot have
one part without having, in some degree and in some manner, all the
rest." See J. Gribomont, "Du sacrament de l'Église et de ses realizations
imparfaits," *Irenikon* 22 (1949), 345–67.

21. Ibid. Christophe Dumont perceived "potential parts" of the single
Church existing in the separated Christian confessions. These parts were
"the essential whole expressing itself partially, and thus deficiently, in
its powers and activities." See C. Dumont, "Unité de l'Église et unité
chrétienne," in *Les Voies de l'unité chrétienne. Doctrine et spiritualité* (Paris,
1954), 123–28.

22. Ibid. Maritain chose "to speak of a 'supernatural created personality of the Church,' present in a virtual and invisible way in the non-Catholic communities." See J. Maritain, *De l'Église du Christ. Sa personne
et ses personages* (Paris, 1970), 47 and 188ff.

Within this emerging climate among prominent theologians in the two decades leading up to Vatican II, a new ecclesiological orientation took shape. On the eve of Vatican II the German Jesuit Heinrich Fries articulated what Congar called "a wider consensus" when he suggested that the notion of participation or communion was a key idea in this context.[23] Congar expressed the emerging agreement thus: "On the eve of the decree on ecumenism, a certain consensus existed among Catholic theologians, in favour of *a theology of the differentiated participation* of the non-Roman communions in the treasure of the single Church, and in favour, too, of an ecumenism of integration which would be something other than 'return,' pure and simple."[24]

The emerging ecclesiology that recognized degrees of communion between all Christians on the strength of the ecclesial elements retained by them was ultimately made possible by the recognition not only of the validity[25] but also of the efficacy of

23. See H. Fries, "Der ekklesiologische Status der evangelischen Kirche in katholischer Sicht," in *Aspekte der Kirche* (Stuttgart, 1963), 123–52.

24. Yves Congar, *Essais oecuméniques* (Paris: Le Centurion, 1984), 212–13 (emphasis added), as quoted in Nichols, 103.

25. Bl. Augustine was the first to develop the idea of what constitutes the "valid" administration and the proper minister of Baptism. Namely, any Baptism that includes the proper element (water) and proper words (invocation of the Holy Trinity) is "valid." The effect of the sacraments was later said to come by the very fact of being administered (ex opere operato). Since it is Christ who operates through them, their effectiveness does not depend on the worthiness of the minister. However, a sacrament may be "valid" without necessarily being efficacious for the recipient owing to the obstacle of sin that has been erected. Therefore, for those outside the unity of the Church, "valid" Baptism does exist but, on account of the sin of schism or heresy, there is no presence of the fruit of Baptism. Contemporary Catholicism teaches that "valid baptism is administered (in principle by anyone) by pouring

the mysteries performed by schismatics and heretics, the first of
which is Baptism. The dissident, it was now claimed, not only
can receive the grace of God at the moment of Baptism but can
preserve it, participate in it, live and grow by it, within and by
means of his church or ecclesiastical communion.

(or sprinkling, or immersion) in natural water, at the same time des-
ignating the act of baptism ('N., I baptize thee . . .') and invoking the
Blessed Trinity ('in the name of the Father and of the Son and of the
Holy Spirit') with the intention of doing what the Church does when
she baptizes" (Karl Rahner and Herbert Vorgrimler, *Concise Theological
Dictionary* [London: Burns and Oates: 1965], 47). When used within the
Orthodox context, the concept of validity carries a meaning very different from that intended by Roman Catholics and Protestants. The corresponding Greek word used by the Orthodox today in this context, χῦρος
(force or authority), could be better translated as authenticity (not validity). The basic Orthodox distinction is not between validity and efficacy
but between authenticatable potential (or "validity," κατ᾽ οἰκονομίαν)
and authenticity ("validity," κατ᾽ ἀκρίβειαν), without, however, the former being recognized as already genuine. The main difference is that
authenticity cannot be acknowledged apart from unity. An authentic
mystery takes place within the bounds of the One Church with full, not
partial, fidelity to the faith and practice of the Church. The Orthodox
resist the compartmentalization and fragmentation that require only
the intention of carrying out a particular sacrament, apart from the
intention to maintain the entirety of the Church's faith and practice.
(See Charles-James N. Bailey, "Validity and Authenticity: The Difference Between Western and Orthodox Views on Orders," *St. Vladimir's
Theological Quarterly* 8 (1964), 86–92.) Note that neither ἐγχυρότητα
(validity) nor χῦρος (force) is found in patristic texts with reference to
the legitimacy of heretical baptism, which only goes to underscore the
uniqueness of Blessed Augustine's views on the subject and the very
different context in which the discussion is carried out today. Likewise,
"the scholastic distinction between *ex opera operato* and *ex opera operantis*
is alien to Greek canon law, which instead presumes *ex opera communionis.*" David Heith-Stade, "Receiving the Non-Orthodox: A Historical Study of Greek Orthodox Canon Law," *Studia canonica* 44 (2010),
399–426 (425).

Before examining the teaching proper to *Unitatis Redintegratio*, it is necessary to step back in time and become familiar with Rome's older teachings on the subject. One can properly appreciate neither the degree of ecclesiological innovation nor the text's continuity with the past if he is not acquainted with pre-conciliar teaching, both those aspects that are unique to the post-schism West and those with roots in the Latin patristic tradition, especially Blessed Augustine. As Karl Becker has written, "It is against precisely this background that the novelties and new concerns of the conciliar doctrine on Baptism become entirely accessible, both as regards their clear content and also in their unresolved questions."[26]

---

26. Karl Becker, "The Teaching of Vatican II on Baptism: A Stimulus for Theology," in René Latourelle, ed., *Vatican II: Assessment and Perspectives, Twenty-five Years After (1962–1987)* (New York: Paulist Press, 1989), 2:49.

2

PRE-CONCILIAR TEACHING:
AN EXPRESSION OF SACRAMENTAL
MINIMALISM

The official teaching of the Roman Catholic Church on Baptism is largely unchanged from the Fourth Lateran Council in 1215 until the Second Vatican Council. The principal points that were already anticipated in the Lateran Council and then developed in the treatise of Thomas Aquinas (1225–1274) "On the Articles of Faith and the Sacraments of the Church"—which was the basis for the important Decree for the Armenians at the Council of Florence and was enshrined and officially confirmed at the Council of Trent in 1545—represented the structure of the teaching in the nineteenth century and early twentieth century.[27]

The neo-Scholastic manuals of theology, universally held to be authoritative during the nineteenth and early twentieth centuries, essentially reproduced this teaching. The content of these manuals was left largely untouched by the Second Vatican Council.[28] With respect to the most fundamental aspects of the mystery, the manuals teach that the institution of the mys-

27. Karl Becker, "The Teaching of Vatican II on Baptism: A Stimulus for Theology," in René Latourelle, ed., *Vatican II: Assessment and Perspectives, Twenty-five Years After (1962–1987)* (New York: Paulist Press, 1989), 2:49.
28. Ibid.

tery is by Jesus Christ; the matter, a washing with water, done either by immersion, infusion, or aspersion; the form, the invocation of the Trinity in Three Persons. The ordinary minister of the mystery is to be a bishop or priest, but in case of need, anyone can baptize. The recipient of Baptism is an adult with a good intention; but also a child before the "age of reason" could be a recipient. The effect of Baptism is the forgiveness of sins and guilt (for the sin of Adam), and the infusion of grace. The council repudiates none of these statements; however, this is because its particular interest is directed toward other aspects of Baptism.[29]

With respect to these fundamental guidelines for Baptism, we must focus on two aspects of the mystery: the minister and the matter, or more precisely, the method. For, in both cases we have views that differ from Orthodox teaching and are the result of centuries of "reduction to essentials," of a "reduction to sacramental minimalism,"[30] which in turn prepared the groundwork for the new ecclesiology of Vatican II.

Baptismal Minister: Baptized or Unbaptized, Believer or Infidel

With respect to the minister of the mystery, it must be noted that from at least the Fourth Lateran Council there ceased to be a distinction between believer and unbeliever in the performance of Baptism in case of need. That is, the Roman Catholic Church claimed that the "right of any person whatsoever to

29. Ibid., 50. Becker adds, "Indeed from time to time, it mentions one or another of them, for example, that everyone can baptize" (LG 17).

30. Maxwell E. Johnson, *The Rites of Christian Initiation: Their Evolution and Interpretation* (Collegeville, MN: Liturgical Press, 1999), 286.

baptize in case of necessity is in accord with the constant tradition and practice of the Church."[31] "Any person" here includes
the unbaptized and unbelievers, such as Jews or Moslems.

The doctrinal testimonials for this teaching, at least those of
a conciliar origin, are all post-schism. Tertullian and St. Jerome
are cited as sources as well;[32] however, they speak of nothing
more than the possibility for a layman to baptize in case of
need. In fact, St. Jerome supports the legitimacy of a baptized
layman baptizing by saying: "for as a person receives, so may
he give."[33] Since an unbaptized person has not received the
mystery, neither can he give it. Therefore, St. Jerome actually
stands in opposition to this teaching.

Blessed Augustine's maxim "It is Christ who baptizes"[34] is
cited as a source for the teaching, although it can be considered
as such only indirectly, for he never expressly acknowledged
that the non-baptized and unbeliever could legitimately baptize. His own confession of faith, however, made at the end of
his longest treatise on the subject, *De Baptismo*, if read apart
from the entire treatise, could be seen to leave room for such
an idea.[35]

31. William Fanning, "Baptism," *The Catholic Encyclopedia*, vol. 2
(New York: Robert Appleton Company, 1907).

32. Ibid.

33. St. Jerome, *Against the Luciferians* 9, NPNF 1.6.

34. See, for example, Book III of St. Augustine's *Answer to Petilian,
the Donatist*, NPNF 4.1.49.

35. "If anyone were to press me—supposing I were duly seated
in a Council in which a question were raised on points like these—to
declare what my own opinion was, without reference to the previously
expressed views of others, whose judgment I would rather follow, if I
were under the influence of the same feelings as led me to assert what
I have said before, I should have no hesitation in saying that *all men
possess Baptism who have received it in any place, from any sort of men*, pro-

St. Isidore of Seville is probably the explicit source of the teaching, as he declares: "The Spirit of God administers the grace of Baptism, although it be a pagan who does the baptizing."[36] Pope Nicholas (858–867) likewise held the opinion that Baptism by a Jew or a pagan is acceptable.[37]

The Fourth Lateran Council in 1215 defended heretical Baptism, teaching: "The mystery of Baptism . . . rightly conferred by anyone in the form of the Church is useful unto salvation for little ones and for adults."[38] With the Decree for the

vided that it were consecrated in the words of the gospel, and received without deceit on their part with some degree of faith." Significantly, he immediately adds: "although it would be of no profit to them for the salvation of their souls if they were without charity, by which they might be grafted into the Catholic Church." *De Baptismo*, 53–102 (emphasis added).

36. Fanning, "Baptism," provides the following source: *can. Romanus de cons.*, iv.

37. Henry Denzinger, *The Sources of Catholic Dogma* (Fitzwilliam, NH: Loreto, 2007), 135. From his responses to the decrees of the Bulgars in November 866, chap. 104, we read: "You assert that in your fatherland many have been baptized by a certain Jew, you do not know whether Christian or pagan, and you consult us as to what should be done about them. If indeed they have been baptized in the name of the Holy Trinity or only in the name of Christ, as we read in the Acts of the Apostles [cf. Acts 2:38; 19:5], (surely, it is one and the same, as Saint Ambrose sets forth) it is established that they should not be baptized again."

38. *Concilium Lateranense IV*, chap. I, *De fide catholica*. See Denzinger-Bannwart, *Enchiridion Symbolorum*, no. 430, p. 190. The first, *Concilium Lateranense*, is found in the second collection of texts by Denzinger, listed in the Bibliography as Denzinger, Henry, *The Sources of Catholic Dogma*. Fitzwilliam, NH: Loreto, 2007. (The English translation of the thirtieth edition of *Enchiridion Symbolorum*, Henry Denzinger, revised by Karl Rahner, S.J., published in 1954 by Herder & Co., Freiburg.). See also Χρ. Παπαθανασίου, *Τὸ «κατ' ἀκρίβειαν» Βάπτισμα καὶ οἱ ἐξ αὐτοῦ παρεκκλίσεις* (Athens: Grigori Publications, 2001), 196. It is interesting to note that this same council, in its fourth canon, condemned

Armenians, the Council of Florence explicitly says: "in case of necessity, not only a priest or a deacon, but even a layman or laywoman, nay even a pagan or heretic may confer Baptism" so long as he preserves the form of the Church and has the intention of doing as the Church does.[39] And, the very important Council of Trent (1545–1563), in its fourth canon on the mystery of Baptism, anathematizes anyone who says "that the Baptism, which is also given by heretics in the Name of the Father and of the Son and of the Holy Spirit, with the intention of doing what the Church does, is not true Baptism."[40] These views are likewise codified both in the 1917 and 1983 Codes of Canon Law.[41] It is, furthermore, supposed in the Catechism of the Catholic Church that support for this teaching stems from "the universal saving will of God and the necessity of Baptism for salvation."[42] According to Thomas Aquinas, it seems reasonable and proper that, owing to the absolute necessity of Baptism for salvation, every man should be made its minister.[43]

This extension of the ability to initiate into the Church to one who is himself not initiated into the Church—that is, to one who is neither a cleric nor baptized, even to one who does not believe in Christ, or, rather, condemns and blasphemes

the already common practice among the Orthodox of baptizing Latins who were converted to Orthodoxy. See Mansi 22:1082: *Baptizatos etiam a Latinis et ipsi Graeci rebaptizare ausu temerario praesumebant: et adhuc, sicut acceptimus quidam opera hoc non verentur.*"

39. Παπαθανασίου [Papathanasiou], 196. See also Denzinger, *Sources of Catholic Dogma*, 221.

40. Ibid. See also Denzinger, *Sources of Catholic Dogma*, 263.

41. See canon 742, in connection with canon 759, in the 1917 Code of Canon Law, and canon 861 in the 1983 Code.

42. *Catechism of the Catholic Church* (New York: Doubleday, 1997), 2.2.1.V, p. 352.

43. Thomas Aqunas, *SummaTheologica*, 3.64.6 and 3.67.3.

Him—should certainly be considered a significant factor in the historical formation of the Second Vatican Council's teaching on Baptism and the Church. For, long established in the dogmatic consciousness of Roman Catholics was a consideration of the mystery of Baptism, albeit exceptional, that reduced it to its barest form, severed from the context of the Church and the faith of the Church. Having accepted the possibility of an infidel as the minister of Baptism and agent of incorporation into Christ in the medieval age, it is not surprising that in the age of ecumenism much more would be ascribed to the sacred acts of the "separated brethren."

Baptismal Method: Immersion, Pouring, and Sprinkling

A second aspect of the teaching on Baptism likewise diminishes the mystery considerably and is a product of the "reduction to sacramental minimalism" that generally afflicted the medieval West. This component of the teaching, which will set the stage for the development of the ecclesiology of Vatican II and also remain untouched in *Unitatis Redintegratio*, is the question of matter, or rather, more accurately, of method: of whether or not the sacrament is performed by immersion, pouring, or sprinkling.

As is well known, and attested to in many ancient texts, the catholic rule already from the first century is that man is to be baptized, that is, submersed, in water.[44] This was also the case in Rome, as is evidenced in the *Gelasian Sacramentary*,[45] up until

---

44. *The Didache*, for example, containing the earliest description of the rites of Christian initiation after the New Testament, prescribes Baptism, that is, submersion, in "living water" as the rule, with pouring being acceptable only in exceptional cases of need, that is, when it is impossible to baptize (immerse) the candidate.

45. This is a work of great importance, inasmuch as it is one of the

the twelfth century.[46] By the thirteenth century, however, affusion (pouring) or, to a lesser degree, aspersion (sprinkling) had grown common and gradually replaced the ancient practice of Baptism.[47] This change in practice was confirmed and officially sanctioned by the Council of Trent in 1545 and included in that council's Catechism in 1566.[48] This change in the mode

few liturgical books in use in the West before the time of Charlemagne that have survived to the present day. J. D. C. Fisher, *Baptism in the Medieval West: A Study in the Disintegration of the Primitive Rite of Initiation* (London: S.P.C.K., 1965; Chicago: Hillenbrand, 2007), 1.

46. Baptism (submersion in water) was the method employed in the West generally, for which we have historical evidence from Milan, Gaul, Germany, and the British Isles, with the exception of Spain, where from at least the seventh century there was also employed a single immersion. See Fisher, 35, 45, 64, 92, and 102.

47. Fanning, "Baptism." This author incorrectly interprets the word "βαπτίζω" as meaning "a washing" or "ablution." The proper meaning of the word is "to dip in or under water" (Liddell and Scott, *Greek-English Lexicon*) or submerge, sink, or plunge (Lampe, *Patristic Greek Lexicon*). Interpreting "βαπτίζω" as "a washing" allows for one to speak of "different forms of ablution," which include not only immersion but infusion and aspersion as well.

48. The relevant passage from the Catechism reads: "According to the common practice of the Church, baptism may be administered by immersion, infusion, or aspersion; and . . . administered in either of these forms it is equally valid. In baptism water is used to signify the spiritual ablution which it accomplishes, and on this account baptism is called by the Apostle, a laver. This ablution takes place as effectually by immersion, which was for a considerable time the practice in the early ages of the Church, as by infusion, which is now the general practice, or by aspersion, which was the manner in which Peter baptized, when he converted and gave baptism to about three thousand souls. It is also a matter of indifference to the validity of the Sacrament, whether the ablution is performed once or thrice; we learn from the epistle of St. Gregory the great to Leander that baptism was formerly and may still be validly administered in the Church in either way." From *The Cat-*

of administering the mystery was part of an increasingly minimalistic approach amidst what liturgical scholars refer to as a process of "disintegration," "dissolution," and "separation" in the medieval West.[49]

Centuries before the Council of Trent, the unitive rites of initiation in Rome and the West had become broken up into entirely separate rites. For infants, who were the vast majority, the threefold initiation of Baptism, Confirmation, and the Eucharist was replaced by a partial initiation in Baptism alone, to be followed years later with Holy Communion and Confirmation.[50] The delay in Confirmation for practical and other reasons,[51] and the decline and eventual disappearance

echism of the Council of Trent, trans. Rev. J. Donovan (Baltimore: Lucas Brothers, 1829), 118–19.

49. See the classic study by J. D. C. Fisher, *Baptism in the Medieval West*, as well as the very thorough and insightful study by Maxwell E. Johnson, *Rites of Christian Initiation*.

50. Aidan Kavanagh, in his very important and influential book (for Roman Catholics) *The Shape of Baptism: The Rite of Christian Initiation*, which criticized Scholastic minimalism and sounded the horn for a return to sacramental exactitude, writes relative to this: "The separation of the old Roman consignation from Baptism—first by the intervening Baptismal Mass, then by Easter week, and later by years as became the case within some three centuries—should be called what it is. It is a dissolution, not a development." Aidan Kavanagh, *The Shape of Baptism: The Rite of Christian Initiation—Studies in the Reform Rites of the Catholic Church*, vol. 1 (Collegeville, MN: Liturgical Press, 1974/1991), 68.

51. Changes over time in the rite, together with the performance of the mystery exclusively by the bishop, meant that much time, even many years, would pass before the baptized infant would be confirmed. This shift gave rise to theological speculation and interpretation in defense of the new practice, such that "confirmation will become a rite and sacrament in search of a theological meaning and interpretation, a meaning and interpretation increasingly supplied by Scholastic theology." Johnson, 208.

of infant communion for a variety of theological and spiritual reasons,[52] meant that "infant initiation eventually became infant Baptism."[53] "What the earlier churches of both East and West kept together in a unitive and integral rite, the Western Middle Ages . . . 'rent asunder' into four separate and distinct sacraments: Baptism, first confession,[54] first communion,[55] and confirmation."[56] The acceptance and persistence of this disunity profoundly altered the understanding of initiation into the Church.

52. The thirteenth-century doctrine of transubstantiation, clericalism, changes in communion practices such as the withdrawal of the cup from the laity and the lack of frequent communion, all led to a decline in the practice of infant communion. "The whole vision of what the Eucharist was, and what its relationship was to the community, had so changed that the process [of the disappearance of infant communion] could take place unresisted." David Holeton, "The Communion of Infants and Young Children: A Sacrament of Community," in *And Do Not Hinder Them: An Ecumenical Plea for the Admission of Children to the Eucharist*, ed. Geiko Muller-Fahrenholz, Faith and Order Paper 109 (Geneva: WCC, 1982), 63, as quoted in Johnson, *Rites of Christian Initiation*, 220.

53. Johnson, 220.

54. The Fourth Lateran Council in 1205, in its twenty-first canon, mandated first confession before first communion.

55. Even today, decades after Vatican II, as is evidenced in the Catechism of the Catholic Church, the medieval practice has not been abandoned: "The Latin Church, which reserves admission to Holy Communion to those who have attained the age of reason, expresses this orientation of Baptism to the Eucharist by having the newly baptized child brought to the altar for the praying of the Our Father." *Catechism of the Catholic Church*, 349.

56. Johnson, *Rites of Christian Initiation*, 220–21. This is also the order in which, generally speaking, the mysteries were received, a fact that likewise reveals the degree of confusion into which the process of initiation had fallen in the West during the high and late Middle Ages.

This is the context within which the ancient practice of Baptism as the norm was, by the end of the Middle Ages, replaced by affusion[57] and, more exceptionally, aspersion. Similar to the process by which the exception of the minister of Baptism was extended first to a layman and then to an unbaptized unbeliever, the exception of affusion in cases of emergency gradually replaced Baptism as the rule. The universality of affusion reached its peak by the end of the nineteenth century, when the authorized ritual of the Latin Church mandated that Baptism must be performed by a washing of the head of the candidate.[58]

This change in baptismal practice, which had not at all gone unnoticed by Orthodox churchmen,[59] is neither a minor aspect

57. Ibid., 217. Although it is true that the practice of "affusion" is also ancient, it was always seen as an alternative *κατ'οἰκονομίαν*, in the case of emergencies, and not as the norm, for, among other reasons, it lacks the correspondence between outward act and inward meaning. It does not communicate the theological meaning of Baptism as burial and resurrection with Christ and the total regeneration of man.

58. Fanning, "Baptism."

59. Eustratios Argenti's work *Ἐγχειρίδιον περί βαπτίσματος καλούμενον χειραγωγία πλανωμένων* [A Manual of Baptism, named a Guide to those in error] (Constantinople, 1756), is the most representative of the Orthodox critiques of this Latin innovation. As Fr. George Metallinos notes, the Kollyvades Fathers shared Argenti's views wholeheartedly: "Neophytos Kafsokalyvitis, the leader of the Kollyvades movement, St. Nikodemos of the Holy Mountain, and Athanasios Parios, in absolute agreement with each other, unreservedly sided in favor of Patriarch Cyril's decision and the theology of Eustratios Argentis" (Fr. George Metallinos, *I Confess One Baptism: Interpretation and Application of Canon VII of the Second Ecumenical Council by the Kollyvades and Constantine Oikonomos* [Holy Mountain: St. Paul's Monastery, 1994]). See also sections 5, 6, 13, and 22 of the *Encyclical of the Eastern Patriarchs*, which speak of this Latin practice as a novelty, absent from the Holy Tradition of the Church.

of the process of disintegration into sacramental minimalism nor unrelated to the new ecclesiology of Vatican II. When, since the thirteenth century, "Latin Baptism, by omitting immersion, [had] destroyed that correspondence between outward act and inward meaning which is essential to the nature of a sacrament,"[60] this cannot but undermine the general perception of what constitutes initiation into the Church, and therefore also the boundaries of the Church. For, when the mystery of initiation, as originally consisting of a unity of three mysteries, is reduced to one mystery and that gutted of theological symbolism, such that it is a mere shadow of its original fullness, the criterion for membership in the Body is also reduced to the least common denominator: the external form of the mystery combined with the necessary matter and a good intention on the part of anyone, anywhere.

The minimum in theory and practice with regard to minister and matter combine to result in a minimum with regard to membership. The ancient exactitude and fullness of the Church with regard to Baptism and Church initiation became ancient history. With such minimal requirements for initiation into the Church, the ground was prepared at Vatican II for the inclusion in the Church, albeit "imperfectly," of just about anyone who called themselves Christian and carried out the required acts with regard to Baptism.

60. Timothy Ware, *Eustratios Argenti: A Study of the Greek Church under Turkish Rule* (Oxford: Clarendon Press, 1964), 92.

3

SACRAMENTAL MINIMALISM AND FULLNESS

Paradoxically, in the new formulations on Baptism and the Church offered in *Unitatis Redintegratio* and the council's ecclesiology we see that two opposing currents meet: the old sacramental minimalism, which ironically serves the broadening of the Church and ecumenical aims, and a new move to return to sacramental maximalism that seeks to restore a holistic view of sacramental worship without actually being conducive to such a broadening. With respect to Baptism, lip service is paid to the latter, while essential theological positions are taken based on the former. This is apparent in the following example.

After decades of scholarship dedicated to uncovering the historical process of dissolution and recovering the unity of the mysteries, there was a hesitating attempt at the Second Vatican Council to reinstate Baptism (immersion) as the norm. Thus, we read in *Lumen Gentium:*

> In that Body the life of Christ is poured into the believers who, through the sacraments, are united in a hidden and real way to Christ who suffered and was glorified. Through Baptism we are formed in the likeness of Christ: "For in one Spirit we were all baptized into one body." *In this sacred rite a oneness with Christ's death and resurrection is both symbolized and brought about:* "For we were buried with Him by means of Baptism into death; and

if we have been united with Him in the likeness of His death, we shall be so in the likeness of His resurrection also" (Rom. 6:4–5).[61]

As the authors of *Lumen Gentium* knew full well, this theology did not (and does not) correspond to the practice of the Latin Church. Nevertheless, in the face of this reality, or perhaps in spite of it and in an effort to energize an overturning of it, they present it as the norm.

The problematic phrase for Latin theology, which, however, is quite consistent with patristic teaching, is that "in this sacred rite a oneness with Christ's death and resurrection is both symbolized (repraesentatur) and brought about." This use of the term *repraesentatur* was accepted by an overwhelming majority of bishops, of whom most were from the Latin-rite church in which affusion (pouring) was without exception the norm.[62] Hence, for these bishops, as Karl Becker has observed, "we cannot speak of a visual representation of dying with Christ and rising again with him in Baptism in their rite. Since, however, the sacraments have their effect by their signification, how can we speak of *efficitur* ('is effected' or 'brought about') with regard to dying and rising again with Christ?"[63]

How is this inconsistency between theology and practice to be overcome? The answer given by Becker, if it is representative of the general approach post–Vatican II, is not encouraging for those who would like to see a return to sacramental

61. LG 7b (emphasis added).

62. Karl Becker, "The Teaching of Vatican II on Baptism: A Stimulus for Theology," in René Latourelle, ed., *Vatican II: Assessment and Perspectives, Twenty-five Years After (1962–1987)* (New York: Paulist Press, 1989), 2:52.

63. Ibid.

maximalism. Such a return necessarily means disassociation with post-schism theology and practice, for, if the practice of pouring is to be defended, it is only by the way of sacramental minimalism that the chasm (which pouring creates) between outward act and inward meaning[64] can be justified, although it cannot be bridged. Bridging the gap here between theology and practice can be accomplished only by way of sacramental maximalism, which means regarding immersion as integral to the mystery. This will become clear with the following case in point.[65]

The theological text that guided medieval Catholicism in its theology of Baptism is the *Summa Theologica* of Thomas Aquinas.[66] Therein, Aquinas says that the action of Baptism is the

64. Or, to speak in the somewhat similar terms of Latin theology: "the sign" and "the effect."

65. The following explanation is taken largely from Becker's article.

66. It is interesting and important to note that, as Maxwell Johnson (*The Rites of Christian Initiation: Their Evolution and Interpretation* [Collegeville, MN: Liturgical Press, 1999]) has shown, Aquinas' *Summa Theologica* was based on earlier texts that had over time subtly altered the understanding of the mysteries. Theological speculation and interpretation arose in defense of new practices—interpretations that then passed into authoritative documents upon which Aquinas based his *Summa Theologica*. In the case of chrismation (or confirmation) an interpretation attributed to St. Faustus of Riez in the fifth century reappeared in the eighth century attributed to a fictitious Pope named Melchiades, then in the papal documents known as the *False Decretals*. From there it passed into the *Decretum Gratiani* in the twelfth century, a legal document that was to serve as the foundation of canon law. From there Peter Lombard would incorporate it into his famous *Sentences*, the basic textbook of theology throughout the Middle Ages. It was on the basis of Lombard's *Sentences* that Aquinas wrote his highly influential *Summa Theologica*. The problem is, however, that on the strength of this interpretation Confirmation emerged as a distinct rite, separate from Baptism itself, as a special sacrament of the Holy Spirit for an increase in grace, and as

bodily washing,[67] which might be performed either by immersion, pouring, or sprinkling.[68] In order to justify these variations he links them to Scripture passages (1 Cor. 6:11, washing; Rom. 6:4–5, immersion; Heb. 10:22, sprinkling; and Ezekiel 36:25, pouring). The reasoning is that each of these expressions indicates one aspect of the effect of Baptism that the other three do not mention explicitly, and, thus, none of them alone fully expresses the effect of Baptism.

Aquinas, however, considers that washing is essential and required, but that alongside it the rite of Baptism must have only one of the three prescriptions (immersion, pouring, sprinkling), for none of the three is required, nor all three together.[69]

a sacrament of "maturity"—an interpretation far from that common in the days of St. Faustus. See Johnson, *Rites of Christian Initiation*, 203–13.

67. See chapter 2, note 47. Aquinas' interpretation of Baptism as a washing is determinative of his subsequent explanation and justification of pouring and sprinkling.

68. Thomas Aquinas, *Summa Theologica*, 3.66.7c.

69. Aquinas' claim that it matters not if Baptism is performed with three immersions is cited and censured by St. Nikodemos the Hagiorite in his commentary on apostolic canon 50 in *The Pedalion* (or Rudder). (Comp. Agapius a Hieromonk and Nicodemus a Monk. First printed and published A.D.1800; trans. D. Cummings, from the 5th edition published by John Nicolaides [Kesisoglou the Caesarian] in Athens, Greece, in 1908 [Chicago: The Orthodox Christian Educational Society, 1957; Repr., New York, N.Y.: Luna Printing Co., 1983]).This canon prescribes three immersions, against the Eunomian baptismal rite, which employed only one. St. Nikodemos refers approvingly to a certain Latin theologian (Cordier) who rejects the "wicked opinion of Thomas Aquinas who holds that it is a matter of indifference whether baptism is performed with three immersions or not." It is interesting to note here Cardinal Humbert's anathematization of the Eastern Church because of Patriarch Keroularios' practice of baptizing Latins who converted to Orthodoxy. The renowned canonist Theodore Balsamon shared the view of Patriarch Keroularios. In 1193 he argued on the basis of Canon 7 of the Second Ecumenical Council that Latin baptisms, based on one

This means that the sign of Baptism that effects the grace does not represent the whole effect symbolically, but only part of it, and thus, according to Becker, that "we must be very cautious in speaking of the sign producing the effect" (as concerns Baptism).[70]

Faced with this problem, the only response possible, if neither pouring nor sprinkling is to be impugned, is to accept that "the action of Baptism makes one or more aspects of the effect of Baptism visible by representation," whereas for the others "the visible action is merely *an occasion that recalls them.*"[71] Affusion (or pouring) is then justified, for it "symbolizes the washing away of sins and the infusion of graces, but secondarily also represents union with the death and resurrection of Christ, and effects what it signifies both symbolically and representatively."[72]

Notably, Becker, in response to this break with tradition and theological inconsistency, wonders out loud if the awareness of the Church or the emphasis of the baptismal doctrine can shift and "whether such shifts may have produced at least some

immersion (as was practiced especially in Spain and accepted in Rome), ought to be considered unacceptable (for $\varkappa\alpha\tau'o\dot{\iota}\varkappa o\nu o\mu\dot{\iota}\alpha\nu$ reception) because of the similarity with Eunomian baptism. See Fr. George Dragas, "The Manner of Reception of Roman Catholic Converts into the Orthodox Church," a paper prepared for the Orthodox–Roman Catholic Dialogue in the United States in 1998.

70. Becker, 53.

71. Ibid. (emphasis added).

72. Ibid. It is unclear how pouring can "represent union with the death and resurrection of Christ," even "secondarily," as Becker claims. Earlier in the same article, he says plainly that "we cannot speak of a visual representation of dying with Christ and rising again with him" in pouring. Is there to be inferred a difference between representing dying and rising and representing a union with the death and resurrection?

change in the 'essential part' of the rite of Baptism from the thirteenth century onward."[73]

In these ruminations one can sense the theological tension present in contemporary Catholicism since the Second Vatican Council between a quest for a return to the ancient Church's sacramental maximalism and the inertia of a millennium or more of sacramental minimalism. The council was faced with the choice of returning to the fullness of the rite, in which alone there is theological consistency, or equivocating and remaining in the inconsistent margins of a minimalistic approach, which lacks the meaning appropriate to the sacrament's content.[74] As was apparent in the preceding excerpt from *Lumen Gentium* and as Karl Becker did in the example just given, even while theoretically acknowledging the rightness of the Church's ancient practice, sacramental minimalism in the form of pouring is justified and remains the standard practice.[75]

73. Ibid.

74. Aidan Kavanagh writes relative to this: "There is nothing mechanical about sacraments. They do not trap God, but they may well convict of tempting Him those who bring to them little or no meaning commensurate with their content. Baptism done anonymously and indiscriminately in a *pro forma* manner with little inconvenience to anyone, with drops of water and dabs of oil, is not merely a regrettable lapse in pastoral taste. It symbolizes and inevitably reinforces a view of the Christian mystery that is vastly at odds with everything the Church knows about the intent of its Lord." (*The Shape of Baptism: The Rite of Christian Initiation—Studies in the Reform Rites of the Catholic Church*, vol. 1 [Collegeville, MN: Liturgical Press, 1974/1991], 172). Could there be a "Baptism" more at odds with the intention of the Lord than that which is performed outside the Church's unity by those standing in opposition or indifference to the Church, or even by the unbaptized and unbelieving, and in a manner that does not express its inner meaning?

75. LG 7b; Becker, 53. This is evident, for example, in the Catholic Catechism: "Baptism is performed in the most expressive way by triple

The long and gradual development and justification of sacramental minimalism—in relation to the baptismal minister and method, and in other ways—while being recognized and rebuked within contemporary Catholicism, was not to be overturned at the Second Vatican Council. Noteworthy changes were made, however, in post-conciliar baptismal practices in an effort to return to a holistic, integrated, and unitive process of Christian initiation.[76] These reforms, being essentially a recovery of what has always been the practice of the Christian East,[77]

immersion in the Baptismal water. However, from ancient times it has also been able to be conferred by pouring the water three times over the candidate's head." *Catechism of the Catholic Church* (New York: Doubleday, 1997), 348.

76. As part of the reforms brought about through the Second Vatican Council, *The Rite of Christian Initiation of Adults* was published in 1972 (widely available online). Aidan Kavanagh commends this document as an important step toward a unitive, holistic view of Christian initiation in this way: "Rather than regarding the sacraments as separate entities, each containing a meaning exclusive to itself and apart from all others, the full rites of adult initiation presume that all the initiatory rites form *one closely articulated whole* which relates intimately with all the other non-initiatory sacraments and rites. The entire sacramental economy is thus viewed not as something divorced from and peripheral to Church life, but as *the very way in which that life is lived in common* and on the most crucial level. The vision is one in which *a sacramental theology and ecclesiology mate to become functions of one another*, producing *in the concrete* a church order of a particular (in this case Roman) kind. Sacraments are a realized ecclesiology in time and place. . . ." Kavanagh, *Shape of Baptism*, 127 (emphasis added).

77. Johnson, *Rites of Christian Initiation*, 222: "The process of ritual and theological disintegration, dissolution, or separation . . . is a *uniquely* Western Christian phenomenon. That the evolution of Christian initiation *could* have gone in a different direction altogether is demonstrated by the rites of the Eastern Christian churches. . . . The earlier integral and unitive pattern, seen already in the great Eastern mystagogues of the fourth and fifth centuries, continued through the centuries—as still

only serve to set in sharp contrast the new ecclesiology of Vatican II, dependent as it is on sacramental minimalism. While baptismal practice is attempting to move away from the dissolution of sacramental minimalism, the new ecclesiology has been based on and developed out of this very same sacramental minimalism. The continuity and discontinuity of the new ecclesiological outlook with this Latin tradition becomes clear when we examine the root and source of sacramental minimalism: the views of Blessed Augustine of Hippo expressed in his struggle against the Donatists.

today—to constitute the ritual process of Christian initiation in its entirety" (emphasis in the original).

4

THE DEEPER ROOTS IN AUGUSTINE:
CONTINUITY AND DISCONTINUITY

As we noted earlier, the roots of the sacramental theology that ascended to precedence at Vatican II reach beyond the medieval West and Scholasticism to Blessed Augustine of Hippo (354–430). The influence of Saint Augustine on sacramental theology in the post-schism West cannot be overemphasized.[78] With regard to Christian initiation, the significance of Blessed Augustine's contribution lay in his theological thought about what constitutes a "valid" sacrament.[79] With regard to the nature of the Church, he reached the point of doing nothing less than "creating a new theology of the church."[80]

It was in his response to the fourth-century Donatist schism[81]

---

78. Maxwell E. Johnson, *The Rites of Christian Initiation: Their Evolution and Interpretation* (Collegeville, MN: Liturgical Press, 1999), 147.

79. Ibid.

80. Philip Cary, *Outward Signs: The Powerlessness of External Things in Augustine's Thought* (Oxford: Oxford University Press, 2008), 195. "With his Platonist inwardness he reconceives the unity of the church and the power of Baptism."

81. In 313, a division occurred among the African Christians that lasted more than a century. Accusing Caecilian, the newly elected bishop of Carthage, of not having ministered to a group of forty-seven Numidian martyrs imprisoned during the persecution of Diocletian (which ended in 311), a Bishop Secundus and seventy others consecrated a rival bishop named Majorinus and, when he died, another named Donatus, who gave his name to the ensuing schism.

that Blessed Augustine developed his ideas on "validity" and
the proper minister of Baptism. Against the Donatists' claim
that they were the legitimate church of North Africa and, as
such, could alone dispense the true sacraments whose authenticity and effectiveness were—so they maintained—dependent upon the worthiness and moral character of the minister,
Blessed Augustine argued that:

> Any Baptism that makes use of the proper element of
> water and the proper word (i.e. the Trinitarian baptismal
> interrogation) is "valid."[82]
> Any sacrament results from "the word . . . added to
> the element" and becomes "itself also a kind of visible
> word."[83]
> Any Baptism, or any sacrament, "consecrated by the
> words of the gospel, is necessarily holy, however polluted
> and unclean its ministers may be,"[84] for Christ, not the
> purity of the minister, makes Baptism effective.[85]

Holding to the "validity" of schismatic or heretical Baptism
does not, however, therefore mean, according to Blessed Augustine, that a "valid" Baptism is necessarily "fruitful." "Augustine himself taught that, although sacraments administered
outside the Church were valid, they were wholly devoid of
the Holy Spirit."[86] Blessed Augustine made a distinction here

---

82. *Contra litteras Petiliani*, 1.6.6. See also Johnson, *Rites of Christian Initiation*, 151.

83. *Tractates on the Gospel of John*, NPNF 80.3; PL 35.1840. Available online at http://www.ccel.org/ccel/schaff/npnf107.iii.lxxxi.html.

84. *On Baptism*, NPNF 3.10.15.

85. Cf. *Tractates on the Gospel of John*, etc.

86. H. E. J. Cowdrey, "The Dissemination of St. Augustine's Doctrine of Holy Orders During the Later Patristic Age," *Journal of Theological*

between validity and efficacy, or in other words, between the sacrament or sign itself (sacramentum) and its reality, fruitfulness, or usefulness (res sacramenti). As Geoffrey Willis states in his study of Blessed Augustine's doctrine of the ministration of the sacraments: "The grace is there [outside the Church], latent and useless, valid but not efficacious to salvation or to the well-being of souls, until it be revivified by the fructifying gift of charity within the fold of the Church."[87]

Blessed Augustine treats "the unity of the church as inward, but the sacrament itself as outward."[88] As Philip Cary puts it: "As a mere sign, the sacrament has no power of its own to accomplish what it signifies (as in the semiotics of *On the Teacher*) and gets its significance from the agreement of will among those who use it rightly (as in the semiotics of *On Christian Doctrine*). Hence when it is found outside the Catholic church it is devoid of salvific power but retains its meaning and holiness, which stem not from its external circumstances but from its ultimate origin in the Catholic communion."[89]

For Blessed Augustine, the schismatics and heretics have "lawful Baptism, but they do not have it lawfully."[90] Although Augustine at times makes the case that he is following his predecessor St. Cyprian of Carthage, this important Augustinian distinction between lawful or valid baptism and having it

Studies, n.s., 20:2 (October 1969), 480.

87. Geoffrey Grimshaw Willis, *Saint Augustine and the Donatist Controversy* (Eugene OR: Wipf and Stock, 2005; reprint of London: S.P.C.K., 1950), 156.

88. Cary, *Outward Signs*, 196.

89. Ibid.

90. *On Baptism*, NPNF 5.7.8. A "lawful" or "legitimate" baptism is synonymous with a "valid" baptism, since, as he writes in this context, "we recognize the sacrament of the Lord in the words of the gospel."

lawfully and therefore fruitfully does not exist in the hieromartyr's letters.[91] For St. Cyprian, the question is whether Baptism
exists at all outside the Church, apart from the Eucharistic
assembly, not whether or not it exists lawfully. For Augustine,
since the proper element of water is used and the "words of
the gospel" have been pronounced, the power of the sacrament remains latent in the sign, and therefore lawful or valid
Baptism is obvious and undeniable. As Augustine writes: "The
word is cojoined to the element and sacrament is constituted,
it itself becoming, in its turn, as it were, a visible word. . . . For
in that very word, whereas the actual sound is transitory, the
power remains."[92]

There is, then, a power *inherent* in the sacrament that brings
to bear upon the recipient the sanctifying work of Christ in
the Holy Spirit regardless of the moral or spiritual status of
the minister. Here the doctrine of instrumental causality subsequently developed by Aquinas is obscurely foreshadowed.
Even more clearly, although incipiently, one can perceive the

---

91. In *On Baptism*, NPNF 5.7.8, Augustine quotes St. Cyprian when
he warns that if the bishops of the Church were to accept "that the baptism with which [the schismatics and heretics] are baptized in heresy
is considered just and lawful, they will think that they are in just and
lawful possession of the Church also, and all its other gifts." Augustine
then writes, "He does not say 'that they will think they are in possession,' but 'in just and lawful possession of the gifts of the Church.' But
we say that we cannot allow that they are *in just and lawful possession*
of baptism. That they are in possession of it we cannot deny, when we
recognize the sacrament of the Lord in the words of the gospel. They
have therefore lawful baptism, but they do not have it lawfully." Although Augustine initially appears to agree with St. Cyprian, he then
states his cornerstone distinction, that they *do* have lawful baptism, but
not lawfully.

92. *Tractates on the Gospel of John*, NPNF 80.3; PL 35.1840.

doctrine that the sacraments work *ex opera operato*. As the sacraments "have their origin in Christ and the spiritual reality they signify is Christ Himself, they possess *an objective intrinsic value and sanctity of their own that cannot be affected or diminished by the personal unworthiness of their human minister*."[93]

For St. Cyprian and the subsequent Eastern tradition none of this would be objectionable if the minister and sacrament in question were *within* the Church, within the eucharistic synaxis. For, as Christ is the author and institutor of the sacraments, and the word that makes the material element a sacrament is the word of faith spoken by the Church through Her representative, how is it that a schismatic or heretic, who is cut off from Christ and not a representative of the Church, can possess legitimate Baptism?

Of course, already in the third and fourth centuries the Church began to accept certain groups of heretics without baptizing them, as is clearly delineated by St. Basil the Great. Nevertheless,

> [It] is clear that in the practice of receiving schismatics and heretics into the Church that which was basic and fundamental was uniting them to the unity and communion of the Church and not the recognition of any "objective" mysteries among the heretics. Thus it is apparent that St. Cyprian's principle that the charismatic and canonical boundaries of the Church coincide continues to be in effect. Indeed, the charismatic and canonical boundaries of the Church are manifest in practice in the one Eucharist of the one true Church, into which those

93. See the introduction to Blackfriars' translation of the *Summa Theologica* of Thomas Aquinas, vol. 56, *On the Sacraments* (London: Blackfriars with Eyre and Spottiswoode, 1975), xvi (emphasis added).

returning now commune and in this way belong to the Church. For, outside of the Eucharist, outside of the Liturgical communion, there is no Church. This is the content and meaning of the entire canonical tradition of the Church.[94]

This synthesis of St. Cyprian's ecclesiology with the subsequent practice of the Church, as is evident in St. Basil the Great's canons, will remain elusive to the post-schism West. It was, rather, Blessed Augustine's teaching on schismatic and heretical sacraments that proved crucial for the whole development of the West after the Great Schism, and even for the Reformers of the sixteenth century.[95] It is indicative of the degree of Blessed Augustine's influence that, of those sources cited for the teaching that the validly baptized in the dissident communities are "genuine members of the one true Church of Jesus Christ," Yves Congar names only one pre-schism source: Blessed Augustine.[96]

---

94. Ἀθανασίου Γιέβτιτς [Athanasius Yevtich], Ἐπισκόπου πρ. Ζαχουμίου καὶ Ἐρζεγοβίνης, "Ὁ π. Γεώργιος Φλωρόφσκυ περὶ τῶν ὁρίων τῆς Ἐκκλησίας" [Fr. Georges Florovsky on the Boundaries of the Church], Θεολογία 81:4 (Oct.–Dec. 2010), 137–58 (151). The manner of reception of heterodox into the Orthodox Church is specified by various canons, including: Apostolic Canons 46, 47, and 50, Canons 8 and 19 of the First Ecum. Council, Canon 7 of the Second Ecum. Council, Canon 95 of the Sixth Ecum. Council, Canon of the Council of Carthage under St. Cyprian, and Canons 1, 5, and 47 of St. Basil.

95. Walter Kasper, "Ecclesiological and Ecumenical Implications of Baptism," *The Ecumenical Review* (Geneva: WCC, 2000), part 3.

96. Yves M.-J. Congar, O.P., *Divided Christendom, A Catholic Study of the Problem of Reunion*, trans. M. A. Bousfield (London: Geoffrey Bles: The Centenary Press, 1939), 230–31. However, Congar's claim of Augustinian support is problematic. The text Congar cites is far from an explicit endorsement of membership in the Church for the Donatist

Moreover, after the Great Schism his theology will clothe the already differentiated stance of Rome with a complex, even if narrow, ecclesiological explanation and thus definitively separate the West from the Orthodox on the question. After medieval modifications, the differences that appear will not be limited to theology alone. The minimalism of the neo-Scholastic manuals of the nineteenth and early twentieth centuries can ultimately be traced back, through Aquinas, to Blessed Augustine's theology. For, as Maxwell Johnson has said, in Augustine's vision and theology of Baptism, "we see the beginnings of a minimalistic approach to rite, interpretation, candidate, minister, and Church and a loss of sacramental and liturgical richness in favor of a concern for sacramental validity."[97] This descent into sacramental minimalism is generated by and further generates theological minimalism and disintegration, such that the catholic understanding of the mysteries as inseparable from the visible Body of Christ is lost.

Blessed Augustine's sacramental theology and ecclesiology represent a break with the patristic consensus before him as expressed from as early as St. Ignatius the God-bearer and up into his own day in the East with St. Basil the Great and St. John Chrysostom, among others. To provide only two examples here:

First, St. Augustine clearly saw any "valid" Baptism performed by schismatics and heretics as the one Baptism of the Church (even if unprofitable for them while they remained

schismatics: "We do not acknowledge any Baptism of yours for it is not the Baptism of schismatics or heretics, but of God and of the Church, wheresoever it may be found, and whithersoever it may be transferred" (*On Baptism*, NPNF 1.14.22.). See our analysis of Augustine's view of membership in chapter 6.

97. Johnson, *Rites of Christian Initiation*, 156.

outside the Church), such that it must not be repeated when and if they returned to the Church.[98] To the contrary, St. Basil the Great, in his second canonical letter to St. Amphilochios,[99] clearly rejected the Baptism of certain schismatics (Encratitæ,[100] Saccophors, and Apotactitæ) even if they kept the form and called upon the name of the Holy Trinity in Baptism, and he directed Amphilochios to baptize them.[101] St. Basil urges

98. See *On Baptism*, NPNF 1.12.18, 1.14.22, 1.19.29, for example.

99. His Canon 47.

100. The Encratite sect, led initially by Tatian, the former disciple of St. Justin Martyr, and later by a certain Severus, held heretical views on marriage, the eating of meat, and drinking of wine, and used water instead of wine in the Eucharist. St. Epiphanius says the following concerning this sect and their mysteries: "They are outside of the truth, 'having the form of godliness, but denying the power thereof.' For if a person neglects any part of a work such as this, through the one part which he neglects he has given up the whole of it. And so it is that their mysteries are celebrated only with water, and are not mysteries but false mysteries, celebrated in imitation of the true ones" (*Panarion*, 4.3.1). *The Panarion of Epiphanius of Salamis*, Books II and III, *De Fide*, trans. Frank Williams (Boston: Brill, 2013; 2nd rev. ed.), p. 5. Available online at: http://www.scribd.com/doc/166106444/Frank-Williams-the-Panarion-of-Epiphanius-of-Salamis-Books-II-and-III-de-Fide-2013#scribd.   St. Epiphanius makes no mention of heretical views regarding the Trinity (*Panarion*, 4.1.1–4.3.1). Eusebius quotes St. Irenaeus' *Against Heresies* on Tatian and this sect, describing him as an "apostate" from the Church but adding nothing in the way of Trinitarian heresy. St. Basil, likewise, lists the Encratites alongside the Cathari and Hydroparastatae as schismatics, not heretics. That is, the Trinitarian form of their baptism was not doubted.

101. Canon 47: "Encratitæ, Saccophors and Apotactitæ all come under the same rule as the Novatians. For a Canon was promulgated concerning the latter, although it varies from place to place; whereas nothing specific has been said regarding the former. Be that as it may, we simply rebaptize such persons. If among yourselves the measure of rebaptizing is banned, as it more surely is among the Romans for the sake

Amphilochios to ignore the practice of the Romans who refuse to baptize on account of some economia, directing him to pay no heed to returning heretics when they say "we have been baptized in the Father and the Son and the Holy Spirit." With this stance, St. Basil ignored and directly contradicted Canon 9 of the Western Council of Arles,[102] which Augustine would later praise repeatedly in his main anti-Donatist work, *On Baptism.*[103]

of some *economia*, nevertheless let what we say prevail. For their heresy is something of an offshoot of the Marcionites who abominate marriage, and disdain wine, and say that God's creation is defiled. Therefore we do not receive them into the Church unless they be baptized in our baptism. And let them not say, 'We have been baptized in the Father and the Son and the Holy Spirit,' when they suppose—as they do in a manner rivaling Marcion and the rest of the heresies—that God is the maker of things evil. Hence if this please you, then more bishops must come together and thus set forth the Canon, so as to afford security to him who performs [rebaptism], and so that he who defends this practice might be considered trustworthy when responding on such matters." Πηδάλιον, τοῦ Ἱερομονάχου Ἀγαπίου καὶ Μοναχοῦ Νικοδήμου (Ἀθήνα: Κωνσταντίνου Γκαρπολᾶ, 1841), 369; English translation by the editors of George Metallinos, *I Confess One Baptism: Interpretation and Application of Canon VII of the Second Ecumenical Council by the Kollyvades and Constantine Oikonomos* (Mt. Athos, Greece: St. Paul's Monastery, 1994), 131.

102. Canon 9, Council of Arles, in C. Munier, *Concilia Galliae a.314–a.506* (Turnhout: Brepols, 1963), 9–13: "it is resolved that if any come to the church from heresy, they question him on the creed (used at his Baptism), and if they consider him to have been baptized into the Father and the Son and the Holy Spirit, let him only receive the laying on of hands so that he receive the Holy Spirit; but if when questioned he does not solemnly confess this Trinity, let him be baptized."

103. Many Western scholars would like to see St. Basil as an exponent of a more "moderate" or "nuanced" view than his predecessor St. Firmillian, akin to that of Blessed Augustine. They are also not prepared to accept the "theory of *economia*" as an explanation for his

Second, St. Augustine taught that one must distinguish the heretics' doctrines from their use of the sacraments, which belong to Christ and the Church (*On Baptism* 1.12.19). St. Athanasius the Great, on the other hand, taught that on account of heretical doctrine, even though the heretics use the Names of the Trinity and perform the rite in an Orthodox manner, their Baptism pollutes rather than redeems. Orthodox faith is

approach, and so with Canons 1 and 47 they are at a loss to make sense of St. Basil's reasoning. However, in this canon it is apparent that St. Basil's Church of Caesarea, if not Asia Minor generally, continued in the tradition and teaching of the councils of Iconium, Synnada, and Carthage. To claim that St. Basil held views akin to those of Blessed Augustine would be as far-fetched as claiming that Rome adopted the views of St. Firmilian and the East. For readings of St. Basil's first canon along these lines, see Will Cohen, "Sacraments and the Visible Unity of the Church," *Ecclesiology* 4.1 (2007), 68–87, Speaking of St. Basil's "incoherent logic," contradictions, lack of theological reasoning, and supposed changes of opinion in his first canon, Mr. Cohen writes: "It is notable that even as his various explanations shift from one basis to another, Basil ends up actually behaving very much in accordance with what Augustine prescribes in *De Baptismo*" (75). See also Walter Kasper, "The Decree on Ecumenism—Read Anew After Forty Years," Pontifical Council for Promoting Christian Unity, Conference on the 40th Anniversary of the Promulgation of the Conciliar Decree "Unitatis Redintegratio," Rocca di Papa, Mondo Migliore, November 11, 12, and 13, 2004. Here Kasper states that, in the East, on the one hand there is the "rigid position" of Cyprian and Firmilian, rejecting the baptism of heretics, while, on the other hand, "there is the nuanced position of Basil of Caesarea," who "did not reject the baptism of schismatics." Kallistos Ware, Metropolitan of Diokleia, holds that "Basil himself is somewhat inconsistent in his usage." He also writes that, while St. Cyprian "is the champion of the 'rigorist' position, the classic exponents of the 'moderate' view are Basil and Augustine." "The Rebaptism of Heretics in the Orthodox Canonical Tradition," published in *Heresy and the Making of European Culture: Medieval and Modern Perspectives,* ed. James R. Simpson and Andrew P. Roach (London and Burlington: Ashgate, 2013).

regarded as sine qua non for the accomplishment of a saving Mystery. Invoking the Names of the Persons of the Holy Trinity is insufficient. There first must come Orthodox teaching, followed by Orthodox faith, and only then the saving Baptism.[104]

This point is often neglected by scholars, or, if admitted, Blessed Augustine's peculiar theories are justified as necessary in order to bring an end to the Donatist schism.[105] However, as C. H. Turner points out, that which was of higher value was the Holy Tradition:

> The historian of Christian doctrine may venture the judgment that in order to achieve this short-cut to reunion Saint Augustine sacrificed something of higher value when *he threw over the inherited tradition of the Church on the subject of sacraments*. The divorce of the theology of the sacraments from the theology of the Church was a heavy price to pay even for the union with the Donatists.[106]

Nevertheless, for the West, Blessed Augustine's position became the criterion. As we have already mentioned, the Fourth Lateran Council, and the councils of Trent and Florence, defended the validity of heretical Baptism on the basis of what was a restatement of the Augustinian doctrine. For medieval Catholicism there was no other position even to consider. The

---

104. See St. Athanasius the Great, *Second Discourse Against the Arians*, PG 26.237b.42–43. See also chapter 13 herein on "Baptism and the Unity of Faith" for further discussion of this patristic position.

105. See Willis, *Saint Augustine and the Donatist Controversy*, 153, for one such example.

106. C. H. Turner, "*Apostolic Succession*," Sect. B, "The Problem of Non-Catholic Orders," p. 143; in H. B. Swete, *Essays on the Early History of the Church and the* Ministry (London: Macmillan, 1918), as quoted in Willis, 167 (emphasis added).

teaching of the Eastern Fathers—Ss. Athanasius, Cyril of Jerusalem, Basil the Great, John Chrysostom, and Gregory the
Theologian—on the question was either unknown or ignored.
For Thomas Aquinas and the Scholastics, the patristic position
was that of Blessed Augustine. Even for the theologians of
Vatican II, who consciously sought a *ressourcement* and return
to the Church Fathers, there was no question of a recovery of
the patristic consensus on this question, only a revisiting of the
teaching of Saint Augustine through the lens of Aquinas.[107]

During the interwar years, there was "a re-discovery of St.
Augustine after the great silence which was a consequence of
the Jansenist controversy"[108] in the seventeenth and eighteenth
centuries. At that time, in response to the provocation of the
Jansenists,[109] Pope Clement XI issued his dogmatic constitu-

107. According to Jurgën Mettepenningen, in his important survey
of the historical development and catalytic texts of the *nouvelle théologie*, all of the pioneers of renewal before Vatican II showed particular
interest in Augustine. It is noteworthy that in Mettepenningen's study
little mention is made of the Eastern Fathers being an object of these
theologians' interest (*Nouvelle Théologie—New Theology: Inheritor of Modernism, Precursor of Vatican II* [London: T and T Clark, 2010)], 145).
Henri de Lubac and Joseph Ratzinger, to give two examples, began their
efforts of *ressourcement* with studies focused on the theology of Saint
Augustine. De Lubac is considered the most eminent representative of
the *nouvelle théologie*, invariably with reference to his book *Surnaturel*, a
historical study of theology related to the supernatural, which critiqued
neo-Scholasticism. In this book, De Lubac showed greater interest in
Augustine, at the expense of Thomas Aquinas, which earned him the
wrath of the neo-Scholastic establishment. Likewise, Joseph Ratzinger's
first dissertation in graduate school was on the subject "The People of
God and the House of God in Augustine's Doctrine of the Church." In
both cases, the ecclesiology of Church Fathers other than Augustine is
not of particular interest.

108. Mettepenningen, *Nouvelle Théologie*, 99.

109. Through the seventeenth century and into the eighteenth, Jan-

tion *Unigenitus,* which was a condemnation of 101 different propositions made in a book by Paschasius Quesnel. Among the propositions condemned was "Outside of the Church, no grace is granted" (no. 29). Indirectly, this was at the same time a condemnation of the teaching of Blessed Augustine that "no man can receive the Holy Spirit, or be a partaker of the divine love, who is not a member of the unity of Christ,"[110] for "essential grace is lacking . . . to all those outside the Church"—that is, "the grace of charity, the first of the Spirit's fruits."[111]

Therefore, in addition to bypassing the patristic consensus on our question, an unmitigated return to Blessed Augustine's

senism was a distinct movement within the Roman Catholic Church, primarily in France, that emphasized original sin, human depravity, the necessity of divine grace, and predestination. The movement originated from the posthumously published work of the Dutch theologian Cornelius Otto Jansen, who died in 1638. It was first popularized by Jansen's friend Jean du Vergier, Abbé de Saint-Cyran, and after Saint-Cyran's death in 1643 was led by Antoine Arnauld. Jansenism was opposed by many in the Catholic hierarchy, especially the Jesuits. Although the Jansenists identified themselves only as rigorous followers of Augustinism, the Jesuits identified them as having Calvinist affinities. The bull *Cum occasione,* issued by Pope Innocent X in 1653, condemned five cardinal doctrines of Jansenism as heresy—especially the relationship between human free will and efficacious grace, wherein the teachings of Augustine contradicted the teachings of the Jesuit School. After a measure of peace in the late seventeenth century, further controversy led to the bull *Unigenitus,* issued by Pope Clement XI in 1713, which marked the end of Catholic toleration of Jansenist doctrine. For their part, the Jansenists insisted that they were simply repeating and following the teachings of Saint Augustine on grace.

110. Willis, 116. See Saint Augustine, Epistle 185, 48–50.

111. Willis, 125. To be more precise, St. Augustine held that it existed among the Donatists but that it was latent or held in suspense and therefore useless (because of their lack of love) and would only be revived upon union with the Church.

theology by the theologians of the *nouvelle théologie* and Vatican II was also ruled out as a result of the Jansenist condemnation. Karl Adam,[112] one of the most important figures in the early twentieth-century renewal of Roman Catholic ecclesiology, explains this departure from Blessed Augustine thus:

> We are not to regard these sacraments [of non-Catholics] thus administered outside the Church as being objectively valid only, and not also subjectively efficacious. Blessed Augustine seems to have held such a view regarding the efficacy of these sacraments. . . . The Jansenists in the seventeenth century followed Blessed Augustine and advocated the same erroneous opinion, setting it up as their principle that "outside the Church there is no grace" (extra ecclesiam nulla conceditur gratia). But again *it was Rome and a pope that expressly rejected this proposition.* The assertion that the Catholic Church of later centuries has developed the ideas of St. Cyprian and Blessed Augustine . . . is *in contradiction* with the plain facts of history. For the truth is that the later Church corrected the original rigorism of the ancient African theologian and maintained that *God's grace worked even outside the Catholic*

---

112. Karl Adam was a renowned scholar of both Christology and ecclesiology in the German inter-war period. He is considered, together with Johann Adam Möhler and Romano Guardini, to be one of the greatest representatives of German theological thought in the nineteenth and early twentieth centuries. These theologians are considered pioneers in the renewal in Roman Catholic ecclesiology, and Adam in particular as a pathfinder to Roman Catholic involvement in ecumenism. Adam's book, *The Spirit of Catholicism* (first published in 1929; then by Macmillan, 1943; Crossroad, 1997), was an attempt to recover the ancient ecclesiology of the patristic age and was very influential for succeeding generations and translated into many languages.

body. Non-Catholic sacraments have the power to sanctify and save, not only objectively, but also subjectively. It is therefore conceivable also, from the Church's standpoint, that there is true, devout and Christian life in those non-Catholic communions which believe in Jesus and baptize in His Name.[113]

Adam touches upon a very important point: Rome, after the Great Schism, expressly rejected Blessed Augustine's view and maintained that God's grace works outside the Church, in the "sacraments" of schismatics and heretics. But, in fact, this view was not peculiar to Blessed Augustine, as much of his ecclesiology was. It is ironic that, precisely on that point on which Blessed Augustine agreed with all his predecessors[114]—that there is no sacramental Grace outside the Church—on that point Rome "expressly rejected" the proposition. This is of the utmost importance, really the basis for the entire post-schism development of Latin theology in regard to this question.

Therefore we see that this aspect of patristic doctrine, hav-

---

113. Adam, *The Spirit of Catholicism*, 191 (emphasis added).

114. We will discuss the early Fathers' teaching on this matter further on. However, let us cite here what G. Willis wrote in his study on St. Augustine and the Donatists when reviewing the teaching of the Holy Fathers before St. Augustine: "Irenaeus . . . holding as he does *with all primitive Fathers* that the Church is the sole fountain of grace, and that outside it none can be assured of salvation or of sacramental grace, would have ruled out as entirely worthless the sacraments of schismatics . . ." (145, emphasis added). Cf. also Ἰωάννου Ζηζιούλα [John Zizioulas], Μητροπολίτου Περγάμου, Ἡ ἑνότης τῆς Ἐκκλησίας ἐν τῇ Θείᾳ Εὐχαριστίᾳ καί τῷ Ἐπισκόπῳ κατά τούς τρεῖς πρώτους αἰῶνας, 1965 (Athens: Grigori, 2009), 132: "Both [St. Cyprian and Pope Stephen] held that the Holy Spirit is not imparted to those baptized outside the Church. . . . [T]his is the consensus of the entire Church in the middle of the third century."

ing been roughly incorporated into the Jansenist dogmatic portfolio, was hitherto officially, if indirectly, rejected.[115] That this rejection of a fundamental feature of patristic ecclesiology did indeed pass into the ecclesiological outlook of the Roman Catholic Church and her theologians is apparent one hundred and fifty years later in the thought of the nineteenth-century Anglican convert to Catholicism John Henry Newman.

In Newman's book *Certain Difficulties Felt by Anglicans in Catholic Teaching,* written years after his conversion to Catholicism, he considers, along with his own English Protestants, the "fearful state" of the Greek people of his day. For them, he says, "faith is but material and obedience mechanical, and religion . . . superstition instead of a reasonable service." And, yet, he happily allows for exceptions, and even if the country is given up to heresy or schism, still it "is far from being in the miserable state of a heathen population: it has portions of the truth . . . and supernatural channels of grace." "Thus, the blessing is inestimable" to England and Greece where "the whole population may be considered regenerate" in "so far as the Sacrament of Baptism is validly administered."

Newman goes on to say: "And further, if we consider that there is a true priesthood in certain countries, and a true sacrifice, the benefits of Mass to those who never had the means of knowing better, may be almost the same as they are in the Catholic Church." Those humble souls who suffer under the effects of the errors of their Communion may still "obtain, as well as we, remission of such sins as the Sacrifice directly effects, and that supernatural charity which wipes out greater ones."[116]

---

115. To be sure, Blessed Augustine's theological explanation was nuanced and complex, whereas the Jansenist reproduction of it was more simplistic.

116. J. H. Newman, "Heretical and Schismatical Bodies no Prejudice

Newman's reflections on the schismatics and heretics of his day reveal those aspects of Blessed Augustine's thought that were retained in his time, and prefigure the development that will ensue with *nouvelle théologie* and Vatican II. Newman agrees with Blessed Augustine that the Sacrament itself is not limited to members of the visible Catholic Church. He departs, however, from the African Father's teaching concerning the efficacy or profitability of the sacrament, viz., that "no grace is available [to those outside], though the empty shell of the sacrament is possessed. If they remain outside the Church all their lives, they receive nothing"[117]; and only if and when they are reconciled to the unity of the Church will the latent grace revive and what was possessed before uselessly or more probably to their damnation be crowned with the gift of love and become life-giving.[118] Newman considers schismatics and heretics to be regenerated by Baptism even while apart from the Church, a point that Blessed Augustine fought hard not to concede to the dissidents of his time, the Donatists.[119]

to Catholicity of the Church," in *Certain Difficulties Felt By Anglicans in Catholic Teaching* (1908), 1: 351–53.

117. Willis, 167.

118. *On Baptism*, NPNF 3.10.13–15 and 1.12.18. See also Willis, 156–60.

119. Ibid. See also Willis, 156. His innovative explanation for how one is baptized but not ultimately regenerated is, however, not consistent with the patristic consensus and, according to Philip Cary, is "one of the strangest arguments Augustine ever made" (*Outward Signs*, 201). It is true that even medieval theologians refused to accept Augustine's explanation for how schismatics can be baptized but have their sins immediately return upon them such that the regeneration they received in Baptism is worthless (see *On Baptism*, NPNF 1.12.18–19 and 5.8.9). Therefore, it may have been inevitable that, gradually, from the medieval theologians' limited admittance of certain kinds of spiritual efficacy connected to every valid sacrament, Latin theology would arrive today

That other Holy Mysteries besides Holy Baptism, such as Ordination and the Holy Eucharist, could be present among the schismatics or heretics, both Newman and Blessed Augustine agree.[120] That they could be fruitful outside the unity of the Church, in this Newman again departs from Blessed Augustine. He likewise grants that the grace of charity is present and active in wiping out the sins of the schismatic or heretic, whereas Blessed Augustine, recognizing the force of the tradi-

at the total acceptance of spiritual efficacy in every valid sacrament performed outside the Church. The question arises: If Augustine's sacramental theology and ecclesiology had been founded upon the rock of Holy Tradition and inspired by the Holy Spirit, would it have been thus abandoned? See Cary's discussion of this in *Outward Signs,* 200–205.

120. In this St. Augustine innovates, departing even from Pope Stephen. "However much Stephen and Cyprian differed about Baptism, it was common ground to them, and it would seem, not only to all their contemporaries but to their successors of the next generations for another hundred years, that no other sacrament could be validly administered in heresy or schism. The gift of the Holy Spirit, whether in confirmation [chrismation] or ordination, was recognized on both sides as reserved to the Holy Church." (Attributed to C. H. Turner, "Apostolic Succession," 160–61, as quoted in Willis, 160). One could also cite the important Apostolic Canon 47 as witness to the common mind of the Church in the late third to early fourth centuries: that the acceptable baptism is that performed by true priests of the Church. The canon reads: "If a bishop or presbyter baptize anew anyone that has had a true baptism, or fail to baptize someone that had been polluted by the impious, let him be defrocked, on the grounds that he is mocking the cross and death of the Lord, and fails to distinguish priests from false priests." Since we know that it was universal practice to reject the ordinations of heretics and to ordain those returning to the Church who had been ordained in the heresy, it is clear that by "fails to distinguish priests from false priests" this canon sees all priests of heretical sects as "false priests," and thus their baptisms as "pollutions of the impious." See Archbishop Peter Huillier, *The Church of the Ancient Councils* (Crestwood, New York: St. Vladimir's Seminary Press, 1996), 60.

tional teaching (as expressed by, among others, St. Cyprian), maintains that only within unity can the grace of charity be possessed.[121]

So it is that Blessed Augustine's step away from the *consensus patrum* was followed later by Catholicism's step away from his theology. Catholicism, in the fallout and milieu of the Reformation and the Jansenist controversy, had solidified its rejection of Blessed Augustine's crucial distinction in sacramental theology and ecclesiology—the distinction between *sacramentum* and *res sacramenti*, or between sacrament and its usefulness, for those outside the Church. This distinction set Catholicism apart from the patristic tradition but also, paradoxically, and in contrast to what was to come, kept it somewhat tied to the tradition. It was Blessed Augustine's own peculiar theory; and, yet, by formally doing away with it Catholicism moved even further away from the pre-Augustine patristic consensus.

Newman and his contemporaries, such as Johann Adam Möhler,[122] and later Yves Congar and his generation, inherited

121. Willis, 159.
122. Johann Adam Möhler (1796–1838), a prominent theologian, Church historian, and leading representative of the Catholic Tübingen School, is today considered by many the father of the modern Roman Catholic renewal of ecclesiology. Möhler followed closely Johann Sebastian von Drey (1777–1853), the founder of this school and his mentor, in seeing the Church Tradition as the necessary focus of historical and theological attention. Möhler's view of Tradition incorporated the notions of change and revelation, such that the development of doctrine is, for him, an undeniable historical fact. As Drey did, Möhler sees the task of theology as the discernment of the eternal from the contingent in its historical manifestations. Möhler, along with Newman, heavily influenced renewal-oriented theologians of the twentieth century, and both are credited for providing the initial theological impetus for Vatican II's new ecclesiology.

this departure from Blessed Augustine's sacramental theology and ecclesiology apparently uncritically. This is because they were viewing Augustine through the lens of Aquinas and his contemporaries, who were among the first to depart from Augustine on the question. Newman, Möhler, and later Congar were not alone in standing apart from Augustine, nor were they breaking radically from establishment thinking on the matter, nor could they. The fact is that the "official" view had, at least since the days of Aquinas, been under continuous development.

5

THE AQUINAN BREAK WITH AUGUSTINE ON THE SIGNIFICANCE OF BAPTISM FOR THOSE OUTSIDE THE CHURCH

I n the writings of Thomas Aquinas on Baptism there are significant changes in understanding from that of Augustine. Aquinas offered a different answer to the question of why schismatic and heretical baptism is valid but not efficacious, and his explanation of the meaning of "baptismal character" differed as well. In this chapter, we see how these changes effected a change in how membership in the Church is understood—a very important point for our understanding of *Unitatis Redintegratio.*

As noted previously, the Roman Catholic teaching on the ability of those outside the church to impart Baptism has remained constant, at least since the high Middle Ages. Heretics, even pagans, can validly baptize under certain basic conditions. What this "valid Baptism" signified, how it accorded with ecclesiology, and whether it could also be fruitfully received unto a life of grace and salvation had, on the other hand, been neither clearly nor consistently presented until Vatican II.

Initially, despite its peculiar view of heretical Baptism, the Church of Rome maintained the patristic consensus on the grace of the Holy Spirit being present only within the mysteries of the Church. Pope Stephan, the fervent adversary of St. Cyprian and the entire East on the question of heretical Baptism, nonetheless expressed the patristic consensus that it was impossible for the Holy Spirit to be sacramentally imparted outside the Church. At the Council of Arles (in Gaul) in 314, in its ninth canon, concerning the Baptism of heretics, the same patristic position was upheld. Although the council introduced as the criterion for acceptance of heretical Baptism the preservation of the baptismal formula (the Trinitarian epiclesis), nonetheless, it did insist on the need for the Church to impart the Holy Spirit to heretics coming to Her.[123] The Pope of Rome from 384 to 398, St. Siricius, in his letter of 385, *Directa ad decessorem*, to Himerius, Bishop of Terracina, continues in the patristic tradition of recognizing the need of imparting the Holy Spirit to heretics joining the Church.[124] And, finally, as we have already noted, Augustine, in spite of his innovative sacramental theology and ecclesiology, maintained that, valid though the sacraments may be outside the Church, the Church is the exclusive vehicle of the Holy Spirit.[125]

Agreement with the patristic consensus that only the Church can impart the Grace of the Holy Spirit continued through the fifth and sixth centuries with the Popes of Rome remaining faithful to the rulings of Arles. From the time of the oft-quoted letter of Pope Innocent I in 414 to Bishop Alexander of Antioch dealing with an organized Arian body, until the time of Pope Pelagius I (556–561) in the sixth century, who adamantly expressed the thinking of St. Cyprian, the Roman Church remained steadfast in this teaching.[126]

123. See chapter 4, note 102.

124. Henry Denzinger, *The Sources of Catholic Dogma* (Fitzwilliam, NH: Loreto, 2007), 37.

125. H. E. J. Cowdrey, "The Dissemination of Blessed Augustine's Doctrine of Holy Orders during the Later Patristic Age," *Journal of Theological Studies*, n.s., 10:2 (October 1969), 451.

126. Ibid., 479.

Pope Pelagius' dedication to St. Cyprian points to a lesser known but very important historical fact: that during this period Blessed Augustine's teaching on schismatic and heretical mysteries, later adopted with great effect on Latin ecclesiology, was almost entirely ignored. When the matter of ordination imparted outside the Church was an issue, the pre-Augustinian position was upheld: a distinction was made between Baptism and the other sacraments, affording no clear grounds for maintaining the validity of the latter. "The sources provide no positive evidence that [from the fifth to the seventh centuries] the Latin West, in general, drew any distinction that was comparable with Augustine's between the sacramentum and the res sacramenti."[127] The West continued to ordain schismatics and heretics coming to the Church.

In *Contra epistolam Parmeniani*[128] and *De Correctione Donatistarum*,[129] among other places, we find Bl. Augustine's treatment of ordination. He drew "an explicit parallel between Baptism and ordination" (of the schismatics and heretics) and allowed that the sacrament need not be repeated in either case.[130] This idea came into direct contradiction with the ancient practice in Rome of the bishop laying hands on returning schismatics for the descent of the Holy Spirit:

> This gift came only with the reconciliation of the baptized person to the Church. Its medium was a laying on of hands, which was not, as a rule, distinguished from confirmation. So far as holy orders were concerned, a parity of argument with confirmation on a fortiori grounds was

127. Ibid., 480.
128. *Contra epistolam Parmeniani* 2.13.28–2.14.32.
129. *De Correctione Donatistarum, Epistolae* 185.44–47.
130. Cowdrey, 479.

inevitable: if the Holy Spirit could not be given outside
the Church in the sacrament of confirmation, how much
more could he not be given in the sacrament of holy
orders?[131]

Augustine's ideas would not rise to dominance until after
the schism, in the twelfth and thirteen centuries. With only one
exception, that of Pope Gregory I (590–604), was the question of reordination addressed in what was tantamount to the
peculiar Augustinian way. Even so, it was an isolated case in
which the authority of Augustine was not even appealed to,
and the West saw no significant change on the matter. The
seven intervening centuries saw "a long history of an underlying uncertainty concerning the legitimacy of sacraments, and
especially of ordinations, administered outside the Church"
(ibid.). The high medieval discussion from Peter Lombard
(1100–1160) to Raymond of Penafort (1175–1275) will succeed
in bringing Augustine's doctrine of holy orders to prominence,
"making it without doubt the generally accepted doctrine of
the Latin West."[132] This delay in the West—until after the Great
Schism—in adopting the full Augustinian view of sacraments
outside the Church corresponds historically with the adoption of a slightly altered view of the sacramental character by
Thomas Aquinas.[133]

131. Ibid.,457.
132. Ibid. 480. See also Bernard Leeming, S.J., *Principles of Sacramental Theology* (Westminster, MD: Newman Press, 1960), 521, where
the author states that only after the thirteenth century did Augustine's
teaching that "neither heresy nor wickedness as such invalidate[s] the
conferring of Orders" come to be "regarded as 'common and certain'
doctrine by all approved authors."
133. Aquinas' notion of sign was mainly gathered from Augustine,
but not only. Aquinas' view of linguistic signification is a result of the

For Augustine, the spiritual power of grace is a social power found only within hearts bound by charity, not in external things, words, or sacraments (signs). The validity of the sacrament belongs to the whole church and does not depend on either the minister or the recipient. The efficacy of the sacrament, however, depends on unity, which alone drives out sin, such that a lack of love, which puts people outside this unity (schism), renders a valid sacrament profitless. The external sacrament (sign) of Baptism is not an efficacious means of grace, for all spiritual efficacy is inward. Grace is not conferred by the sacred sign of Baptism, only marked outwardly.

This "seal" or character is an external sign of belonging, which, however, can be falsified if not accompanied by the good disposition of love and submission to the Church. When, and if, this sign of belonging, existing outside the Church, is united to true unity and communion, it need not be re-issued; that is, the schismatic need not be baptized. Augustine illustrates this point by analogy with the military mark, something like a tattoo given to soldiers when they are inducted into the army. The externality of Christian Baptism (as with the military character) is, therefore, a key feature of Augustine's theory.

Thomas Aquinas, in developing the medieval doctrine of baptismal character,[134] cites this argument of Augustine. Aquinas' use of the term "character" is, however, quite different than Augustine's. For Aquinas, character is an indelible mark

addition of Aristotle to Augustine (see Mark Jordan, *Ordering Wisdom: The Hierarchy of Philosophical Discourses in Aquinas* [Notre Dame: University of Notre Dame Press, 1996], 22). Also of great influence on Aquinas' thought is the teaching on sacramental character found in the writings of the Areopagite (discussed in the Introduction to the *Summa Theologica*, volume 56, *On the Sacraments*, p. xvii).

134. Cf. Aquinas, *Summa Theologica*, 3.63.1; 3.66 (esp.) a.9; 3.69.

on the soul,[135] which can never be removed.[136] For Augustine it is an external sign. He is "referring quite literally to a mark on the body, and using it as an analogy to explain the validity of the sacred sign of Baptism."[137] His theory is based upon the idea that the external sign of Baptism can be possessed by someone who is actually internally alien to the body of the Church and so bereft of the sacrament's effectiveness. This difference has grave implications for the meaning of sacramental efficacy.

For Aquinas the baptismal character produces spiritual effects and is sealed on the soul of all who are validly baptized. The sign, therefore, simply on account of being externally valid, brings about an enduring effect on the soul. This is exactly what does not happen in Augustine's theory: valid sacraments can be and many times are totally without spiritual efficacy.[138]

135. Ibid., 63.1.
136. Ibid., 63.5. As John P. Yocum writes concerning Aquinas' view of the indelibility of character as opposed to grace in the soul of the recipient of the sacraments: "Thomas distinguishes the two effects of the sacraments, grace and character, according to their permanence. The character is a kind of deputation to the service of divine worship, in which one is empowered to give or to receive the sacraments. As such it is indifferent to good or evil use, and may be misused, but is not effaced (Aquinas, *Summa Theologica*, 3.63.2, 3.63.4). While grace, he says, is in the soul as a form it is changeable as long as the soul itself is changeable; that is, it is subject to the effects of the exercise of free will, because its subject is the person who receives it. The character, however, is a kind of instrumental power and its subject is the principal agent, Christ, whose priesthood lasts forever." John P. Yocum, "Sacraments in Aquinas," in *Aquinas on Doctrine: A Critical Introduction*, ed. Thomas G. Weinandy et al. (London: T and T Clark, 2004), 172–73.
137. Philip Cary, *Outward Signs: The Powerlessness of External Things in Augustine's Thought* (Oxford: Oxford University Press, 2008), 201.
138. Ibid.

In this teaching of Aquinas we may have the first step toward the full, conciliar acceptance at Vatican II of the presence and workings of the Holy Spirit in the mysteries with regard to schismatics and heretics.[139]

As with Augustine, whose "new theology" of the Church was intended as a guarded development of the patristic consensus expressed before him, but who nevertheless laid the first foundation stone for much greater innovations, Aquinas can also be said to have laid the groundwork for later theological development.

In his *Summa Theologica*, question 64, answer 9, Aquinas does maintain in principle what Vatican II will later abandon

139. In contrast to both Augustine's and Aquinas' understanding of the term "seal," for the Church Fathers of the East, according to John D. Zizioulas, "the term σφραγὶς [seal] would never acquire . . . a strictly ontological meaning in the sense of πρᾶγμα [thing]; it would be understood rather as σχέσις [relation], which is usually *contrasted* by them with πρᾶγμα." (*Being As Communion: Studies in Personhood and the Church* [Crestwood, NY: St. Vladimir's Seminary Press, 1993], 235). It is also important to note that the unique Aquinan development of "character" or "seal" is totally absent in the sacramental theology of St. Nicholas Cabasilas, who sees "seal" as essentially synonymous with "anointing" and the other terms used to describe Baptism: "Baptism is called 'anointing' because on those who are initiated it engraves Christ, who was anointed for us. It is a 'seal' which imprints the Savior Himself. As the anointing is actually applied to the whole form of the body of him who is anointed, so it imprints on him the Anointed One and displays His form and is really a sealing. By what has been said it has been shown that the seal has the same effect as the birth, just as the clothing and the plunging [Baptism] effect the same as the sealing. Since the free gift, the illumination, and the washing have the same effect as the new creation and the birth, it is evident that all the nomenclature of Baptism signifies one thing—the baptismal washing is our birth and the beginning of our life in Christ." Nicholas Cabasilas, *The Life in Christ* (Crestwood, NY: St. Vladimir's Seminary Press, 1974), 69.

with regard to the "separated brethren," namely the Augustinian distinction between the "sacrament" and the "reality" of
the sacrament. Therein he states that there are heretics who
"observe the form prescribed by the church" and that they
"confer indeed the sacrament but not the reality." He is referring, however, as he stresses, to those "outwardly cut off from
the Church," such that one who "receives the sacraments from
them, sins and consequently is hindered from receiving the
effect of the sacrament." Their sin in receiving the sacrament
from known heretics is what obstructs their reception of the
reality, not the impossibility of the sacramental reality being
imparted outside of the Church.

Aquinas writes that anyone who receives the sacraments
from one excommunicated or defrocked "does not receive the
reality of the sacrament, unless ignorance excuses him." Thus,
for Aquinas, the obstacle to efficaciousness and the reality of
grace in the mystery is not necessarily the lack of unity, as Augustine would have it, but knowingly participating in the sin
of disobedience and rebellion. "The power of conferring sacraments" remains with the schismatic or heretical cleric, such
that one ignorantly receiving Baptism from him has not only
received a true sacrament, but has also received the spiritual
reality of Baptism, which includes initiation and incorporation
into Christ.

Aquinas writes the same in his *Commentary on the Sentences of Peter Lombard*, holding that "heretics and those cut off
from the Church confer true sacraments, but that no grace is
given, *not from defect in the sacraments, but because of the sin of
those who receive sacraments from such against the prohibition of
the Church*."[140] This is the most crucial point and that point

---

140. Leeming, 541 (emphasis added).

which separates post-schism Catholicism from Augustine and the pre-schism Church in the West. When, with Vatican II's re-evaluation of schismatics and heretics as "separated brethren," the council will not only lift any such prohibition but even encourage limited intercommunion, then the "life of grace" will be seen as springing from the dissidents' liturgical life and prayer, a life that opens up access to the assembly of those being saved (UR 3c).

It is precisely on this point of efficaciousness by way of ignorance and in seeing "character" as the sign of ecclesiastical membership that the fashioners of the new ecclesiology will form their new view of schism, heresy, and the Church. Aquinas provided, as it were, the building blocks with which to shape the new vision of the Church. The most important of these is that which would have every valid sacrament producing spiritual effects for all but those who knowingly commune with schism and heresy. Hence, following Aquinas, Bernard Leeming could state, even in 1960, before the advent of Vatican II, that, "if the sacrament is valid, its fruitfulness depends exclusively upon the disposition of the recipient."[141]

In this abolition, in practice, of the distinction between the sign and its fruitfulness the raison d'être of Augustine's ecclesiology ceases to exist. That is because Augustine's theological and pastoral efforts were entirely directed toward a return of the schismatics to the unity of the Church precisely because in schism he considered their sacraments to be empty and powerless.

Owing to the massive influence of Aquinas' theology, his understanding of baptismal character and efficacy was widely adopted. In the texts of the Council of Florence in the fifteenth

141. Ibid., 542.

century his influence is striking. The entire instruction on Baptism contained in the Decree for the Armenians of the Council of Florence is taken almost word for word from Aquinas' work "On the Articles of Faith and the Sacraments of the Church" (De articulis fidei et Ecclesiae sacramentis).

The council embraces Aquinas' teaching that through Holy Baptism "we are all made members of Christ and of the body of the Church." "True Baptism" is administered not only by a priest but also by "a layman or a woman, yes even a pagan and a heretic . . . so long as he preserves the form of the Church and has the intention of doing as the Church does." This sacrament "effects the remission of sins" and makes possible the attainment of the "kingdom of heaven and the vision of God."[142] Here Augustine's qualifications for a spiritually efficacious Baptism, namely charity within the unity of the Church, are conspicuously absent. It does seem that the only possible reading of the text is that the sacrament, simply on account of being externally valid, produces its effects: cleansing, incorporating, and opening the door to heaven.

The Council of Florence produced another document, however, which touts an Augustinian ecclesiology[143] and appears to contradict Aquinas' sacramental theology in the Decree for the Armenians. In the Bull *Cantate Domino*, Decree in behalf of the Jacobites, we read:

> [The holy Roman Church] . . . firmly believes, professes, and proclaims that those not living within the Catholic

142. Papal Bull, *Exultate Deo*, Decree for the Armenians (Nov. 22, 1439), in Denzinger, *Sources of Catholic Dogma*, 221.

143. The relevant sections of the decree are taken straight from the work *On the Truth of Predestination* by Augustine's sixth-century disciple Fulgentius of Ruspe (468–533).

Church, not only pagans, but also Jews and heretics and schismatics cannot become participants in eternal life... unless before the end of their life the same have been added to the flock; and that the unity of the ecclesiastical body is so strong that *only to those remaining in it are the sacraments of the Church of benefit for salvation* . . . [N]o one can be saved unless he has remained in the bosom and unity of the Catholic Church.[144]

The Augustinian prerequisite of living and remaining in the unity of the Church is predominant here, ruling out the possibility that external validity brings fruitful participation in the grace of God. Clearly, this decree does not consider heretics and schismatics to be a part of the flock, living members of the Church. But, then how is this to be reconciled with the Decree for the Armenians, which calls heretical Baptism not only "true" and capable of effecting remission of sins, but also capable of initiating the heretic into Christ and the Church? The two understandings appear to be irreconcilable.

In fact, this was the very dilemma faced by Augustine in his polemic against the Donatists. As we've already seen, medieval theologians did not entirely follow Augustine in his most crucial distinction: between the sacrament itself and its use or effect.[145] They went beyond Augustine and connected certain kinds of spiritual efficacy to every valid sacrament.[146] In the face of the long-held and universal connection of Baptism and regeneration, Augustine was also forced to make a similar con-

---

144. Papal Bull, *Cantate Domino,* Decree in behalf of the Jacobites (1441), in Denzinger, *Sources of Catholic Dogma,* 230 (emphasis added).
145. Cf. *On Baptism,* NPNF 3.10.13.
146. Cary, *Outward Signs,* 201.

cession; but, again, his peculiar solution was not adopted by Scholastic theologians.[147]

Augustine accepted that since valid Baptism was present among the schismatics, spiritual rebirth is there, as well. However, this power of rebirth is a gift that belongs to the Catholic Church—not to the schismatics. So, although regeneration can happen anywhere, not all to whom the Church gives birth belong to her unity, which alone saves.

This solution has its problems. Most remarkable of all is the idea that there is a Baptism that regenerates but does not save. Or, as Philip Cary puts it: "spiritual rebirth in Christ which has no salvific power. It is like a riddle. When does efficacy have no efficacy? . . . When it is attached to a valid sacrament outside the Catholic Church."[148]

The solution to this new problem takes Augustine into even deeper waters of peculiarity. How was Augustine going to explain regeneration without the Holy Spirit? And, secondly, if schismatics are truly "born again" in Christ, how can it be denied that their sins are also forgiven? This is how Russian New Martyr St. Hilarion Troitsky describes Augustine's solution:

> Augustine makes the strange assumption that presumably at the moment of Baptism, and only at that moment, the Holy Spirit operates outside the Church as well [in their mysteries]. The sins of the person being baptized— so goes Augustine's reasoning—are forgiven but return

147. See *On Baptism* NPNF 1.12.18–19 and 5.8.9 for St. Augustine's explanation for how schismatics can be baptized but have their sins immediately return upon them such that the regeneration they received in Baptism is worthless. See also Cary's discussion of this in *Outward Signs*, 200–205.

148. Cary, *Outward Signs*, 203.

upon him at once. He who is baptized outside the Church passes as it were through a narrow zone of light and again enters darkness. While he passes through the zone of light, he is cleansed of his sins, but since immediately after Baptism he returns to the darkness of dissent, his sins return immediately upon him.[149]

No one, neither the Scholastics nor, of course, St. Hilarion and the Orthodox, can accept this idea. St. Hilarion, continuing in the patristic tradition, asks rhetorically, "Why is the Church's Baptism to be found among the schismatics, although only at the moment of its accomplishment? For the schismatic is converted not to the Church, but to the schism." Medieval theologians simply evaded the question, took Augustine as speaking hypothetically, and firmly rejected "the possibility of 'the return of sins.'"[150] Yet, short of returning to the patristic consensus and consistency of St. Cyprian, the only other option was to accept a clean break of the sacrament from the forgiveness of sins: to accept that "there is no necessary connection between the external sign and the inward spiritual benefit of grace. . . ."[151] Whether one chose the first bizarre solution (a return of sins) or the second (no sure connection), Augustine's intended outcome was the same: "the remission of irrevocable sins does not follow from Baptism, unless a man not only have lawful Baptism, but have it lawfully."[152]

149. New Hieromartyr Hilarion (Troitsky), Archbishop of Verey, *The Unity of the Church* (Montreal: Monastery Press, 1975), 29–30 (English translation from the Russian, originally written in 1917).

150. Cary, *Outward Signs*, 204.

151. Ibid.

152. *On Baptism*, NPNF 5.8.9.

Having come full circle, we see that Augustine, while creating "a whole new theology of the Church," nevertheless strove
earnestly to remain true to the patristic dictum: *extra ecclesiam
nulla salus*. The problem was that, since he didn't go about
it "lawfully," by following the Holy Fathers before him, but
rather innovated, his ecclesiology was destined to serve the
undermining of the boundaries of the Church.

The moment that medieval Western theology connected certain kinds of spiritual efficacy to every valid sacrament, including those outside the unity of the Church, that ever-so-tenuous
wall erected by Augustine was doomed to tumble. This is apparent when we examine the question of membership in the
Church.

6

THE MEANING OF MEMBERSHIP
IN THE CHURCH

K arl Becker, in his noteworthy essay "The Teaching of Vatican II on Baptism," provides us with examples of how medieval and post-Reformation Catholicism saw membership. The Scholastic manuals, so authoritative for Catholicism before Vatican II, essentially followed a Thomistic line of thought. It is not surprising then that in them we find "constant repetitions of the statement that Baptism makes a person a member of the Church because it confers a character."[153] This is the same idea of character that originated with Aquinas and the Scholastics, as we have seen, and differs substantially from Augustine's understanding.

An authoritative source for how pre–Vatican II Catholicism understood membership in the Church is Canon 87 of the 1917 Code of Canon Law. This canon is based on a brief of Pope Benedict XIV (1740–1758),[154] who in turn depends on the Jesuit theologian Francisco Suárez[155] (1548–1617), who depends

153. Karl Becker, "The Teaching of Vatican II on Baptism: A Stimulus for Theology," in René Latourelle, ed., *Vatican II: Assessment and Perspectives, Twenty-five Years After (1962–1987)* (New York: Paulist Press, 1989), 2:69.

154. The brief is Benedict's Letter *Singulari* of February 9, 1749.

155. Suárez was a Spanish Jesuit theologian and philosopher who made a major contribution to the philosophy of law. The work Becker cites is Suárez's *Defensio Fidei Catholicae*.

on Augustine's treatise *On Baptism*. Although one is said to be following the other, three different answers are provided as to the nature of membership.

Suárez says that one becomes a member of the Church by a properly administered Baptism, since he receives the righteousness and faith of Christ and the character of Christ. He uses the following passage from Augustine's treatise *On Baptism* as his basis:

> We do not say to those [in schism] whom we see them on the point of baptizing, "Do not receive the Baptism," but "Do not receive it in schism." For if anyone were compelled by urgent necessity, being unable to find a Catholic from whom to receive Baptism, and so, while preserving Catholic peace [i.e. unity] in his heart, should receive from one without the pale of Catholic unity the sacrament which he was intending to receive within its pale, this man, should he forthwith depart this life, we deem to be none other than a Catholic.[156]

Becker sees Augustine as positing faith, an act of Christian faith, as the key that, along with the act of Baptism, opens the door of membership. Suárez includes "infused faith" (or *habitus fidei*) in this, saying that the same holds true for a baby baptized by a heretical minister at the request of heretical parents. He also mentions baptismal character, which isn't even mentioned by Augustine.

Both Becker and Suárez have misunderstood Augustine. Augustine was not reducing membership in the Church to either simply the external, "valid" Baptism or "an act of faith" that was intended as an act of Christian faith, or even these two

156. *On Baptism*, NPNF 1.2.3.

together. Rather, faith and Baptism have to be united within "Catholic peace," by which Augustine meant unity[157]—even if this was only "preserved . . . in [one's] heart." We can take issue with this as not being consistent with patristic ecclesiology, which centers on the concreteness of the Incarnation, the "scandal of the particular"; however, insomuch as he does not depart from the necessity of unity, in this he is following the Fathers. Indeed, Augustine repeats his well-known, peculiar principle only a few lines later, that, even though Baptism can be received elsewhere, it "cannot profit elsewhere." Profit is only gained in unity, and unity means membership.

Benedict XIV cites Suárez and his mention of the *habitus fidei* approvingly; however, he links membership to the validity of Baptism. He supports this by pointing out that if the proper form and matter were employed for the Baptism then the character was received. "Thus," as Becker concludes, "here membership of the Catholic Church is now linked only to the character."[158]

The process of disintegration described earlier with regard to the rites of initiation is apparent here, again, with regard to the theology of initiation and membership. In Augustine, membership was located within the threefold unity of faith, Baptism, and "Catholic peace" or Church unity. In Suárez, who refers back to Augustine but misunderstands him, it was faith, righteousness, and baptismal character. In Benedict XIV, who refers back to Suárez, it is now only baptismal character, which—it is important to stress—depends only upon "the proper form and matter" (validity).

---

157. Cf. Ludwig Hertling, S.J., *Communio: Church and Papacy in Early Christianity*, trans. Jared Wicks, S.J. (Chicago: Loyola University, 1972), 18–23.

158. Becker, 70.

The initial, more restrained sacramental minimalism of Augustine has undergone such a "development of doctrine" as would be unrecognizable to Augustine himself. Augustine would be appalled at the depths to which later theology took his "narrowing down" to the essentials of validity, especially since his purpose was to unite the dissidents to the unity of the Church, which, of course, presupposed maintaining the unity of the Church. He would certainly have thought that by reducing membership to external validity, true spiritual, inward unity is discarded for literally nothing, the external mark (character) being no conduit of spiritual power and easily falsified. Here unity in truth and love is traded in for a simple sharing in externals, which are powerless, void of salvific efficacy.[159]

That this disintegration is a post-schism phenomenon in the West is apparent when one considers, as Becker does in his article, that "if we go back from the eighteenth to the twelfth century, we can even find an opinion that does not so much as mention the character (indeed, this concept had not yet made its appearance)."[160] Becker is speaking of Hugh of St. Victor (1096–1141), French philosopher and theologian, highly influenced by Blessed Augustine's writings. Hugh of St. Victor remains true to the basic patristic vision of initiation, stressing the unity of the mysteries, connecting Baptism and the Eucharist as together necessary for initiation into the Church.[161]

Hugh of St. Victor is also one of a handful of theologians in the twelfth-century West who continued in the ancient be-

159. Philip Cary, *Outward Signs: The Powerlessness of External Things in Augustine's Thought* (Oxford, UK: Oxford University Press, 2008), 196.

160. Becker, 70.

161. Hugh of St. Victor, *De Sacramentis christianae fidei* 2.2.2, in PL 176.416b.

lief that schismatic and heretical celebrations of the Eucharist were invalid.[162] According to Bernard Leeming, it was only well after the Great Schism, in the thirteenth century, with the rise of Scholasticsm and the writings of Thomas Aquinas, that the worth of any sacrament, even the Eucharist, regardless of the faith and uprightness of the minister was universally admitted and defended. In Leeming's words: "Since the middle of the thirteenth century it has been generally accepted in the [Roman] Church that lack neither of due faith nor of moral goodness affects the validity of the sacraments, provided there is due matter, form, and intention."[163]

It is clear, then, that the catholic vision of initiation and membership—that is, of the unity of the mysteries of Baptism, Chrismation, and the Eucharist, still held in the West up until the twelfth century—is not and could not be the foundation upon which the recognition of the Baptism of schismatics and heretics is placed. The two views are irreconcilably opposed. Although Augustine departed from the patristic consensus in his new theory of the sacraments, he nonetheless strove to construct his new ecclesiology within this most crucial bound-

162. Other prominent theologians of the twelfth century who stood with Hugh of St. Victor on this point were Honorius of Autun (d. 1135), Geroch of Ratisbon (d. 1169), Gratian, and Peter of Lombard (see Bernard Leeming, S.J., *Principles of Sacramental Theology* [Westminster, MD: Newman Press, 1960, 540). Leeming claims that from the time of Augustine onward opposition to the validity of schismatic or heretical sacraments existed only for a short period, "principally in the eleventh and twelfth centuries, when theological studies were not at their best" (541). Leeming joins Congar and other Vatican II theologians not only in ignoring the teaching of the Eastern Fathers on this matter, but also in ignoring the change in justification for "valid but inefficacious" sacraments among schismatics and heretics from Augustine to Aquinas.

163. Leeming, 538–39.

ary: only the mysteries within the Church have the Holy Spirit; and only within "Catholic peace," where Baptism is united to Chrismation and the Eucharist, is Baptism salvific and is one made a member of the Church.

Yves Congar, in contrast, presents Augustine as agreeing with, even being one of the sources for, Vatican II's uniquely post-schism teaching on what constitutes membership. Congar sites Augustine as his only pre-schism source for this teaching—a fact that alone testifies to its late, post-schism origins. However, the passage from Augustine's writings that Congar cites as supporting the claim that schismatics and heretics are members of the Church isn't supportive at all.

Congar claims that Augustine is a source for "traditional teaching," which is "clear and unanimous": "children validly baptized in the separated Churches or dissident communities are genuinely members of the one true Church of Jesus Christ."[164] Augustine is supposed to be supportive of this when he writes: "We do not acknowledge any Baptism of yours; for it is not the Baptism of schismatics or heretics, but of God and of the Church, wheresoever it may be found, and whithersoever it may be transferred."[165]

As we have seen, however, Augustine maintained that one could have the outward sign, the sacrament, with its meaning and holiness, without having the inward, salvific power, which alone existed within the unity of the Church. Clearly, membership for Augustine was not a matter simply of powerless outward signs. To belong to Christ, to "put Him on" in Baptism,

---

164. Yves Congar, *Divided Christendom, A Catholic Study of the Problem of Reunion*, trans. M. A. Bousfield (London: Geoffrey Bles: The Centenary Press, 1939), 230.

165. *On Baptism*, NPNF 1.14.22. (cited in *Divided Christendom*, 231).

is a spiritual event and reality that cannot happen outside the unity and love of "the One Dove," as he referred to the Church. He expressly denied to the schismatics and heretics spiritual profit from their Baptism, precisely those spiritual principles that Congar says flow from the Baptism of schismatics and heretics: "sanctifying grace, infused faith and charity," which, Congar says, dispose him for "the profession of the true faith, participation in the sacraments, and the full flowering of his Christian life in the Church. . . ."[166]

Blessed Augustine, for all his expansion and originality, never extended the dignity of membership in the Church to schismatics and heretics. In numerous references[167] throughout his massive treatise *On Baptism*, alongside his insistence on heretics possessing Baptism but without salvation, he declared that they stand not on the rock and thus "are aliens from the Church" and do "not belong to the members of the dove."[168] For Augustine the unique dove is all the saints united by love in Christ, by the Holy Spirit, and within the unity of the Faith.

The power that unites, the uniting power of love, which is the Holy Spirit, draws men into the bond of peace, charity, and unity (Eph. 4:3, Col. 3:14). That which holds together, which unites, is, in fact, the very power of the Holy Spirit. So, as Philip Cary has written, "The fundamental ontological point here is that"—for Augustine—"being and unity are not ultimately distinguishable. 'To be is nothing other than to be one thing,' Augustine says, adding that 'insofar as anything achieves unity, it exists.'"[169]

---

166. Congar, *Divided Christendom*, 231.
167. See, for example, *On Baptism*, NPNF 4.3.5, 4.5.8, 5.3.3.
168. Ibid., 6.40.78.
169. Cary, *Outward Signs*, 197.

It should be clear then, that Augustine could never countenance the idea of belonging to the Church, of being a member of the Church, outside the unity and charity of the Church. For him, to be is to be in unity, "to be one thing." Baptism, on the other hand, as an outward sign, an external thing, "can be misused, stolen, and possessed by people who have no right to it."[170] Their possession of it, for Augustine, only means it need not be repeated when, and if, they finally are united to the Church, at which time they become spiritual participants in, and living members of, the Body of Christ.

If we retain Augustine's understanding of sacrament and character, Congar not only misses Augustine's teaching here, he goes on, and Vatican II with him, to invert it. For Augustine it was possible for one outside the unity of the Church to gain an external sign of belonging to the Church without there being any internal, spiritual reality accompanying this sign, nor thus any true unity. For Congar, one who is manifestly separated from the Church can, by way of an external sign, gain an internal, spiritual reality that unites him to the Church internally, invisibly, but not externally.

Besides quoting Augustine as support for the teaching, Congar cites nine post-schism sources. Six are authoritative decisions from 1439 to 1925—from the Council of Florence (1439), the Council of Trent (1545–1563), a brief of Benedict XIV (1749), a letter of Pius IX (1873), an encyclical of Leo XIII (1899), and an encyclical of Pius XI (1925). He also cites the writings of Albert the Great (1206–1280) and Thomas Aquinas (1225–1274), as well as canonical regulations showing that the Church, in issuing censures against schismatics and heretics, did so because these were regarded as part of the body.[171] These

170. Ibid., 196
171. Congar, *Divided Christendom*, 230–31.

sources, as would be expected, view membership as conferred by sacramental "validity" or "baptismal character" alone, the latter being a concept unknown not only to Augustine but to the entire Western Church before the thirteenth century.

Of all the sources, Congar gives the most weight to the views of Thomas Aquinas. To substantiate his claims of membership for those baptized in heresy, he quotes from Aquinas' *Commentary on the Sentences:*

> Although a heretic *may* not be a member of the Church through right faith, nevertheless insofar as he keeps the custom of the Church in baptizing, he bequeaths the Baptism of the Church; from whence *he regenerates sons for Christ and for the Church,* not for himself or for his heresy. As Jacob gave birth to sons through free women and slaves, thus does Christ through Catholics and heretics, good men and bad men, as Augustine says.[172]

Here, although Aquinas does not state clearly and unequivocally, as Congar does, that heretics are members of the Church, neither does he qualify, as Augustine does, the scope of the regeneration bequeathed in the Baptism imparted by the heretic. Augustine's peculiar idea that regeneration occurs in heretical baptism only to be immediately nullified with a complete return of previous sins is absent. Rather, Aquinas states unconditionally that those outside the unity of the Church are regenerated. Aquinas' views here once again show his subtle

---

172. IV Sent., lib. 4d. 6q.1a.3 qc. 2 ad 2: *Quamvis haereticus per fidem rectam non sit membrum Ecclesiae, tamen inquantum servant morem Ecclesiae in baptizando, Baptismum Ecclesiae tradit; unde regenerat filios Christo et Ecclesiae, non sibi vel haeresi suae. Sicut enim Jacob genuit filios per liberas et ancillas, ita Chistus per Catholicos et haereticos, bonos et malos, ut Augustinus dicit* (emphasis added).

but substantial distancing from Augustine and place him as the origin of the teaching developed later by Congar and Vatican II on schismatic and heretical Baptism.

Congar's claim to present the "traditional teaching" of the Magisterium on this subject can only be accepted as meaning a post-schism teaching that began with Aquinas and evolved slowly and inconspicuously. It is clear, then, that on this question of heretical baptism and membership, the effort of *ressourcement*, of returning to the Fathers, or even to Augustine, is shown to be nonexistent.[173]

173. This is also quite evident when considering the theological approach of Augustin Cardinal Bea, the first head of the Secretariat for Promoting Christian Unity and one of a handful of Vatican officials who were instrumental in shaping the Second Vatican Council's ecumenical agenda. See chapter 8 for discussion of Bea's important contribution.

7

CONGAR, BLESSED AUGUSTINE, AND THE FORMULATION OF THE NEW ECCLESIOLOGY

A s we have already suggested, Yves Congar should be considered the father of the Second Vatican Council's ecclesiology. According to the American Jesuit theologian Avery Dulles, "Vatican II could almost be called Congar's Council."[174] With the death of Pius XII and the election of John XXIII Congar returned from virtual exile to become, "by most estimates, the single most important theological influence on Vatican II."[175] More than that of any of his contemporaries, his thought, ecumenical orientation, and tone became the council's thought, ecumenical orientation, and tone. "His prodigious ecclesiological programme was translated directly into the documents of Vatican II."[176] With regard to the new ecclesiology, he was the primary author behind the texts, the central thinker

174. Avery Dulles, S.J., "Yves Congar: In Appreciation," *America* 173 (15 July 1995), 6–7.

175. Paul Lakeland, *Yves Congar: Essential Writings* (Maryknoll, NY: Orbis, 2010), 21.

176. Gabriel Flynn, *Yves Congar's Vision of the Church in a World of Unbelief* (Burlington, VT: Ashgate Publishing, 2004), 18. Congar noted with joy the council's adoption of his theology: "I was filled to overflowing. All the things to which I gave quite special attention issued in the council: ecclesiology, ecumenism, reform of the Church, the lay state, mission, ministries, collegiality, return to the sources and Tradition." Ibid.

behind the council's thought. To be sure, he was but one of several theologians in the *nouvelle théologie* movement[177] who went on later to leave their mark on Vatican II's theology. However, as his area of expertise and main contribution was in the field of ecclesiology, and Vatican II was chiefly concerned with this, the mark he left on its theology was the most pronounced.[178] For this reason, then, Congar's approach and aim are of especial interest to us and will shed greater light on how the Baptism and ecclesial status of those outside the Roman Catholic Church came to be formulated in *Unitatis Redintegratio.*

Congar was deeply concerned that the true visage of the Church had been obscured, even lost.[179] He wrote that "it is necessary to restore fully to the mystery of the Church its human and divine dimensions."[180] In order to combat the apostasy and unbelief arising from this loss, Congar called his fellow religionists to a return to the sources. "[His] intentions were to return to the teaching of the Fathers, to, as he is quoted as saying, 'd'enjamber quinze siècles,' or 'skip fifteen centuries.'"[181]

177. Flynn, *Yves Congar's Vision*, 34–35. Flynn, focusing on the French quarter of the movement, divides it there into two groups, Dominican and Jesuit, singling out Chenu, Congar, and André Marie Dubarle in the former and Danielou, de Lubac, and Henri Bouillard in the latter. Of these, Congar was the specialist in ecclesiology.

178. "Congar's stamp can be seen most clearly on the central document of the Council, Lumen Gentium." Lakeland, 21.

179. He lamented that the true face of the Church had been lost and acknowledged that it needed to again "assume its true face," to become again "very simply the Church." Éric Mahieu and Bernard Dupuy, *Yves Congar: Mon journal du Concile* (Paris: Cerf, 2002), 1:257 (entry for November 24, 1962); cited in Flynn, 25.

180. Yves Congar, *Sainte Église: études et approaches ecclésiologique* (Paris: Cerf, 1963), 552; cited in Flynn, 25.

181. Romano Amerio, *Iota Unum: A Study of Changes in the Catholic Church in the XXth Century* (Kansas City, MO: Sarto House, 1996), 114.

The return to the sources had as its aim a practical outcome: to combat the reasons for the growing apostasy of Europe and the West, of the very peoples under the spiritual leadership of Rome. Roman Catholics, he said, were partly to blame for the apostasy, which arose "from the fact that the Church shows men a face which belies rather than expresses her true nature."[182] The Living God, Who comes with power,[183] Who lives in and connects men to Himself and to one another and in this way reigns in and among them had ceased being an experience and become an idea.[184] This explains why one encounters in Congar's writings a complex sense of loss and oft-expressed lament of distance from the Holy Fathers and great need to return to them.

Congar exhibits a clear recognition of a gap existing between the ecclesiology of the Holy Fathers and that of Tridentine Catholicism. Above all, what had been lost to Western theology was unity, the unity "it enjoyed in its golden days of the Middle Ages," before "the dissociations introduced by Nominalism, the Reformation, the theology of the seventeenth century, Rational-

---

For this phrase and desire he is severely criticized by those within Catholicism intent on following the established practices and tradition inherited after the schism and especially after the Council of Trent.

182. Yves Congar, *Dialogue Between Christians: Catholic Contributions to Ecumenism*, trans. Philip Loretz (London: Geoffrey Chapman, 1966), 23.

183. See Luke 9:1; 24:49; Acts 1:8.

184. Congar cites as the main reason for unbelief among Roman Catholics the lack of manifestation of the fruit of the experience of the grace of God: "The greatest obstacle which men encounter today on the road to faith is in the lack of any credible demonstrable connection between faith in God and the prospect of his reign. . . ." (Congar, *Dialogue*, 23).

ism and Modernism."[185] The search for wholeness is the defining feature of Congar's theology, the "golden thread that helps to bind together all his theological projects."[186] The drive for reform was a blatant judgment upon the juridical ecclesiological schemas of the late Middle Ages,[187] which Congar pejoratively labeled "hierarchology" and claimed were impotent in drawing men back to the Church.[188]

Therefore, for Congar the answer to the crisis of apostasy was a "renewal of our presentation of the Church and above all, in order to achieve this, a renewal of our own view of the Church transcending the juridical idea of her which has been dominant for so long."[189] This is, in fact, what happened at

185. Yves Congar, *A History of Theology*, ed. and trans. Hunter Guthrie (New York: Doubleday, 1968), 195.

186. Flynn, 75. Flynn records the opinion of Jean-Pierre Jossua that "this concern for wholeness or totality may be attributed to the Orthodox influence on Congar's theology. [I]t was Congar's contact with the Orthodox Church that enabled him to move beyond strict Latin conceptualism" (78). See Jean-Pierre Jossua, "Le Père Congar: la théologie au service du peuple de Dieu," *Chrétiens de Tous les Temps* 20 (Paris: Cerf, 1967).

187. "A Christian reform is always a judgment on a certain state of things, in the name of a re-examination of the sources and of the Principle. . . ." Yves Congar, "Comment L'Église sainte doit se renouveler sans cesse," *Irenikon* 34 (1961), 342, as quoted in Flynn, 77.

188. "My aim . . . was to recover for ecclesiology the inspiration and the resources of an older and deeper Tradition than the juridical and purely hierarchological schemas that prevailed in the first anti-conciliar polemic, then anti-Protestant, and lastly during the revival under the pontificates of Gregory XVI and Pius IX, schemas which also dominated modern manuals of apologetic. Henceforth the Church would no longer appear as merely *societas perfecta* or *societas inaequalis, hierarchica* but as the Body of Christ wholly and intimately inspired by his life." Congar, "My Path-findings in Theology of Laity and Ministries," *Jurist* 32 (1972), 170, as quoted in Flynn, 78.

189. Congar, *Dialogue*, 23.

Vatican II: ultimately for pastoral and practical reasons, the face of the Church was overhauled, and "in a single short quadrennium, the tendencies of four centuries [were] decisively reversed."[190] This reversal is forceful testimony to the influence of Congar on the council.

In the approach and aims expressed by Congar one cannot but bring to mind the approach and motivations of another renowned Western theologian in another decisive time of turmoil and change: Blessed Augustine. The parallels are many and astounding. Even a brief comparison will help shed light upon the motivations and aims behind the development of the new ecclesiology.

The Donatists of Saint Augustine's day were, for the most part, lay people, ignorant of the theological issues at stake, who inherited the schism by "accident" of birth and upbringing. As inheritors of schism, they were not implicated in the full culpability of being its originators, nor were they inclined to thoughtfully examine the matter on a theological level. Saint Augustine's teaching, therefore, had to be calculated to win such people over to the Church. In an innovative move unheard of in Africa, or anywhere else, Saint Augustine sought to receive not only the Donatist laymen without baptizing them but also the Donatist clergy without ordaining them.[191] It was in accordance with this practical outlook, which carried great weight with him, that he conceived his immensely significant

190. Albert Outlet, *Methodist Observer at Vatican II* (Westminster, MD: Newman Press, 1967), 19.

191. "There is no sign that before Saint Augustine any theologian had worked out the theory, or any church had adopted the practice, of the general recognition of orders conferred outside the Catholic Church." C. H. Turner, quoted in Geoffrey Grimshaw Willis, *Saint Augustine and the Donatist Controversy* (Eugene, OR: Wipf and Stock, 2005), 161.

new distinction between the sacrament and its use and benefit.

Saint Augustine was quite well aware of the established doctrine of Christian antiquity, that Christ had imparted the authority to administer the mysteries to the Apostles and through them and their successors to the bishops and priests of the Church in every age, such that it was only within the Church that the mysteries were imparted. Yet, "he felt compelled in the circumstances of his time to seek a wider basis for the doctrine of the ministration of the sacraments."[192] In order to discover a position that broadened the basis and opened the door for return of the schismatics, without, however, slipping into ecclesiastical relativism, meant he had to make distinctions. He found the now famous distinction between *sacramentum* and *res sacramenti*, which satisfied him, and on this basis sought to forge the hoped-for reunion and peace in the Church in Africa.

There can be little doubt that earlier Fathers, and those in the East who followed them, if they had read Blessed Augustine's texts, "would have been most uncomfortable with his position."[193] In addition to the divorce of the theology of the Church from the theology of the mysteries they would have been dumbfounded by the idea that the inherited tradition and theology of the Holy Fathers could be supplanted by new theories in order to achieve practical, pastoral aims—even the reunion of schismatics. To be sure, Fathers in the East were willing on a case-by-case basis to exercise pastoral economy

192. Willis, 166.

193. Ibid., 168. See, for example: Ignat. Eph. 5; Tral. 7; Smyr. 8; Clem. Alex. PG 8.280B and 281; Iren. *Adv. Haer.* III, xvii, 2, xxiv, 1; IV, xviii, 5, xxxviii, 7; Tert. *De bapt.* XV; Cypr., *Ep.* LXIX, 2; LXXIII, 10, 11; Athan. Meg., PG 26.237.16; Cyr. Jerus., *Procat.* 1.7; Ioan. Chrys., PG 61.73; 61.250–51; 61.622; 61.624; PG 62.26; 62.83.10; 62.84–85; 62.85.38; 62.86A; 62.344.36; 63.131.39; Max. Conf., PG 90.297; 91.705B.

and proceed with discretion in cases of repentant schismatics and heretics. However, they never developed a new theology or divorced sacramental theology from ecclesiology in order to envision anew the Church and the status of the dissidents. This feat belongs to Blessed Augustine alone, who "ended up creating a new theology of the church."[194]

It is impossible to say that he set out with the intention to create a new theology of the church, but one did nonetheless develop within the intense and prolonged struggle to bring the Donatists into unity. "His doctrine of unity and schism, of Church, ministry and sacraments, [was] inevitably molded by the schism, and forged under its pressure."[195] A return of the schismatics to the Church was the aim of all of Blessed Augustine's activity, the principle above all others which he kept in view.[196] His theology was put at the service of his pastoral aims, and thus it sought to account for everything and to be comprehensive. However, such inclusiveness can slip into relativity and minimalism and produce far greater evils than it was originally meant to prevent and "in the hands of lesser men [it] was destined to be productive of great evils."[197]

Blessed Augustine today is often hailed, not for "following the holy fathers" but, rather, because he did not follow them, instead striking out as a "theological pioneer" whose principles dominated thought in later ages.[198] "Learned critics, such as

194. Philip Cary: *Outward Signs: The Powerlessness of External Things in Augustine's Thought* (Oxford, UK: Oxford University Press, 2008), 2.

195. Willis, 170.

196. Ibid., 172.

197. This is how Geoffrey Grimshaw Willis ends the chapters of his classic study of Saint Augustine and the Donatists.

198. Willis, 187. He concludes: "Truly he was a theological pioneer, and the history of Christian doctrine could never have been quite the

Harnack, have called Augustine 'the first modern man,' and in truth, he so molded the Latin world that it is really he who has shaped the education of modern minds."[199] "For in him we see the transition from primitive to later notions" on all subjects related to the Church, her mysteries and relations with the world.[200] The broad transformation in Western theology that eventually followed in the wake of Blessed Augustine's theological exploration and discoveries led to a particular Western theological vision of the Church and of grace.

Like Saint Augustine and his times, Yves Congar and his fellow theologians of Vatican II were faced with a world in crisis and disintegration. Division in Christendom, the onslaught of atheism and materialism, and the threat of further dissolution were forcing them to confront anew the problem of "the dissidents" and the possible pathways to reunion. As with a consideration of Saint Augustine's theology, when considering these new theologians' doctrines of the sacraments and of the Church we must keep in mind their fervent desire for the reunion of separated Christians.[201]

Like Saint Augustine, who consciously diverged from the established ecclesiology before him, Congar and his colleagues believed that the older, established consideration of the Church vis-à-vis the dissidents was inadequate and would not serve

---

same had he not been raised up to bear his witness to the faith at such a critical period as the turn of the fourth century."

199. Eugène Portalié, "Teaching of St. Augustine of Hippo," *The Catholic Encyclopedia*, vol. 2 (New York: Robert Appleton Company, 1907).

200. Willis, 187.

201. "In the doctrine of the sacraments as of the Church, we have to bear constantly in mind the ardent desire of Augustine for the reunion of African Christians" (Willis, 152).

the cause of unity.[202] Ecumenism begins, according to Congar, when the older consideration of the dissidents as individuals is replaced with a consideration of their ecclesial communities as such. By reflection, by his own personal encounters with the dissidents, and in accordance with practical considerations of the day, Congar was led to suggest his own particular idea that schismatic communities retained elements of the Church and that on this basis there already existed unity, which was, however, imperfect.

With this new concept, Congar was taking a great and bold step forward,[203] moving the discussion from individuals to communities and recognizing in these communities elements of the Church that make them participants in the Mystery of the Church as communities.[204] The circumstances of his time were pushing him and many others to seek a wider, more inclusive

202. See Yves Congar, *Divided Christendom, A Catholic Study of the Problem of Reunion*, trans. Philip Loretz (London: Geoffrey Chapman, 1966), 225–26; and Aidan Nichols, *Yves Congar* (London: Morehouse-Barlow, 1989), 102. Congar says that he and other theologians were "returning to the early manner of approaching the question" (226), but it is unknown what this "early manner" is that he is referring to. References to early Church Fathers or other patristic sources are not provided.

203. One of Saint Augustine's "great steps" was to extend the application of his principle to other sacraments than Baptism. "In smoothing the path for returning Donatists, Augustine and his supporters promised Donatist clergy who submitted that they should retain their orders. This was contrary to the general practice of the Western Church" (Willis, 160–61).

204. Traditional Roman Catholic teaching, following Saint Augustine, held that schismatic or heretical communities cannot in and of themselves be means of salvation in any way. The individual Christian may indeed be saved in a separated community, but not through it. Congar's innovation will pass into UR 3.

basis for the doctrine of the Church. The principle that was to guide all others was that of unity as expressed in degrees of communion. Whereas Saint Augustine broadened the basis for the doctrine of the sacraments without recognizing the Donatist body as such as in any way connected with or expressive of the Church, Congar was, in fact, broadening the basis for the doctrine of the Church itself, granting to the dissident bodies themselves a share in the expression of the One Church. All of this was accomplished for the sake of forging unity, for the sake of an "ecumenism of integration."[205]

As with Saint Augustine, Congar's "vision was oriented to the attainment of a goal—specifically the regeneration of ecclesiology in order to construct a renewed Church."[206] Like Saint Augustine, he was a "theological pioneer" who paved the way for a new, broader idea of the Church.[207] It would not be an overstatement to say that Congar, like Saint Augustine, was indeed successful in "constructing" a "new theology of the Church"—which later largely became the new ecclesiology of Vatican II.

The foregoing foray into the approaches of Yves Congar and Saint Augustine has been necessary in order for us to see the new ecclesiology of Vatican II in proper perspective. The council's notion of the Church arose neither spontaneously within the deliberations of the council nor without a studied practi-

205. Yves Congar, *Essais oecumeniques* (Paris: Le Centurion, 1984), 212–13, as quoted in Nichols, 103.

206. Flynn, *Yves Congar's Vision*, 79.

207. According to Klaus Wittstadt, many of the council fathers were indebted to Congar for a broadening of their notion of the Church. "On the Eve of the Second Vatican Council (July 1–October 10, 1962)," in *History of Vatican II*, ed. Giuseppe Alberigo, English version ed. Joseph A. Komonchak (Maryknoll: Orbis; Louvain: Peeters, 1995), 1:459.

cal, pastoral purpose. It was for the most part the result of the visionary Congar's program for internal renewal and return of the "dissidents" by way of ecclesiological renovation. It was, moreover, a response to the "signs of the times," an answer to the ecumenical challenge, and, just as Blessed Augustine's sacramental theology can only rightly be understood in reference to the Donatist controversy, so the new ecclesiology of Vatican II can only rightly be understood in reference to the ecumenical movement.

8

SIDESTEPPING *MYSTICI CORPORIS:*
CARDINAL BEA'S OVERTURE
ON THE EVE OF THE COUNCIL

A fter Congar, the man most responsible for transforming Roman Catholic ecclesiology to include schismatics
and heretics by way of their Baptism alone was Augustin Cardinal Bea.[208] A Vatican insider and intimate counselor to
both Pope Pius XII and Pope John XXIII, Bea's support was
crucial if the new orientation was to be accepted by the "old
guard" loyal to Pius XII's anti-modernist and anti-ecumenist
outlook, and he indeed played the decisive role in converting
the focus and emphasis of ecclesiological research from the
"exclusivity" of *Mystici Corporis Christi* (1943) to the "inclusiveness" of *Lumen Gentium* and *Unitatis Redintegratio.*

Both supporters and detractors of Vatican II agree that these
decrees represent a great reformation in Roman Catholic views
of the Church and sacraments. This becomes especially clear
when one considers the prevailing views of pre–Vatican II Ro-

208. Augustin Bea (May 28, 1881–November 16, 1968), a member
of the order of the Jesuits, was a German scholar at the Gregorian University specializing in biblical studies. He was the confessor of Pope Pius
XII and a highly respected counselor to the Pope. In 1959 Pope John
XXIII made him a cardinal and soon thereafter appointed him as the
first president of the newly created Secretariat for Promoting Christian
Unity.

man Catholicism and the radical redirection taken by the newly created Secretariat for Promoting Christian Unity under the direction of Augustin Cardinal Bea.

The pre-council reality was that the official Vatican stance left no room to speak of an ecclesial reality in other Christian churches, let alone concede that the Holy Spirit vivifies therein.[209] Protestants were considered to be Christians in spite of, not because of, the "churches" they belonged to. The gifts of the Gospel and the Baptism they received were not theirs by right but belonged properly to the Roman Catholic Church; "what they received from their own 'churches' was only the set of errors that constitute the principle of division."[210] According to the teaching of Pope Pius XII in his encyclical *Mystici Corporis Christi*, although the existence of Christians outside the Catholic Church is acknowledged, they are not regarded as "really and truly" members of the Church, "nor can they be living the life of its own divine Spirit."[211] As we have seen above, these views were consistent with the "Augustinian" ecclesiology as it was expressed in the late Middle Ages. Clearly, in such a context "the new ecumenical spring" would have remained an impossibility.

Indeed, with this stance and his subsequent encyclical *Humani generis* in 1950, Pius XII was striving to stave off the growing tide of "modernist" and ecumenically friendly theo-

---

209. Gregory Baum, O.S.A., "The Ecclesial Reality of the Other Churches," in *The Church and Ecumenism* (New York: Paulist Press, 1965), 66. It seems that here Baum is referring to the Protestants alone. Consideration of the status of the Orthodox as schismatics was more nauanced but also more ambiguous and debated.

210. Ibid.

211. Henry Denzinger, *The Sources of Catholic Dogma* (Fitzwilliam, NH: Loreto, 2007), 616 (no. 228b).

logical speculation. And, yet, the seeds of the very innovations Pius XII was intent on crushing were already present in his own writings. That is why opposing theologians could, without directly challenging the legitimacy of *Mystici Corporis,* adopt those aspects of Pius XII's encyclicals that supported their preferred strain of thought drawn from the post-schism Latin tradition. For in Pius XII's encyclical *Mediator Dei* he acknowledges as legitimate the key tenet of the emerging ecclesiology—an efficacious Baptism for those outside the church—even if the implications of this recognition are ignored in deference to a consistent "Augustinian" ecclesiology. The same tension and confusion we saw existing in the documents of the Council of Florence—between an Augustinian ecclesiology and a Thomistic baptismal theology—are present in Pius XII's encyclicals.

At Vatican II the supporters of ecumenical involvement aimed for this tension to give way entirely to a united ecclesiology and baptismal theology that was inclusive of the separated brethren. Their main objective was to convince the council fathers to follow the implications of every baptism being the one Baptism to its logical conclusion: because the baptized are incorporated into Christ, Baptism delineates the boundaries of the Church, so that wherever a valid Baptism, there the Body of Christ. This would necessitate a new theory of Church incorporation, or membership, measured in degrees of communion regardless of an orthodox profession of faith.

With the announcement of the council and the formation of a special secretariat to promote ecumenism, its first chief, Cardinal Augustin Bea, would emerge as the "focal point for the inauguration of the Roman Catholic phase of the worldwide Ecumenical Movement."[212] At the outset of his leadership of

212. Jerome-Michael Vereb, *"Because He Was a German": Cardinal Bea*

the Secretariat, he listed as the most urgent item on the agenda that of Church membership of non-Catholic baptized people (239). Bea broke with Pius XII's view of membership and challenged the Vatican establishment, and yet he did this by citing this same Pope's views, expressed in another encyclical that Bea is largely credited with authoring. And, moreover, he did so with the new Pope's blessing. Pope John had charged Bea with the following task: mobilize the rank-and-file faithful in favor of the non-Catholic baptized; make the council from an internal event to an inter-Christian event. Bea sought to create a new atmosphere to achieve this and chose "the presentation of Baptism as the essential experience for all Christians and the basis for all unity" (252).

Long before taking the helm of the ecumenical campaign, "Bea had traced the importance of the Sacrament of Baptism as the gateway to many things, but most especially, as the gateway to understanding the Church" (281). Bea moved within the milieu of German Catholicism, which, especially during the inter-war years, pioneered Roman Catholic involvement in ecumenism. In regard to his views on Baptism and the Church he was highly influenced by one German cleric, Monsignor Josef Hofër of the University of Paderborn. Hofër was one of the few outspoken critics of the encyclical *Mystici Corporis*. According to Hofër, the encyclical was "mono-Christic in scope, in that it did not show sufficient attention to the dynamic action of the Holy Spirit, who is not confined to the action of love within the Godhead, but who reaches deep into the creation and draws all persons into Christ . . ." (138–39).

and the Origins of Roman Catholic Engagement in the Ecumenical Movement (Grand Rapids, MI: Eerdmans, 2006), 1. The following quotations are from this source with page numbers given in text.

Hofër's sharpest criticism, however, was reserved for paragraph 22 of the encyclical, which attempts to answer the question, Who is a member of the Church? Paragraph 22 reads:

> Actually only those are to be included as members of
> the Church who have been baptized and profess the true
> faith, and who have not been so unfortunate as to separate
> themselves from the unity of the Body, or been excluded
> by legitimate authority for grave faults committed. "For
> in one spirit," says the Apostle, "were we all baptized into
> one Body, whether Jews or Gentiles, whether bond or
> free." As therefore in the true Christian community there
> is only one Body, one Spirit, one Lord, and one Baptism,
> so there can be only one faith. And therefore, if a man
> refuse to hear the Church, let him be considered—so the
> Lord commands—as a heathen and a publican. It follows
> that *those who are divided in faith or government cannot be
> living in the unity of such a Body, nor can they be living the
> life of its one Divine Spirit.*[213]

In response, Josef Hofër felt that this statement "does not
take into consideration the new dispensation of the glorified
Risen Christ, in which the Holy Spirit is active to assemble the
body of the Church." "Hofër identified the lacuna of *Mystici
Corporis:* the need to refine [membership] for the sake of a
Spirit-given inclusiveness in the Universal Church" (141). He
"sought an inclusivity which had not yet been addressed by
magisterial authority" (139). And, it was Hofër who presented
to Bea the need to find a corrective to paragraph 22 and who
claimed that "it was he who made Cardinal Bea an ecumenist"
(ibid.). Bea, the scholar, will never forget the question or its
importance.

213. Emphasis added.

Monsignor Hofër's preoccupation with the question of Church membership, in the light of *Mystici Corporis*, would in-fluence Bea to make common Baptism the basis for the "over-arching theory" of his secretariat and the *locus theologicus* of the Vatican's ecumenical efforts. It was clear that until the question of who is a member of the Body of Christ was answered anew it would be impossible for "the concept of ecumenism to be developed from a Roman Catholic perspective" (143). Within twenty years of its publication, it had become necessary for the unprecedented Papal document on ecclesiology, on account of how it addressed the all-important question of membership, to be by-passed and replaced without appearing to be rejected outright. The irony of the new situation is striking: between Bea and the new Pope's ecumenical agenda for the Church stood the last Pope's celebrated encyclical on the Church.

This was clearly a theological challenge of the first order to Cardinal Bea's ecumenical mission. The Christological con-sistency and orthodoxy in Pius XII's ecclesiology had to be circumvented without being undermined. A deeper, more fun-damental unity, within a broader, more inclusive context need-ed to rise and overshadow the narrow environs of Pius XII's Church. What was sought was the least common denominator upon which an essential Christian unity existed in spite of all the divisions.

It did not take Bea long to come to the conclusion that "the incommensurable grace of Baptism, which consists of in-destructible bonds, is stronger than all our divisions" (224). "Above all . . . Bea was anxious to showcase the irrevocability of the gift of Baptism upon which all else is based" (259). By Baptism, so Bea argued, those separated by schism or heresy "have *become members of the Mystical Body of Christ* and, by that very fact, the Church's children: even though some are deprived of the full use of their rights, because they *are visibly separated* from her."[214]

The need for members of the Body of Christ to profess the true faith, a requirement both ancient and, indeed, explicit in *Mystici Corporis,* is swept aside as a casualty of history. Today's schismatic or heretic is, according to Bea, unlike his equivalent in ancient times in that he is a victim of history, an innocent inheritor of his ancestors' errors. As he cannot be considered culpable for his delusions, they are irrelevant—and the true faith as well—when determining his status as a member. If obstacles do still exist, they do not impede membership per se, much less the authenticity of the sacrament, but only the full exercise of "all the privileges and rights conferred on him by Baptism, in the unity of the one, holy, and visible Church."[215]

To answer the question whether Orthodox or Protestants are outside the Church, Bea again said nothing of the need to profess the true faith, but rather pointed to the concepts of Word and Sacrament. He "identified the ecclesial elements which are shared by all Christians, Sacred Scripture and the celebration of the sacrament of Baptism as the fundamental rite of Christian initiation. . . . [T]his disclosure of the Church, by Word and Sacrament, provided a methodology that could be viable in the future . . ." in ecumenical dialogue (265). "According to Bea's speculation, neither the present-day Protestant communities nor the Orthodox Churches have made any effort to concoct heresy or promote schism. Children of their families are also children of history. They were in fact born into their

214. Cardinal Augustin Bea, *The Unity of Christians* (New York: Herder and Herder, 1961), 67 (emphasis added).
215. Vereb, *"Because He Was a German,"* 237–38. The following quotations are from this source with page numbers given in text.

current religious traditions" (258). Bea strongly insisted that, "Accepting in good faith the inheritance handed on by their parents, these non-Catholics can sincerely believe that they are on the right path" (ibid.).

Basing himself on these stern facts of history, Bea, far from tearing down the image of *Mystici Corporis*, simply and shrewdly sidestepped its provisions of paragraph 22.[216] Potentially paralyzing questions of ecclesial ontology, either theoretical or functional, were, in the quest for unity, simply bypassed for the simple and helpful narrative of "that particular unity inherent in the Sacrament of Baptism" (272). By emphasizing what was shared, Bea is said to have avoided the approach of *Mystici Corporis*—an approach now considered to belong to an antiquated outlook. As J. M. Vereb writes, *Mystici Corporis* held up everyone to "the standards of objectivized reality, as it were, a theological extrinsicism. Instead, he operated from a twofold intrinsicism, to resolve the problem of *Mystici Corporis*, No. 22 . . ." (265).

The new inclusiveness and "situational ecclesiology" does not mean, however, that an appeal to the past, to tradition, has lost its significance. As Cardinal Bea was charged with easing

216. On Bea's views, Peter Hebblethwaite, author of Pope John XXIII's biography, wrote: "[T]he meaning was clear: this was a decisive move from an ecclesiology that excluded other Christians to one that embraced them; it was based on an older tradition that regarded Baptism as the common bond between all who invoke the name of Christ; it by-passed *Mystici Corporis* and left it stranded in the pages of Denzinger [the collection of papal documents], a curious historical monument from 1943." (Peter Hebblethwaite, *Pope John XXIII* [Garden City, NY: Doubleday, 1985], 382). It is unclear what Hebblethwaite means by "older tradition," since Bea cites Pius XII elsewhere to support the common Baptism idea. The subsequent quotations are from this source with page numbers given in text.

the Roman Catholic Church into the ecumenical movement, it was critical that new ecclesiology be seen as an acceptable development of thought and not as a sharp break with previous thinking. He sought to ground the new inclusive ecclesiology in the opinions of past Popes who were revered within traditionalist circles. Even if these Popes held an exclusivist ecclesiology, they expressed a Thomistic baptismal theology that served the new inclusiveness:

> [T]he Sovereign Pontiffs, beginning with Leo XIII (1810–1903), have repeatedly shown what "traces of Christ and gifts of the Holy Spirit" are found among our non-Catholic brothers, and this because of their Baptism itself and grace, which flows from Baptism. And anyone who assails this way of acting automatically attacks the Sovereign Pontiffs from Leo XII to Paul VI. (229)

Cardinal Bea was, in style and methodology, a true Vatican churchman. In order to anticipate and mollify potential detractors, he used language that could be stylized as Ultramontane, even if the heart of his doctrine was the opposite of a centralized, exclusivist ecclesiology. The focus of his attention and source of his general theory was the significance and irrevocability of Baptism, by which the narrow limits of a total acceptance of faith, government, and sacraments for Church membership could be circumvented in favor of a vision based upon the fruitful dynamic of the Holy Spirit, which is showered upon "all who are baptized (and who) are indeed baptized in Christ Jesus (Eph. 3:6)" (230).

In a particular reference to a text he himself helped pen, Bea would repeat the following words from Pius XII's *Mediator Dei* often, making it the cornerstone for his "overarching theory":

Nor is it to be wondered at, that the faithful should be raised to this dignity. *By the waters of Baptism, as by common right, Christians are made members of the Mystical Body of Christ the Priest*, and by the "character" which is imprinted on their souls, they are appointed to give worship to God. Thus they participate, according to their condition, in the priesthood of Christ (No. 88).[217]

The Thomistic baptismal theology is evident here in the idea of there being "a character" that "is imprinted on their souls." In this passage, Pope Pius XII and Cardinal Bea are following Canon 87 of the 1917 Code of Canon Law, which, as we've noted above, is based upon the brief of Pope Benedict XIV, who in turn relies on the theologian Francisco Suárez, who cites Augustine but is following Thomas Aquinas. Although Blessed Augustine has been cited as support for this teaching, in fact, it was Aquinas, not Augustine, who first taught that the baptismal character produces spiritual effects and is "sealed" on the soul of all who are validly baptized. For Aquinas, the sign, simply on account of being externally valid, brings about an enduring effect on the soul. In claiming, as Bea did, that every validly baptized person received the sacramental character, he knew he was not only basing himself on the solid ground of Pius XII's teaching, but, more important, on Aquinas' baptismal theology.[218]

Bea was, therefore, right in concluding that, at least in this passage, "Pius XII was teaching that, through Baptism, every-

217. Emphasis added.
218. See *Summa Theologica*, 3.63 ("On whether the sacrament imprints a character on the soul"), 64.a9: ("On whether faith is required of necessity in the minister of a sacrament"), and 69 ("On the effects of Baptism").

one who receives the saving waters is made Homo Christianus, a person in Christ: 'Through the general title of Christian, man becomes a member of the Mystical Body of Christ the Priest.' All share in this identity—the priestly dignity of human life ... 'in Christ.'"[219]

Yet, although Bea was not distorting or misquoting Pius XII, he was reading him selectively, picking and choosing: picking passages reflective of an "inclusive" Thomistic baptismal theology while choosing to leave aside thought reflecting an "exclusivist" Augustinian ecclesiology.

In a famous speech in 1961, delivered at a major ecumenical event in Rome,[220] Cardinal Bea sought to build on his selective reading of Pius XII's encyclicals by reference to the Apostle Paul's teaching on Baptism. He sought to equate the Thomistic tradition and the relevant passage from Pius XII's encyclical with the great Apostle's baptismal theology and ecclesiology: "[T]he teaching of Mediator Dei and St. Paul is *unqualified:* it states what is always effected by the actual reception of Baptism, provided, of course that [it] is valid. So this must somehow hold good for our separated brethren also, even though they are separated from the Holy See as a result of heresy or schism inherited from their ancestors."[221] Cardinal Bea makes the case for continuity here, not only with the last Pope or recent Popes, but even with the "mouth of Christ" himself, the great Apostle Paul. He will also go on to make his case before the Second Vatican Council and be victorious, with *Unitatis Redintegratio* as a witness of this success. The "significance" at-

219. Ibid., 282.
220. This speech was given before the Church Unity Octave at the Dominican Faculty at the Angelicum in Rome.
221. Bea, *Unity of Christians,* 30 (emphasis added).

tributed to Baptism by Cardinal Bea would be recognized by nearly all, both in the council and in the ecumenical movement as a whole in due time.

Yet, there are a number of assumptions made that, if they are shown to be erroneous, call into question the entire new ecclesiology. What if there are qualifications to be made to St. Paul's teaching on Baptism? What if it is a matter not only of external "validity" but of authenticity, of unity, as well? If, in his selective reading of not only Pius XII but also of the Apostle Paul, Cardinal Bea has omitted an essential element—orthodox faith, the criterion of the authenticity of the mysteries—can his theory stand, or that of the Second Vatican Council?

Cardinal Bea and the Second Vatican Council have built their new ecclesiological edifice upon the cornerstone of a common Baptism. If it is shown that this foundation is hollow, that the house has not, in fact, been built upon the Rock but upon disparate and incongruous clods of earthly ideas, the whole structure will come tumbling down. An examination of the meaning attributed to Baptism and the Church in the official conciliar text, *Unitatis Redintegratio,* reveals most clearly of what the new ecclesiology consists.

II

Baptism and the Church According to the
Decree on Ecumenism, *Unitatis Redintegratio*

The Second Vatican Council

The designation of *Unitatis Redintegratio* as a "decree" signifies that it chiefly, but not exclusively, contains instructions of a practical nature that are based on doctrinal teaching expressed elsewhere.[222] *Lumen Gentium* is said to provide the main doctrinal basis for the decree.[223] Nevertheless, the document's doctrinal content is significant, and its detailed application of the ecclesiology expounded in *Lumen Gentium* brings important illumination to the subject.[224] When promulgating the decree at the end of the third session of the council, Pope Paul VI stated that the "Decree explained and completed the Constitution on the Church,"[225] thus linking the two documents together in terms of their significance for the dogma of

222. In response to some who claimed that Vatican II's decrees, including UR, were of a purely pastoral nature, Yves Congar replied, "Vatican II was undoubtedly doctrinal" (Yves Congar, "A Last Look at the Council," in *Vatican II by Those Who Were There*, ed. Alberic Stacpoole [London: Geoffrey Chapman, 1986], 347). And elsewhere he wrote that, "The first objective of the Council is doctrinal: to protect the doctrine, the deposit." Éric Mahieu and Bernard Dupuy, eds., *Yves Congar: Mon journal du Concile* (Paris: Cerf, 2002), 210.

223. See the last paragraph of article one of UR.

224. According to Cardinal Walter Kasper, "*Unitatis Redintegratio* . . . indicates the approach to take in explaining the assertations of *Lumen Gentium* (an attitude of openness on more than one point)." See Kasper, "The Fortieth Anniversary of the Vatican Council II Decree *Unitatis Redintegratio*," Information Service of the Pontifical Council for Promoting Unity, no. 115 (Vatican City: 2004), 20.

225. "[E]a dotrina, explicationibus complete in Schemate 'De Oecumenismo' comprehensis . . ." Ench. Vat., Vol. 1, *Documenti del Concilio Vaticano II* (Bologna, 1981), 178.

the Church. The two documents should therefore be read and understood together.[226]

Contents and Aim of the Decree

Unitatis Redintegratio consists of an introduction and three chapters, which are in turn divided into twenty-four articles.[227] The introduction consists of one article. Chapter 1, entitled "Catholic Principles on Ecumenism," contains three articles (2–4). Chapter 2 is entitled "The Practice of Ecumenism" and contains eight articles (5–12). Chapter 3 is entitled "Churches and Ecclesial Communities Separated from the Roman Apostolic See" and is divided into sub-chapters, "The Special Position of the Eastern Churches" (articles 14–18) and "The Separated Churches and Ecclesial Communities in the West" (articles 19–24).

There are three distinctive, interrelated features of the ecclesiology expressed in *Unitatis Redintegratio* that pertain to our topic. Taken as a whole they express a new understanding of the status of other Christians and of the nature of the Roman Catholic Church itself. This new understanding comes from a recognition "of the signs of the times": in a surprising "about face," the previously rejected ecumenical movement is deemed a result of the "inspiring grace of the Holy Spirit."[228] As Cardinal Edward Cassidy has written: "In a clear and radical departure from pre-council teaching, the council presents the ecumenical movement as being 'fostered by the grace of the Holy Spirit,' and desires in this document 'to set before all Catholics the ways and means by which they too can respond

---

226. *Commentary on the Documents of Vatican II*, 2:57.
227. The Decree is roughly 7000 words.
228. UR 4a.

to this grace and to this divine call."[229] Throughout this text the influence of the ecumenical movement is obvious.

The first distinguishing feature of the Decree is the discovery and declaration of a "universal brotherhood of Christians."[230] The Decree refers to other Christians as "brothers." This brotherliness is of a sacramental nature; it refers not only to fellow followers and believers in Christ, but also to all those who have "put on Christ,"[231] who have become His members through Baptism.[232] In other words, this "brotherhood" is not based solely on man's common humanity or convictions, but on the theanthropic communion shared by all Christians in Baptism, which incorporates them into Christ.[233]

This communion in Christ, established through Baptism, is imparted by the churches that exist apart from the Roman Communion. The Decree stresses that the "Churches and ecclesial communities" as such are conveyers of grace and "means of salvation."[234] Sacraments performed in the "Churches and

229. UR 1. Cardinal Edward Idris Cassidy, *Ecumenism and Interreligious Dialogue: Unitatis Redintegratio, Nostra Aetate* (New York: Paulist Press, 2005), 13.

230. UR 3a and 5a. Cardinal Cassidy continues: "In his encyclical letter *Ut Unum Sint* (On Commitment to Ecumenism), Pope John Paul II presents 'brotherhood rediscovered' as one of the principal fruits of the ecumenical dialogue that had taken place" (ibid.).

231. UR 3a; Gal. 3:37; and Rom. 13:14.

232. 1 Cor. 12:27.

233. UR 3a. Two sentences in this section especially stress this: "For men who believe in Christ and have been truly baptized are in communion with the Catholic Church" and "even in spite of [obstacles to full communion] it remains true that all who have been justified by faith in Baptism are incorporated into Christ, and have a right to be called Christian, and so are correctly accepted as brothers by the children of the Catholic Church."

234. UR 3d: "It follows that the separated Churches and Communi-

ecclesial communities"[235] separated from Rome, once thought of as valid in spite of being performed by the non–Roman Catholic communion,[236] are now considered fruitful because they are carried out within such churches and ecclesial communities.[237] Baptism incorporates them into the Church of Christ, first, as members of their particular church, and second, as Christians in imperfect communion with Rome.[238] Thus, the new ecclesiology envisions a "Church of Christ" that includes within it both the Roman Catholic Church and the "Churches and ecclesial communities" separated from it.[239]

ties *as such*, though we believe them to be deficient in some respects, have been by no means deprived of significance and importance in the mystery of salvation. For the Spirit of Christ has not refrained from using them *as means of salvation* which derive their efficacy from the very fullness of grace and truth entrusted to the Church" (emphases mine). This point will be discussed in detail further on.

235. UR 3. These are new terms for the communities of the "separated brethren" and are meant to have ecclesiological significance.

236. See Augustine, *On Baptism*, NPNF 1.10.14. See also Francis A. Sullivan, S.J., *Salvation Outside the Church: Tracing the History of the Catholic Response* (New York: Paulist Press, 1992; Eugene, OR: Wipf and Stock, 2002), 28–35, 149.

237. UR 3d.

238. Fr. Jorge A Scampini, O.P., *"We acknowledge one Baptism for the forgiveness of sins,"* a paper delivered at the Faith and Order Plenary Commission in Kuala, Malaysia, July 28–Aug. 6, 2004; pdf available online: "We are incorporated into the Church through the concrete Christian community in which the sacrament is administered. In other words, through Baptism we become Christians who are also Catholic, Orthodox, Anglican, or whatever." See also *Directory for the Application of Principles and Norms on Ecumenism* (www.vatican.va/roman_curia/pontifical_councils/chrstuni/ general-docs/rc_pc_chrstuni_doc_19930325_directory_ en.html): "While by Baptism a person is incorporated into Christ and his Church, this is only done in practice in a given Church or ecclesial Community" (no. 97, p. 33).

239. As UR 15a clearly states in reference to the "Eastern Church-

This brings us to the second distinguishing feature of the new ecclesiology. In order to be consistent with this new view of the separated churches, *Lumen Gentium* dropped an absolute and exclusive identity between the Church of Christ and the Roman Catholic Church, as had been traditionally asserted.[240] The simple identification of the Church of Christ with the Roman Catholic Church, as stated in papal encyclicals,[241] but also in pre-conciliar versions of the Constitution,[242] was replaced with the statement that "the Church of Christ *subsistit in* the Catholic Church" (LG 8). The Latin term *subsistit in* is gener-

es": "[T]hrough the celebration of the Holy Eucharist in each of these Churches, the Church of God is built up and grows in stature." See also Francis A. Sullivan, S.J., "The Significance of the Vatican II Declaration that the Church of Christ 'Subsists in' the Roman Catholic Church," in René Latourelle, ed., *Vatican II: Assessment and Perspectives, Twenty-five Years After (1962–1987)* (New York: Paulist Press, 1989), 2:283: "[T] here is one Church of God that embraces the particular churches of East and West, even though at present they are not in full communion with one another."

240. The official explanation given to the bishops by the Theological Commission to explain this change shows that it was made to agree with the new consideration of the non–Roman Catholic mysteries and communions as such. The Commission said the change was made "so that the expression might better agree with the affirmation about the ecclesial elements which are found elsewhere." Sullivan, "Significance," 274.

241. For example, Pope Pius XII, in both *Mystici Corporis* (1943) and *Humani generis* (1950), made it very clear that the Mystical Body of Christ, the Church of Christ, and the Roman Catholic Church were one and the same thing.

242. The preparatory commission to the council in its opening session of 1962 made the following statements in the schema *De Ecclesia:* "The Roman Catholic Church is the Mystical Body of Christ . . . and only the one that is Roman Catholic has the right to be called Church." See Sullivan, "Significance," 273.

ally interpreted as follows: while the unity of the Church and the fullness of the Grace and gifts of God exist within the Roman church alone, in the ecclesial communities "the one sole Church of Christ is present, albeit imperfectly . . . and by means of their ecclesiastical elements the Church of Christ is in some way operative in them."[243] An imperfect ecclesial unity and an imperfect communion exist binding all the baptized and their communities together in the one Church of Christ.[244] Even though this imperfect unity and communion is not the express will of Christ (κατ'εὐδοκίαν), it is allowed (κατά παραχώρηση) by Him to exist;[245] and because no one can be Christ's without

243. This is how the *Relatio*, the official explanation of the use of these terms, puts it (AS, III/2, 335). This text is cited in Sullivan, "Significance," 282. The well-known theologian Alois Grillmeier writes that, with the change from "est" to "subsistit," "it is stressed that the Church of Rome as a local church is only one part of the whole Church. . . . A wholisitic, exclusive view of identity is no longer stated." See Grillmeier's commentary on the tenth chapter of the Dogmatic Constitution on the Church in: LthK. Erg.-Bd. I, p. 175, cited in Στυλιανός Χ. Τσομπανίδης, *Ἡ Διακήρυξη Dominus Iesus καὶ ἡ Οἰκουμενική Σημασία της* [*The Declaration "Dominus Iesus" and Its Ecumenical Significance*] (Θεσσαλονίκη: Πουρναράς, 2003), 183.

244. Suffice it to say here that there are two tendencies among Roman Catholic theologians in interpreting the meaning of *subsistit in*, one that would broaden the proposition, and the other that would like to restrict it. Joseph Ratzinger is seen by many as the most vocal in seeking to restrict the meaning and see it as entirely consistent with previous papal encyclicals. The late Cardinal Willebrands, one-time prefect of the Secretariat for Promoting Christian Unity, the theologian Edward Schillebeeckx, and Francis Sullivan, S.J., among others, all contend that the term does not imply exclusivity.

245. UR 3e: "[O]ur separated brethren, whether considered as individuals or as Communities and Churches, are not blessed with that unity which Jesus Christ wished to bestow on all those who through Him were born again into one body, and with Him quickened to newness of life."

belonging to the Church, the limits of the Church coincide with the circumscription of all those belonging to Christ,[246] that is, all the baptized. This is definitely a new and unprecedented view of the Church.

This brings us to the third primary feature of the new ecclesiology, which is also the core of the teaching of the Second Vatican Council on the Church: the communio ecclesiology.[247] Communio ecclesiology is said to be the guiding concept, the key to understanding the new ecclesiology and ecumenism of Vatican II.[248] It refers to the sharing in the goods of salvation, in the sancta or the sacramenta, a communio "formed as it were as an icon of the Trinity in the image of the Trinitarian communio."[249] Integral to this idea is Baptism, the sacrament of faith, whereby "those who have been baptized belong to the one body of Christ which is the church."[250] In this way, then,

---

246. This is how Cardinal Willebrands expressed his understanding of the dogmatic meaning behind the transition from *est* to *subsistit in*. See Cardinal Johannes Willebrands, "Vatican II's Ecclesiology of Communion," *Origins* 17 (1987), 28.

247. This is also referred to as a "eucharistic ecclesiology," retaining the name given it originally by Orthodox theologians. *Communio* is the Latin form of the Greek word "κοινωνία," which does not mean community, as some wrongly interpret it, but participation. We will use the term "communio ecclesiology," to differentiate the two, for "communio" ecclesiology has important differences with that of the Orthodox.

248. Cardinal Walter Kasper, "Communio: The Guiding Concept of Catholic Ecumenical Theology," in *That They May All Be One: The Call to Unity Today* (London/New York: Burns and Oates, 2004), 50–74.

249. Cardinal Walter Kasper, "The Decree on Ecumenism—Read Anew After Forty Years," Pontifical Council for Promoting Christian Unity, Conference on the 40th Anniversary of the Promulgation of the Conciliar Decree "Unitatis Redintegratio," Rocca di Papa, Mondo Migliore, November 11, 12, and 13, 2004.

250. Ibid.

the "separated brethren" are not considered to be outside the one Church, but to already belong to it in a most fundamental way.[251] "The new and ecumenical insight, therefore, is that among the baptized there already exists a fundamental unity or communio, so that the distinction is not between full unity and no communio at all, but between full and incomplete communio (UR 3)."[252] On the basis of this communio created by the one common Baptism, ecumenism is seen as having an "ontological foundation and an ontological depth," being an event of the Spirit.[253]

What unites each of these new features is the recognition of certain ecclesiological ramifications emerging from a common Baptism. Traditionally, schismatic or heretical Baptism was considered to be "valid" but "unfruitful" (at least for adults) owing to the grave sin of schism or heresy. Through ecumenical involvement, however, Catholicism has been led to presume that those formally known as schismatics and heretics are not guilty of sin in remaining true to their confessions. Hence, their Baptism is accepted as both valid and fruitful of grace and salvation.

This new recognition is the cornerstone upon which the whole edifice of the new ecclesiology rests. The loss of this basis of communio ecclesiology would mean not only that the ecumenical bridge would be broken, but that the new ecclesiological framework of the Roman Catholic edifice itself would collapse. For, according to this vision, the Church of Christ extends beyond the borders of Roman Catholicism on the authenticity of the mysteries of the "separated brethren," first of which is Baptism.

251. See LG 11 and 14; UR 22.
252. Kasper, "Communio," 51.
253. Kasper, "Decree on Ecumenism."

The Pastoral Expediency Behind the Decree

In contrast to the reasons why the ecumenical councils were called—in order to resolve matters of doctrine and establish ecclesiastical order—the Second Vatican Council had as its main raison d'etre the "bringing up to date" (aggiornamento) of the Church, which meant first of all a profound spiritual renewal—"a renewal that included reaching out to the churches separated from Rome." "The Council was to be pastoral rather than dogmatic" and rather than proclaiming new dogmas, the task of the council was to "find new ways of expressing the old."[254] In the spirit of renewal, the council was to bring about a series of progressive changes in liturgical, pastoral, institutional, cultural, and ecumenical matters.[255]

It is therefore not surprising that the unabashed aim of *Unitatis Redintegratio* was to reorient Roman Catholics toward their "separated brethren" and the ecumenical movement.[256] Although officially the text is written as a pastoral decree for Roman Catholics, the authors clearly had in mind the reception it would enjoy among the non–Roman Catholics. For, it is acknowledged that *Unitatis Redintegratio* "would have been unthinkable prior to the existence of the ecumenical movement"[257] and that it "formed a part of the ecumenical movement which had arisen outside of the Catholic Church."[258] It is apparent,

254. Raymond F. Bulman, "Introduction: The Historical Context," in *From Trent to Vatican II: Historical and Theological Investigations*, ed. Raymond F. Bulman and Frederick J. Parrella (Oxford, UK: Oxford University Press, 2006), 11.

255. Ibid.

256. See the Introduction, notes 8 and 9.

257. Cardinal Joseph Ratzinger, *Theological Highlights of Vatican II* (New York: Paulist Press, 2009), 101.

258. Kasper, "Decree on Ecumenism.

then, that *Unitatis Redintegratio* and relevant portions of *Lumen Gentium* were "decisively influenced" by the ecumenical movement.[259]

Hence, along with the Roman Catholic faithful, the "separated brethren" should be considered as co-recipients of the document, for they also influenced the way in which the document was written, and how it refers to those outside the Roman Catholic Church. The conviction that contemporary Protestants and Orthodox "cannot be accused of the sin involved in the separation"[260] and that the traditional stance vis-à-vis schismatics and heretics cannot and does not apply[261] determined the pastoral and theological stance that would be taken. This perceived lack of culpability contributed greatly to a reconsideration of their ecclesiological status.[262] In short, historic circumstances and pastoral aims helped spearhead a theological re-conception of the Church.[263]

259. Ratzinger also points out that many of the views expressed in the Decree were the result of the Church "listening" to the ecumenical movement: "Ecumenism was also to be found in the view of ecclesiastical offices as ministry, of laymen as within the framework of the unity of the holy People of God, and of holiness as a gift God continually gives to a Church in constant need of forgiveness." *Theological Highlights*, 101.

260. UR 3a.

261. The traditional stance is that of Blessed Augustine, namely, that both those who caused schism and those who belonged to the schismatic or heretical group in subsequent centuries are guilty of grave sin, although the latter group less grievously. See *On Baptism*, NPNF 1.5.6. See also Sullivan, *Salvation Outside the Church*, 151: "Vatican II presumes the absence of the culpability that would mean exclusion from salvation for those 'outside' the Catholic Church."

262. See UR 3a, where the recognition of a lack of blameworthiness is immediately followed by recognition of Baptism and Communion, albeit incomplete.

263. Johannes Feiner in his "Commentary on the Decree," in com-

This is the inescapable conclusion from the statements made by the Decree's authors and implementers. Key aspects of the new ecclesiology were developed consciously and purposefully in order to further the pastoral aim of rapprochement, so that one can rightly speak, not of the theological method, but of the pastoral and ecumenical expediency behind the texts. Concepts and changes key to the new ecclesiology, such as the insertion of *subsistit in* to replace the previous *est* in *Lumen Gentium* 8, the rejection of the concept of "members of the Church," and the promotion of the phrase "People of God"[264] were introduced precisely for their ecumenical effect and reception.

Yves Congar, who was involved in the formation of the council's new ecclesiology more than anyone else, explained the reason behind the insertion of *subsistit in* to replace *est* in *Lumen Gentium:* "By expressing the matter in this way, the Council established the possibility of recognizing other Christians as truly belonging to the Body of Christ and of speaking of the relation of other Churches and ecclesial communities

menting on Article 3 of the Decree, says the following: "If a reorientation of the attitude of Catholics to their fellow Christians is to take place, such as the decree is striving for, the relationship which exists between non-Catholic Christianity and the Catholic Church must first be redefined in theological terms. Here the picture of the Church and its unity set out in the previous article is applied, and makes possible statements which have never previously been known from the Church's magisterium." Feiner, in *Commentary on the Documents of Vatican II* (London: Burns and Oates, Ltd., 1968), 2:69. See also Χαρκιανάκι, Στυλιανοῦ, Ἀρχιμ., Τὸ Περὶ Ἐκκλησίας Σύνταγμα τῆς Β´ Βατικανῆς Συνόδου. Θεσσαλονίκη, 1969,140–45.

264. See Yves Congar, *Die Kirche als Volk Gottes*, Conc (D) 1 (1965), 5–16, citation at 11: "The advantage of the concept of the People of God for ecumenism is indisputable, especially for the dialogue with the Protestants."

with the Catholic Church in terms of a real, although imperfect communion."[265]

Cardinal Walter Kasper offers a similar explanation for the change: "In the course of the Council the 'subsistit in' took the place of the previous 'est.' It contains *in nuce* the whole ecumenical problem. . . . It wished to do justice to the fact that there are found outside of the Catholic Church not only individual Christians but also elements of the church, indeed churches and ecclesial communities which, although not in full communion, rightly belong to the one church and possess salvatory significance for their members."[266]

Concepts that had previously been a mainstay of Roman Catholic ecclesiology were intentionally put aside in order to widen the notion of the Church and ease rapprochement. Concerning the phrase "members of the Church" Cardinal Joseph Ratzinger wrote:

> One wondered if the image of the Mystical Body might be too narrow a starting point to define the many forms of belonging to the Church now found in the tangle of human history. If we use the image of a body to describe "belonging" we are limited only to the form of representation as "member." Either one is or one is not a member, there are no other possibilities. One can then ask if the image of the body was too restrictive, since there manifestly existed in reality *intermediate degrees of belonging*. The Constitution on the Church found it helpful for this purpose to use the concept of 'the People of God.' It could describe the relationship of non-Catholic Chris-

---

265. Yves Congar, "What Belonging to the Church Has Come to Mean," trans. Francis M. Chew, *Communio* 4 (1977), 150.

266. Kasper, "Decree on Ecumenism."

tians to the Church as being "in communion" and that of non-Christians as being "ordered" to the Church where in both cases one relies on the idea of the People of God (LG 15, 16). In one respect one can say that the Council introduced the concept of "the People of God" above all as an ecumenical bridge.[267]

Yves Congar, speaking from his experience on the drafting committee of *Lumen Gentium*, concurs with this reading of the change: "The council intentionally avoided speaking of 'membris.' The council fathers had in fact perceived that this vocabulary led to difficulties for which no solution could be found. In the subcommittee of the doctrinal Commission, in which we participated, it was realized that the way in which one spoke of the membership of Catholics in the Church implied a particular concept of the Church."[268]

The principal question was: How can we express a vision of the Church that will serve to further ecumenical relations? That this was the reasoning lurking behind the changes is confirmed by the fact that ideas and definitions of the Church utilized in the past that did not serve this goal were dropped.[269]

267. Joseph Ratzinger, "The Ecclesiology of Vatican II," a talk given at the Pastoral Congress of the Diocese of Aversa (Italy), Sept. 15, 2001, http://www.ewtn.com/library/CURIA/CDFECCV2.HTM (emphasis added).

268. Congar, "What Belonging to the Church Has Come to Mean," 150. See also Maximilian Heinrich Heim, *Joseph Ratzinger: Life in the Church and Living Theology: Fundamentals of Ecclesiology with Reference to Lumen Gentium*, trans. Michael J. Miller (San Francisco: Ignatius Press, 2007), 241–42.

269. Ratzinger, *Theological Highlights*, 103–104. The following commentary and quotations are from this source with page numbers given in text.

Here we will cite three such concepts or formulations of which the young theologian Fr. Joseph Ratzinger spoke as not meeting ecumenical standards, so they were then discarded: (1) the formula that saw membership in the Church as dependent on the joint presence of three prerequisites: Baptism, profession of the same faith, and acceptance of the hierarchy headed by the bishop of Rome (102); (2) the concept of the votum Ecclesiae, which meant that non-Catholics belonged to the Church by virtue of their "desire" to be a part of it (103); and (3) the previously mentioned expression "member of the Church," even if "hallowed by long usage in Catholic theology" (ibid.). "Shedding this terminological armor . . . made possible a much more positive presentation of the way Christians are related to the Church as well as positive Christian status for Christians separated from Rome" (104).

The Significance of the Decree for the Ecumenical Movement

As will become clear, *Unitatis Redintegratio* presents a view of the Church that is consistent neither with prior post-schism understandings of Roman Catholicism nor with a return to the *consensus patrum*, nor even to the views of Blessed Augustine, but is rather a sharp departure from them. In spite of this, the document is hailed by many Roman Catholics and Protestants and even some Orthodox as "historic," "ground breaking," and yet nevertheless "not a radical departure from the genuine Patristic tradition."[270]

270. John Zizioulas (Metropolitan of Pergamon), "Unitatis Redintegratio: An Orthodox Reflection," in *Searching For Christian Unity* (New York: New City Press, 2007), 39: "This opening up of the boundaries of the Church beyond her canonical limits was not a radical departure from the genuine Patristic tradition, indeed of the West itself, since it

The universal approbation of the document in ecumenical circles is, however, not surprising, for Baptism as the connecting link between "ecclesial communities" is one of the foundation stones of the modern ecumenical movement. The broad, positive reception of *Unitatis Redintegratio* undoubtedly stems from its acceptance, based on a common Baptism, of the ecclesial nature or "ecclesiality" of the non-Roman communions. This new position, more than any other, brought Catholicism into close harmony with the prevailing views in Protestantism[271] and into the ecumenical movement itself.[272] *Unitatis Redintegratio* was the first major ecumenical document to develop the implications of a common Baptism into an ecclesiology of communion.

To this day it serves as an inspiration and guide for many in the ecumenical movement. Two examples of ecumenical initiatives are: The Faith and Order convergence text *Baptism, Eucharist and Ministry* (BEM), of which the section on Baptism was the most positively received part; and the paper "Called

was in fact a return to St. Augustine's ecclesiology which, contrary to that of St. Cyprian, distinguished clearly between the canonical and the charismatic limits of the Church."

271. "Protestant churches have long understood that their common Baptism reflects a unity which is more fundamental than their differences." Thomas Best, "Baptism Today: Showing Forth our Unity in Christ," in *Baptism Today: Understanding, Practice, Ecumenical Implications* (Collegeville: WCC Publications, 2008), vii.

272. Ibid. This essential agreement of post–Vatican II Roman Catholic theology and Protestant theology is most apparent in the ecumenical document of the Joint Working Group of the World Council of Churches and the Roman Catholic Church entitled *Ecclesiological and Ecumenical Implications of a Common Baptism* produced in 2004. See "Information Service" of The Pontifical Council for Promoting Christian Unity (Vatican City), No. 117 (2004/IV), 188–204.

to Be the One Church," which was adopted by the member churches of the World Council of Churches in Porto Alegre, Brazil, in 2006. In both documents the mutual recognition of Baptism is the central point.

The success of these texts could not have been possible if an underlying ecclesiology of communio had not also been widely embraced in ecumenical circles.[273] However, the ecumenical movement did not originally focus on this ecclesiology. Rather, from the beginning it considered a variety of "unity concepts." The earliest concept, which was the most straightforward and also the most consistent with Orthodox ecclesiology, was the concept of organic unity. Namely, that in each place there should be one fully committed communion, which would be united in faith, sacraments, the apostolic preaching, and mission. This concept was somewhat refined in the 1960s and 1970s and renamed conciliar fellowship: "truly united" local churches possess in conciliar fellowship "the fullness of catholicity" and the "fullness of truth and love."[274]

It wasn't until the Second Vatican Council that the concept of communio was broadly considered within the ecumenical movement. By the end of the 1980s, however, communio was the concept upon which most ecumenical discussion of unity centered.[275] The World Council of Churches seventh assembly in

---

273. "With *koinonia* as the central concept of unity, it is only natural that holy Baptism has come into prominence, since it is the foundational sacrament of the church, the portal through which one passes in becoming part of the *koinonia* that is the church." S. Anita Stauffer, "Baptism and Communio," *The Ecumenical Review* (Geneva: WCC, April 2000).

274. Ibid.

275. Ibid. It is also true that the Second Vatican Council was heavily influenced by earlier texts of the ecumenical movement. As Stylianos

Canberra (1991) officially accepted the concept of communio,[276] to which the fifth World Council of Faith and Order in Santiago de Compostela (1993) likewise subscribed. This particular understanding of communio is in accord with and largely dependent upon the "communio ecclesiology" declared to be "the central and fundamental idea" of the documents of the Second Vatican Council.[277] "[A]lthough different models of ecumenism, such as the federal and the conciliar, continue to compete for influence, the communio model is increasingly dominant in ecumenical circles today,"[278] not only among Roman Catholics but also among Anglicans, Protestants, and some Orthodox.

Having, then, briefly introduced and touched upon the contents and intended purpose of *Unitatis Redintegratio*, let us now turn to the Decree itself and examine what is presented therein concerning Baptism and the Church.

Tsombanidis notes: "It is easy for anyone to understand just how similar the texts of the Second Vatican Council are to the Statement of the WCC made in Toronto (1950). . . . Similarity is also evident in the Statement made by the Third General Assembly of the WCC in New Dehli in 1961. In fact, this text is practically identical with [that of] the Second Vatican Council. . . ." (Τσομπανίδης, Ἡ Διακήρυξη *Dominus Iesus*, 69).

276. See the Roman Catholic contribution of Emmanuel Lane, "A Catholic Perspective," in *The Unity of the Church as Koinonia. Ecumenical Perspectives on the 1991 Canberra Statement on Unity*, ed. G. Gabmann and J. Radano, Faith and Order Paper 163 (Geneva: WCC, 1991), 4–18.

277. Roman Catholic Church, Synod of Bishops, "The Final Report," *Origins* 15:27 (Dec. 19, 1985), 444–50 (p. 448).

278. Avery Dulles, "Ecumenism without Illusions: A Catholic Perspective," *First Things* (June/July 1990).

9

BAPTISM AND THE UNITY OF THE CHURCH IN *UNITATIS REDINTEGRATIO*

In *Unitatis Redintegratio* we read that non–Roman Catholic Christians,[279] those "men who believe in Christ and have been truly baptized," are considered to be "in communion with the Catholic Church," even if "this communion is imperfect" (3a). For, "all who have been justified by faith in Baptism are incorporated into Christ." If they are thus incorporated into Christ, it follows, of course, that they "have a right to be called Christian," and as Christians they are "accepted as brothers by the children of the Catholic Church" (3a).

If, then, these baptized Christians, truly brothers in Christ, are in communion with the Church, even if somehow only "partially," it follows that not only some, but "even very many" of the "elements and endowments" that "build up and give life to the Church" "exist outside [its] visible boundaries." These "elements" include "the written word of God,"[280] "the life of

279. Although it is not explicitly stated, we presume that this would include the Orthodox, Old-Catholics, Monophysites, Nestorians, the many different Protestant confessions, and others, with the exception of groups like the Mormons or Unitarians, who are not considered to be Trinitarian Christians. Thirty-seven years after Vatican II, on June 5, 2011, the Congregation for the Doctrine of the Faith in fact did issue a ruling denying the validity of the Baptism performed by Mormons on account of their non-Trinitarian faith and understanding of Baptism.

280. Although it is beyond the scope of this work to address wheth-

grace," "the interior gifts of the Holy Spirit," and many others (3b).

This "life of grace" springs from the liturgical life and prayer of the "separated brethren" and is a life that opens up access to the assembly of those being saved (3c). It follows, then, that, in spite of their deficiencies, the "separated Churches and Communities" are in and of themselves[281] important "means of sal-

---

er or not Holy Scripture can be common to both the Church and the heterodox, suffice it to say that Tradition and Scripture are expressed in a perfect harmony only within the living and ever-present organic reality of the Church. Taken separately, apart from the context of the unity of faith in the Church, they are a "closed book" and of a purely external nature. Their internal, spiritual meaning is intelligible only to those living in the Holy Spirit. Hence comes the famous stance of Tertullian that the Scriptures do not belong to those outside the Church, that there is no common ground with them on the basis of the Scriptures, and that the Apostle admonishes us not to dispute with heretics but to admonish them. (Cf. *De praescriptione haereticum*, 15–19). See also the brilliant and extensive treatment of this subject by the New Hieromartyr Hilarion (Troitsky), "Holy Scripture and the Church," *The Orthodox Word*, nos. 264–65 (Platina, CA: St. Herman Press, 2009); English translation by Igor Radev.

281. It is important to note that the very significant meaning of UR 3d, which states that the churches and ecclesiastical communities *themselves* are means of salvation, is lost in the three existing Greek translations of the Decree (*Typis Polyglottis Vaticanis*, 1965; Γραγείον Καλού Τύπου, 1970; and Ἀποστολικὸ Βικαριᾶτο, Θεσσαλονίκης, 2012) because of the omission of the Latin pronoun *ipsae*. The original Latin states: "Proinde *ipsae* Ecclesiae et Communitates seiunctae, etsi defectus illas pati credimus, nequaquam in mysterio salutis significatione et pondere exutae sunt." *Ipsae* is the nominative plural of the definitive pronoun of *ipsa* (femine gender) and should be translated as *themselves*. The English translation, which has not omitted the term *ipsae*, reads, "It follows that the separated Churches and Communities *as such* . . . ," thereby communicating the sense that the churches and communities in and of themselves are means of salvation.

vation," spiritually fruit-bearing because of their participation
in the Church's "fullness of grace and truth" (3d).

The "sharing of divine life" (22a) to which the "separated
brethren" have been admitted comes to them on the strength
of their "duly administered" Baptism; by it they have been
"truly incorporated into the crucified and glorified Christ." It
is because of their true Baptism that a "sacramental bond of
unity"[282] has been established "linking all who have been reborn by it" (22b).

These statements encapsulate the Decree's teaching on the
Baptism of the "separated brethren," as well as the implications
of this Baptism for both individuals and their church or community. In *Unitatis Redintegratio*, the standing of the "separated
brethren" has been extraordinarily enhanced. Recognition of
participation in the life of the Church was extended to them on
essential levels. The Augustinian stance of only recognizing the
validity of schismatic and heretical Baptism definitively became
a relic of the past. The council abandoned this Augustinian
legacy, which earlier had such a deep impact on Latin theology,
and recognized the efficaciousness of schismatic and heretical
Baptism per se (UR 3a). Insomuch that this new view was
recognized in an ecumenical council, it was an unprecedented
move which then opened up the possibility of recognizing the
schismatic and heretical assemblies as "churches" per se (UR
3d).

On the strength of possessing "ecclesial elements," the first
and foremost of which is Baptism, schismatic and heretical

282. LG likewise emphasizes the bond that links all the baptized,
thus: "The Church recognizes that in many ways she is linked with
those who, being baptized, are honored with the name of Christian,
though they do not profess the faith in its entirety or do not preserve
unity of communion with the successor of Peter."

communions as such were now accepted as arks of salvation. As Cardinal Kasper has written, "for Vatican II, Baptism is the foundation for recognizing an ecclesial quality in the non-Catholic churches and church fellowships; it is the basis for the Catholic Church seeing itself as being in a real but not a full communion with the non-Catholic churches and communities."[283] And, as Fr. Francis Sullivan has stressed, *Unitatis Redintegratio* grants "explicit recognition of the salvific role not only of the ecclesial elements and 'sacred actions of the Christian religion' found among our separated brethren (UR 3 b–c), but also for their churches and ecclesial communities as such (Ipsae Ecclesiae et Communitates)."[284]

Threefold Recognition

An important contributor to the theology of Vatican II, Bishop Christopher Butler, referred to as the "voice of the English [Roman Catholic] Church," summarized well the implications of *Unitatis Redintegratio* and the important place that Baptism holds for the recognition of ecclesiality among the non–Roman Catholics. He wrote:

> The decree forces us to acknowledge, outside the visible unity of the Catholic Church, not only "vestiges" of the Church, not only individuals who, especially if they are baptized, have some communion with the Church and, if

283. Cardinal Walter Kasper, "Ecclesiological and Ecumenical Implications of Baptism," *The Ecumenical Review* (Geneva: WCC, 2000), part 3.

284. Frances A. Sullivan, S.J., "The Significance of the Vatican II Declaration that the Church of Christ 'Subsists in' the Roman Catholic Church," in René Latourelle, ed., *Vatican II: Assessment and Perspectives, Twenty-five Years After* (New York: Paulist Press, 1989), 2:281.

incorporated in Christ, are in some degree incorporated in his mystical body which is the Church, but *Christian communions of an ecclesial character* which, at least if they have "the genuine and complete substance of the eucharistic mystery" (*De Ecumenismo*, n. 22) which is the food of the mystical body, and of which the unity of the mystical body is, says St. Thomas, the *res* can truly be called "Churches."[285]

There is a logical progression from the recognition of Baptism, which somehow and to some degree incorporates the baptized into the Church, to the recognition that those baptized exist as communions of an ecclesial character, or even, in some cases, as "true Churches." Regardless of how far the recognition reaches in each case (Protestants, Orthodox, etc.), the essential point of departure for the new ecclesiology shaped at Vatican II was the recognition of schismatic and heretical Baptism per se. This is, as it were, the first of three pillars supporting the new ecclesiology. The second stems from it: the recognition of the presence and sanctifying energy of the Holy Spirit more generally among the schismatics and heretics. The final pillar is the recognition of "ecclesiality," or the character or nature of a church, among the schismatics and heretics. Three groundbreaking recognitions, then, had paved the way for a fourth and final recognition: of the Una Sancta as consisting of both the Roman Catholic Church and the schismatic and heretical assemblies. This new ecclesiology was slowly formed over centuries, but it was only at Vatican II that the entire edifice was completed, revealed, and promoted as one coherent vision of the Church.

285. Butler, Christopher, *The Theology of Vatican II* (London: Darton, Longman and Todd, 1967, rev. ed. 1981), p. 119 (emphasis added).

The idea that schismatics and heretics were "baptized" and therefore received the "baptismal character," an indelible mark on the soul, and thereby became members of the Church, had long been assimilated into canon law and papal decrees.[286] Its implications for ecclesiology, however, were heretofore undeveloped. Aquinas had stated this view of Baptism in his sacramental theology but, since ecclesiological thought was essentially stuck in an Augustinian paradigm, no overall ecclesiological theory had been drawn up incorporating the Thomistic idea as it applied to schismatics and heretics. The first step for reformers like Congar before and at Vatican II was to explain the ecclesiological implications for this recognition of membership—first of all as it pertains to the new ecumenical outlook embraced by the council.[287]

As we have seen, fewer than twenty years before Vatican II, Pope Pius XII, working within an Augustinian paradigm, had restated the ancient Christian principle that it is within the unity of the Church alone that one experiences the life of the Holy Spirit. In article 22 of his encyclical *Mystici Corporis* he wrote: "those who are divided in faith or government cannot be living in the unity of such a Body, *nor can they be living the life of its one Divine Spirit.*"[288] *Unitatis Redintegratio,* on the contrary, states plainly that "the life of grace" (3c) and the "interior gifts of the Holy Spirit" (3b) exist among the "separated brethren." *Lumen Gentium,* echoing *Unitatis Redintegratio,* could hardly have contradicted Pope Pius XII more directly when it stated: "They also share with us in prayer and other spiritual benefits. Likewise we can say that *in some real way [the separated*

286. See chapters 5 and 6.
287. See chapters 6 and 8.
288. Emphasis added.

brethren] are joined with us in the Holy Spirit, for to them too He gives His gifts and graces whereby He is operative among them with His sanctifying power. Some indeed He has strengthened to the extent of the shedding of their blood."[289]

In stating that the unifying and fructifying energy of the Holy Spirit is not present in schismatic and heretical assemblies and sacramental acts, Pope Pius XII was not being original or innovative. He was, rather, simply restating the ancient patristic consensus that the Holy Spirit acts to purify, illumine, and sanctify in the Church alone. The early *consensus patrum* on this question is clear and indisputable: the Holy Spirit is not given in the "Baptism" of those outside the Church.[290] This was the teaching, not only of St. Cyprian of Carthage, St. Firmilian, St. Athanasius, and St. Basil, among many others, but also of the first protagonist in the Baptism controversy, Pope Stephen of Rome. In fact, there was total unanimity on this point in the first millennium.[291]

Even when Pope Stephen provoked a crisis in the Church in the third century by attacking St. Cyprian for his refusal to recognize the Baptism of schismatics and heretics, he did not claim that the Holy Spirit was given in their Baptism.[292]

289. LG 15 (emphasis added).

290. Ζηζιούλα, Ἡ ἑνότης τῆς Ἐκκλησίας, 132

291. It was not until the twelfth century, after Rome had split from the Orthodox Church, that this teaching began to be diluted in the West. For the first millennium there was unanimity: schismatics and heretics lose the grace of the Holy Spirit in the mysteries when they depart from the Church. See part 1 of this study and also H. E. J. Cowdrey, "The Dissemination of St. Augustine's Doctrine of Holy Orders During the Later Patristic Age," *Journal of Theological Studies*, n.s., 20:2 (October 1969), for the case that not even Blessed Augustine's view of orders was accepted in Rome until after the schism.

292. Some Roman Catholic scholars attempt to make the case that

Along with the entire Church, "he acknowledged that heretics and schismatics have fallen away from the Church, that they are outside her, that outside the Church they cannot have the Holy Spirit."[293] In fact, all of St. Cyprian's opponents agreed with him that the Holy Spirit is not at work mysteriologically outside the Church.[294] As already discussed, this includes Saint Augustine 150 years later in the fifth century.[295]

The question of the action of the Holy Spirit outside the Church was, already from the controversy over "rebaptism" in the third century, directly tied to the status of heretics and their "mysteries." As chapter 10 shows, this was not a question of whether or not the Spirit moves within creation or among men to lead them to the Truth. This was not doubted, for the Lord will have all men to be saved, and to come unto the knowledge

Pope Stephen did not, in fact, speak of the absence of the Holy Spirit among schismatics and heretics, but that St. Cyprian only ascribed it to him, so to speak, in the heat of polemics. That claim might have stood if it weren't for the existence of a treatise by an anonymous African Bishop with the title *De ReBaptismate*, written about 257, which makes a detailed case against St. Cyprian's views on Baptism. These views can be seen as expressing the views of the Church of Rome and its Bishop Stephen, for he comes to the same conclusion that Baptism is not necessary for converting heretics. See Ζηζιούλα, Ἡ ἑνότης τῆς Ἐκκλησίας, 131–32. See also, New Hieromartyr Hilarion (Troitsky), Archbishop of Verey, *The Unity of the Church* (Montreal: Monastery Press, 1975), 29–30 (English translation from the Russian, originally written in 1917), 36.

    293. Troitsky, ibid.

    294. Everett Ferguson, *Baptism in the Early Church: History, Theology, and Liturgy in the First Five Centuries* (Grand Rapids, MI: Eerdmans, 2009), 387, 389. For Pope Stephen's position, see St. Cyprian's Letters 73.6.2 and especially St. Firmilian's Letter included therein, 75(74).5.4.

    295. See Saint Augustine, *On Baptism*, NPNF 3.16.21. See also Saint Cyprian, Letter 69.2, To Januarius; *Anonymous Treatise on Re-Baptism*, 10.

of the truth (1 Tim. 2:4). This was a question of the purifying, illuminating, and deifying energies of the Holy Spirit in the mysteries and whether they are at work in schism and heresy. It was a question of the working of the grace of the Holy Spirit in the mysteries and thus of the presence of the Church among schismatics and heretics.[296]

The response of St. Cyprian to Pope Stephen has been well preserved, and its fundamentals have passed into the self-awareness of the Church.[297] If the heretic or schismatic is lacking in one (the Holy Spirit), he is necessarily lacking in the other (forgiveness of sins in Baptism). The gifts of the Spirit belong together and cannot be separated: "The Holy Spirit is not given by measure, but is poured out altogether on the believer," as St. Firmilian wrote.[298] St. Cyprian argued strenuously for the unity of the mysteries. As E. Ferguson has written, "He wanted to keep all the acts together as one unified ceremony."[299]

296. This is clear in St. Firmilian's reply to Pope Stephen, contained in the corpus of St. Cyprian's letters, in which he says: "although [the heretics] confess that they are in sins, and have no grace, and therefore come to the Church, you take away from them remission of sins, which is given in Baptism, by saying that they are already baptized and *have obtained the grace of the Church outside the Church*" (Letter 75[74].23). St. Firmilian here is not contradicting St. Cyprian and saying that Pope Stephen himself accepted the Holy Spirit to be imparted outside the Church, but rather that his acceptance of Baptism outside the Church necessarily leads to such a conclusion.

297. See Troitsky, *Unity of the Church*, 39; and Fr. Georges Florovsky, "The Boundaries of the Church," in *Ecumenism I: A Doctrinal Approach (Vol. 13 of the Collected Works of Georges Florovsky* [Vaduz, Europa: Büchervertriebsanstalt, 1989]), 36.

298. Letter 75.14.1.

299. Ferguson, 354. See also G. W. H. Lampe, *The Seal of the Spirit* (London: S.P.C.K., 1967), 170–78 (cited by Ferguson).

Far from being simply an insistence on church order, a limited, legalistic vision of the Church, or much less a "contribution to Donatism,"[300] St. Cyprian's views are a continuation of the Eucharist-centered ecclesiology of St. Ignatius of Antioch and St. Irenaeus. St. Cyril of Jerusalem and later St. Nicholas Cabasilas will continue in this same view. Indeed, "the link between baptism as the initiation into the covenantal communion and Eucharist as the participation of covenantal communion is already established in 1 Corinthians 10:1–4 and perhaps also 1 John 5:6. The early church linked baptism and eucharist which were the empirical foundation (lex orandi) of ecclesiology."[301] As a faithful son of the Church, then, St. Cyprian kept the mysteries together within the context of the Eucharistic assembly.[302]

300. E. W. Benson, *Cyprian, His Life, His Times, His Work* (London: Macmillan, 1897). The claim that St. Cyprian's Orthodox teaching on the Church supported, contributed to, or even is to be identified with the Donatist moralistic ecclesiology is unfounded. St. Cyprian did not rule out the mysteries of schismatics or heretics on account of subjective imperfections in the minister but rather because the Mysteries of the Church cannot exist above or outside the Church, for the Church is the Mystery of Christ. As he wrote: "The Church is one and cannot be within and outside (que et intus esse et foris non potest)." St. Cyprian laid stress on the unity of the Church and not on the moral character of the ministers.

301. David Heith-Stade, "Receiving the Non-Orthodox: A Historical Study of Greek Orthodox Canon Law," *Studia canonica* 44 (2010), 403.

302. Fr. Georges Florovsky writes concerning the ancient Church's consensus on this point: "In the Early Church the rite of Christian initiation was not divided. Three of the sacraments belong together: Baptism, the Holy Chrism, and the Eucharist. The Initiation described by St. Cyril [of Jerusalem], and later on by [St. Nicholas] Cabasilas, included all three. . . . The sacramental life of believers is the building up of the Church. Through the sacraments and in them, the new life of Christ is extended to and bestowed upon the members of His Body." Fr. Georges Florovsky, *Creation and Redemption, Vol. 3 of the Collected Works of Georges Florovsky* (Belmont, MA: Norland, 1976), 156, 158–59.

His persistence in this is, indeed, at the core not only of his ecclesiology but of the entire early Church.

For the Hieromartyr, all the gifts and mysteries of the Church are revealed and lived within the mystery of the Eucharistic synaxis of the Church, as unity of faith and communion of the Holy Spirit. "St. Cyprian emphasized the connection between baptism and Eucharistic communion since he saw the church as the communion of the Holy Spirit: if the dissidents had left the Eucharistic communion of the church they had rejected the Holy Spirit and consequently their baptism was not sanctified by the Spirit of God."[303]

He connects "the grace of the one Baptism of the Church" (unici ecclesiastici baptismi gratiam) with "the unity of the Church" (Ecclesiae unitatem) and the "inseparable mystery of unity" (inseparabile Unitatis sacramentum) with the Eucharist, as the Body and Blood of Christ, where "the Christian unanimity is linked together with itself by a firm and inseparable charity, as even the Lord's sacrifice declares" (unianimitatem christianam firma sibi adque inseparabilio caritatem conexam etiam ipsa Dominica sacrificial declarant).[304] Thus, for St. Cyprian, the "one Baptism" is inseparable from the unity of the Church in the Eucharist.[305]

If Baptism is inseparable from the Eucharist, it follows that the various aspects of the mystery of Baptism are also indivisible, such as the water and the Spirit. Seeing, then, that as recipients of the Holy Spirit we are spiritually reborn in Baptism, it is nonsensical to claim that he who has "put on Christ" is unable to receive the Holy Spirit Whom Christ sent. "Otherwise,"

---

303. Heith-Stade, David, "Receiving the Non-Orthodox," p. 404.

304. Letter 76(75).6.

305. See Γιέβτιτς, Ἀθανασίου, "Ὀπ. Γεώργιος Φλωρόφσκυ περὶ τῶν ὁρίων τῆς Ἐκκλησίας," 145.

St. Cyprian continues,

> He who is sent will be greater than Him who sends; so that one baptized without may begin indeed to put on Christ, but not to be able to receive the Holy Spirit, as if Christ could either be put on without the Spirit, or the Spirit be separated from Christ.[306] Moreover, it is silly to say, that although the second birth is spiritual, by which we are born in Christ through the laver of regeneration, one may be born spiritually among the heretics, where they say that the Spirit is not. For water alone is not able to cleanse away sins, and to sanctify a man, unless he have also the Holy Spirit. Wherefore *it is necessary that they should grant the Holy Spirit to be there, where they say that Baptism is;* or else there is no Baptism where the Holy Spirit is not, because there cannot be Baptism without the Spirit.[307]

At the Second Vatican Council the opponents of St. Cyprian not only conceded that the Holy Spirit is given anywhere

306. St. Firmilian echoes this in his own letter to St. Cyprian and in response to Pope Stephen, writing: "But if he has put on Christ, he might also receive the Holy Spirit, who was sent by Christ, and hands are vainly laid upon him who comes to us for the reception of the Spirit; unless, perhaps, he has not put on the Spirit from Christ, so that Christ indeed may be with heretics, but the Holy Spirit not be with them." Letter 75(74).12.

307. Letter 73.5. St. Firmilian says the same: "let them consider and understand that spiritual birth cannot be without the Spirit" (Letter 75[74].8). Jaroslav Pelikan writes of these words of St. Cyprian: "Whatever the precise moment of the coming of the Holy Spirit may have been thought to be, Cyprian was expressing [here] a catholic doctrine." *The Christian Tradition: A History of the Development of Doctrine, Volume 1: The Emergence of the Catholic Tradition (100–600)* (Chicago: University of Chicago Press, 1973), 166 (emphasis added).

Baptism is validly imparted, they made it a pillar of the new ecclesiology. With the concession of the Holy Spirit, the Church will also necessarily be conceded to heretics and schismatics and then the total inversion of the early patristic vision of the Church will come to pass.

The teaching of the council is clear that all who are considered baptized—within or outside the Roman Catholic Church—"have been incorporated into Christ and His Church,"[308] regenerated to participate in divine life.[309] They are considered to have been baptized into the one single body,[310] and thus "a sacramental bond, a unity in grace, has been formed between them."[311] Hence, on the basis of Baptism, unity is said to "transcend the visible boundaries of the Catholic Church and embrace all Christians,"[312] a real but incomplete communion existing between them, despite divisions.[313]

Jorge Scampini, speaking on behalf of the Roman Catholic Church before the Faith and Order Commission of the World Council of Churches in 2004, succinctly presents the established view: "The reality of a sacrament cannot be seen as lying exclusively in its validity, and it is necessary to bear in mind that the rite itself produces certain effects and that they have consequences." Further on, he continues, citing the ecclesiological implications of recognition of the fruitfulness of non–Roman Catholic Baptism:

308. Fr. Jorge A Scampini, O.P., *"We acknowledge one Baptism for the forgiveness of sins,"* address given at the Faith and Order Plenary Commission in Kuala, Malaysia, July 28–August 6, 2004. See also UR 3a–c.

309. LG 11.1, 14.1, and UR 3a–c.

310. LG 7.2.

311. Scampini, *"We acknowledge one Baptism."*

312. Ibid.

313. UR 3a

> The Council does not only recognize the validity of Baptism administered in other Christian communities, but it also maintains *that this sacrament produces all its fruits and is a source of grace.* This recognition is not limited to Christians as individuals, but *entails ecclesiological consequences: it is within their own communities that other Christians have been incorporated into Christ.* That is why the Catholic Church accords such great importance to Baptism when it engages in ecumenical debate and it cherishes well-founded hopes for an explicit recognition of it.[314]

Aquinas' investment of "character" with permanent spiritual content in every Baptism, within or outside the Church, is evident in Scampini's statement that "the rite itself produces certain effects," whereas the use of this idea in the realm of ecclesiology is apparent in the new-found "ecclesiological consequences" flowing from a now fruitful and grace-giving rite. Ever since Aquinas maintained that an indelible spiritual "character" was imparted in every valid Baptism the path opened for Rome to accept that heretics enjoy the life of grace of the Holy Spirit. This rather legalistic view imagines that the activity of the Holy Spirit depends upon purely external factors—the proper form and matter (validity)—without any connection to catholic agreement in faith, apostolic faith and succession, or the Eucharist. The idea that the execution of the rite alone, albeit with good intentions, produces ecclesiological consequences, namely the presence of the Church of Christ, can rightly be labeled a principle of magic whereby God is seen to be obligated to act because the rite has been properly carried out.

---

314. Scampini, *"We acknowledge one Baptism"* (emphasis added).

The uniquely Augustinian principle that heretics had the *sacramentum* (sign) but not the *res sacramenti* (the reality it conveys) has been surpassed by an even more perplexing idea: baptized into perfection, they are yet imperfect in communion. For, if the various groups of baptized have Christ as their common bond—the axis through which they are in communion—and since Christ is perfect and imparts perfection, how is their communion with Him and between themselves imperfect? They are in communion as a gift not as a merit, so what they personally lack cannot be the cause of an incomplete ecclesiastical communion. If the "church" is lacking, the ultimate implication is that Christ is lacking, for the Church is the Body of Christ. An imperfect communion can only mean, then, an imperfect Church, a Body of Christ that is lacking and unable to be truly catholic. This is precisely what the council and contemporary Latin theology have concluded.

Unitatis Redintegratio states that "the divisions among Christians prevent the Church from attaining the fullness of catholicity proper to her, in those of her sons who, though attached to her by Baptism, are yet separated from full communion with her. Furthermore, the Church herself finds it more difficult to express in actual life her full catholicity in all her bearings" (UR 4J).

Likewise, Cardinal Kasper has written: "The separated communities have on occasion better developed individual aspects of the revealed truth, so that the Catholic Church, under the circumstances of division, is unable to fully accomplish its intrinsic catholicity (UUS 14). Therefore the church is in need of purification and renewal, and must constantly walk the path of penance."[315]

315. Cardinal Walter Kasper, "The Decree on Ecumenism—Read Anew After Forty Years," Pontifical Council for Promoting Christian

For the Fathers, however, such as St. Maximus the Confessor, "Christ *enlightens totally* all the Christians, and each Christian shows forth the same light of Christ."[316] Summarizing the teaching of St. Maximus on the Church, Fr. George Dragas writes that all the baptized receive from the Church,

> in equal measure one divine form and name, because they all come to exist and to be called Christians from the one Christ. The Church gives all these people one simple (incomposite) and undivided relation of Faith . . . because all are related to it and meet it in a catholic way. They all come to coinhere with each other and be cojoined to one another in the one simple and undivided grace or power of the Faith. That is exactly what Acts 4:32 expresses, when it says of the early Christians "the heart and soul of all was one." They were many and different members, says St. Maximus, but they constituted one visible body, worthy indeed to be the body of the Very Christ, their true Head.[317]

In the new ecclesiology, which admits an "incomplete communion" among the baptized, it cannot be said that all are related to the Church in a catholic way, or that they all are united in one, simple, undivided way. That is, however, precisely what the grace of the Holy Spirit accomplishes in the Baptism and Eucharist of the Church. That is also why schismatics and her-

Unity, Conference on the 40th Anniversary of the Promulgation of the Conciliar Decree "Unitatis Redintegratio," Rocca di Papa, Mondo Migliore, November 11, 12 and 13, 2004, Section IV, paragraph 7.

316. Fr. George Dion Dragas, "The Church in St. Maximus' Mystagogy: The Problem and the Orthodox Perspective," *Theology* 1 (1995) (emphasis added).

317. Ibid.

etics are necessarily not recipients of this grace and not worthy to be the Body of the Very Christ.

In conclusion, the understanding of Baptism in and of itself, outside the Church, producing the effects of grace and having ecclesiological consequences, was critical for the formation of the new ecclesiology. Largely on the basis of autonomous "externals," Vatican II sought to forge the unity of the Church. With such sacramental minimalism at the base of Church identity, the tragic though inevitable result was the loss of one of the four marks of the Church, as confessed in the Nicene Creed; for how can She remain truly "catholic" if "divisions among Christians prevent the Church from attaining the fullness of catholicity proper to her"? A church that admits the purifying and sanctifying presence of the Holy Spirit among schismatics and heretics, and also admits that divisions and delusions are compatible with communion in Christ (even if this communion is labeled "incomplete"), cannot be catholic, but rather is unavoidably "wounded" and lacking. In short, such a body cannot be the Body of Christ, the fullness of him that filleth all in all (Eph. 1:23).

Ecclesiastical Unity through "Elements"

The crucial assumption underlying and supporting the entirety of the new ecclesiology is the idea that "elements" of the Church, such as Baptism, can be extracted from the whole and still have life to give. In UR 3b and c, elements—Baptism and "liturgical actions"—are given magical power to "engender a life of grace" and give "access to the community of salvation." This power serves as the basis for recognizing, in UR 3d, the "separated Churches and Communities as such" to be "means of salvation." This theory of autonomous ecclesiastical elements accepted by *Unitatis Redintegratio* and Vatican II has its origins in none other than John Calvin's doctrine of *vestigia Ecclesiae*, which was developed and presented by Yves Congar with a slight change of emphasis.[318] Once again, the claim that *Unitatis Redintegratio* represents a return to patristic sources proves to be empty.

Congar developed Calvin's theory in the following way. He states that Christ has entrusted to the Church various "principles" of reconciliation between God and man. Although these principles—principles also of the Church's unity—are "an ordered fullness, living and organic" and, "so ordered as to complete and explain each other, they can to some extent be

318. See John Calvin, *Institutes of the Christian Religion* 4 (1559 ed.), 2: 11–12; and Yves M.-J. Congar, *Divided Christendom, A Catholic Study of the Problem of Reunion*, trans. M. A. Bousfield (London: Geoffrey Bles: The Centenary Press, 1939), 224–48. See also the recent study by Sandra Arenas, "Merely Quantifiable Realities? The 'Vestigia Ecclesiae' in the Thought of John Calvin and Its Twentieth-Century Reception," pp. 69–89 in *John Calvin's Ecclesiology: Ecumenical Perspectives (Ecclesiological Investigations)*, ed. Gerard Mannion and Eduardus Van der Borght (London: T and T Clark, 2011). Calvin develops his theory of *vestigia Ecclesiae* as a part of his reflections on the nature of the Church and critique of Roman Catholicism. In spite of asserting that the Roman Catholic Church holds false dogmas and practices, he nonetheless concedes the existence of some ecclesiastical elements in it, elements he calls *vestigia Ecclesiae*. Calvin concludes that on the strength of Baptism the papal institution contains certain *vestigia* of the ancient church which testify to the presence of God, however, since "those marks [of the true church] . . . are effaced, I say that the whole body, as well as every single assembly, want the form of a legitimate Church" (*Institutes*, 4.2, 11–12). See also Walter Kasper's essay "Decree on Ecumenism," where he informs us that this idea "was first brought into play in an *extension* of the anti-Donatist position of Augustine by Y. Congar" and that, "[i]n the Toronto Declaration (1950) it also entered into the usage of the World Council of Churches."

realized in separation."[319] For him who lives [fully] by these principles of reconciliation there is "perfect membership" in the Church. For "one who lives only by one or other of the principles of new life" there is "imperfect membership." The dissident who lives in separation from the institutional Church will never be able to find in his church the organic fullness of the principles of life in Christ that make for the unity of the Church. Nevertheless, according to Congar:

> In so far as [the dissident] does discover these principles he is, by virtue of them a member of the Church, that is, by his Baptismal character through grace and supernatural charity and sacramental graces (so far as sacraments exist in his communion); though not by an explicit profession of faith, a full sacramental life, or the inward inspiration of Catholic communion in faith and love, which, regulated by the Catholic hierarchy, is the ultimate seal of unity. In this way it is that the Church includes members who appear to be outside her. They belong, invisibly and incompletely, but they really belong. They belong to the Church in so far as they belong to Christ, because what unites them to Christ is a fibre of His Mystical Body [i.e. Baptism], a constituent element of His Church.[320]

Such is the foundation of the new ecclesiology as laid down by Congar. Why can the principles or elements of the Church's life and unity be lived in separation? There is no answer given except the idea that as long as the "form and intent" of a rite of Baptism is preserved, the mystery is valid and membership extended. These principles, however, were said to be inseparable

---

319. Congar, *Divided Christendom*, 227.
320. Ibid., 234.

from the living, organic reality of the soul of the Church. How is it that they can retain life when ripped from the living organism of the Body of Christ? Congar claims the sheer quantity of the gifts makes a partial or incomplete participation possible: "It is because the benefits of the New Covenant are many that it is possible to belong to the Church in varying degree and to claim membership of it on various grounds."[321]

The chasm between the patristic understanding of St. Cyprian and the Holy Fathers and Congar's theory should now begin to become clear. The heart of the difference between the two opposing views is this: in the first, the Church as the Body of Christ, that is Christ Himself, reconciles man to Himself, giving Himself to man in the mysteries; in the second, principles of reconciliation are derived from Christ, which, although meant to function within the ordered fullness of the Una Sancta, nevertheless, can and do work outside this fullness in varying ways and degrees to incompletely incorporate men into the Church. In the first, the Body of Christ is not and cannot be divided, mysteries cannot operate autonomously, and membership cannot be had invisibly. In the second, the Body of Christ is mutilated, possessing incomplete members, with "sacraments" retaining their power self-sufficiently, with an invisible membership in the Body of Christ. Congar's theory is

---

321. Ibid., 227. Congar's justification recalls the arguments of the anonymous third-century author of *De Rebaptismate*, the first tract written in Africa against St. Cyprian's ecclesiology. The unknown writer claims that, as Bernard Leeming summarizes, "although it is normal that there should be a unity between Baptism and the indwelling of the Holy Spirit, nevertheless they may be found separated. The action of the Holy Spirit is too various to be confined merely to the one baptismal rite." Bernard Leeming, *Principles of Sacramental Theology* (Westminster, MD: Newman Press, 1960), 175.

a magical conception of the mysteries that imagines them to be self-powered vehicles of salvation operating autonomously from the visible Body of Christ on the strength of the most minimal and external bases.

Again, the cornerstone of this novel ecclesiology is the acceptance of schismatic and heretical Baptism per se. As the New Martyr Hilarion (Troitsky) has written, "If the grace-giving Baptism of the Holy Spirit is permitted outside the Church, then it is completely impossible to preserve the unity of the Church."[322] This is so because the visible and invisible Church constitutes one continuous reality.[323] If the Holy Spirit is accepted to be active—purifying and illuminating those outside the Church through various "ecclesiastical elements," the first among which is Baptism—it follows that "ecclesiality," the possession of the character or nature of the Church, must also be conceded. For, the Church is apostolic; only the apostolic Church is one and holy; "only onto the apostles did 'the Holy Spirit descend'[324] . . . and through them 'into a union of everyone summon.'[325]"[326]

When the mysteriological operations of the Holy Spirit are granted to schismatics and heretics, the Church must necessarily be there as well, according to the words of the Apostle: "For in one Spirit are we all baptized into one body and have been all made to drink into one Spirit" (1 Cor. 12:13). For the

322. Troitsky, *Unity of the Church*, 39.

323. John S. Romanides, "The Ecclesiology of St. Ignatius of Antioch," *The Greek Orthodox Theological Review* 7:1 and 2 (1961–62), 53–77.

324. Aposticha of Vespers for Pentecost.

325. Kontakion of Pentecost.

326. Fr. Georges Florovsky, "The House of the Father," in *Ecumenism I: A Doctrinal Approach, Vol. 13 of the Collected Works of Georges Florovsky* (Vaduz, Europa: Büchervertriebsanstalt, 1989), 66.

Church is "one body, and one Spirit" (Eph. 4:4), and "he that is joined unto the Lord is one spirit" (1 Cor. 6:17). Saint John Chrysostom, in his commentary on 1 Corinthians 12:13, explains this further:

> [T]hat which established us to become one body and regenerated us, is one Spirit: for not in one Spirit was one baptized, and another, another. And not only is that which hath baptized us one, but also that unto which He baptized us, that is, for which He baptized us, is one [the Church]. For we were baptized not so that several bodies might be formed, but that we might all preserve one with another the perfect nature of one body: that is, that we might all be one body, into the same were we baptized. So that both He who formed it is one, and that into which He formed it is one. And he said not, "that we might all come to be of the same body"; but, "that we might all be one body."[327]

The Spirit of Christ does not form several bodies, distinct and separate. The One Spirit works to establish us as one body and to regenerate us. Not only did One Spirit baptize us, but we were baptized into One Church—at once visible and indivisible. This was, indeed, the aim of our Baptism: to preserve the perfect nature of one body, to all be one Body of Christ.

327. St. John Chrysostom, Homily 30 on 1 Corinthians, 1–2; PG 61, 250–51.

The Visible and Invisible Church

There was no doubt, already in the early Church, "that the ecclesial reality of the new covenant was visible; the later Augustinian and Protestant notions of a distinction between visible and invisible church would have been alien to the Christianity of the first centuries. The church of the first centuries perceived itself as the Spirit-filled visible communion (koinônia) of the saved, united by baptism and the Eucharist, who would inherit the kingdom of God."[328]

The visible and invisible aspects of the Church do not refer to a twofold reality among those still struggling against the devil, such that there is a visible, concrete manifestation of the Church and a broader Church of Christ, the boundaries of which surpass the visible Church and are ultimately indeterminate. "The Church is invisible and visible at one and the same time, that is, it consists of those who are enrolled for the struggles on the earth and those who are in heaven experiencing the triumph of the glory of God."[329] There is one visible Church and it consists of the baptized who are struggling against the devil by their unity in the life-giving human nature of Christ, a unity that is manifested not in a common Baptism alone, but in all the mysteries together, especially the Eucharist.[330]

There are no grounds, therefore, to speak of sacramental action outside the "visible limits" of the Church, as this would

328. David Heith-Stade, "Receiving the Non-Orthodox," 403.

329. John S. Romanides, *An Outline of Orthodox Patristic Dogmatics* (Rollinsford, NH: Orthodox Research Institute, 2004), 77.

330. See St. Ignatius of Antioch, Letter to the Ephesians, 1, 7, 19, and 20, in *The Apostolic Fathers*, vol. 1, *I Clement. II Clement. Ignatius. Polycarp. Didache. Barnabas* (Greek text edition), ed. Kirsopp Lake, Loeb Classical Library (New York: Macmillan, 1913; repr. 1997: Christian Classics Ethereal Library), http://www.ccel.org/ccel/lake/fathers2.html

imply that there are "invisible limits" of the Church, or a portion of the Church that is invisible (LG 8b, 15, and UR 3d). For, if there are "invisible limits" of the Church, how could they be determined? And if indeterminable, how can they be limits? The same problem applies with reference to a "visible unity" of the Church, the implication being that there could be a unity of the Church that is invisible and indeterminable.

The Body of Christ is in the world (John 1:10) as the light of the world (John 9:5), which cannot be hidden (Matt. 5:15–16). Unity is the Church's very being, tied intimately to Her being the Body of Christ, which is made of flesh and blood and dwells in the world (John 1:14). Just as the Incarnate Word was visible to all who approached Him when He walked incarnate as *Theanthropos*, so too is His Body visible in the flesh and blood of Her members, the baptized faithful who participate in the mystery of the Eucharist—to all who have eyes to see (Ezek. 12:2, Matt. 13:15–16).

The unity of the Church presupposes the union of the members of the Church with the Head of the Body. This union is most certainly apparent to the unified, just as its absence in others who purport to be co-unified with them is most certainly apparent to them. This union takes place and is maintained in the mysteries, which are quite visible: "The Church is known in the mysteries."[331] "The Church exists and is continuously formed in the mysteries and through the mysteries. Those who live their lives outside the mysterial life of love are outside the body of Christ."[332] The divinity of the Lord was

---

331. Nicholas Cabasilas, *A Commentary on the Divine Liturgy*, 38; PG 150:452C. See Μεταλληνοῦ, π. Γ.Δ., Δοκίμια Ὀρθόδοξης Μαρτυρίας [Essays Giving an Orthodox Witness] (Athens: Athos, 2001), "Ἐξ ὕδατος καὶ πνεύματος" [Of Water and the Spirit], 67–87.

332. John S. Romanides, *The Ancestral Sin* (Ridgewood, NJ: Zephyr, 2002), 173.

made manifest to the people by the miracles that He worked, without this meaning that wherever "signs and wonders" were worked the Lord was necessarily present: "And no marvel; for Satan himself is transformed into an angel of light" (2 Cor. 11:14). Likewise, the Theanthropic Body of the Lord is made manifest in the mysteries, without this meaning that wherever a "mystery" is performed the Lord is necessarily present: "We ordain that any bishop or presbyter or deacon who accepts the baptism or sacrifice [i.e., eucharist] of heretics is to be deposed: 'For what agreement has Christ with Belial? Or what has a believer in common with an unbeliever?' (2 Cor 6:15)."[333]

Father John Romanides sums up the patristic teaching as presented by St. Ignatius of Antioch, which is the perennial, unchanging understanding of the Church, thus:

> The visible Church is composed of only those who continuously share in the corporate Eucharistic life. . . . Beyond the life of unity centered in the corporate Eucharist as an end in itself there is no Church and only God can know if there is any salvation. Where the Church is not locally manifested and being formed by God *epi to auto*[334] there is the rest of humanity being carried to and fro by the prince of this world. "I pray not for the world, but for them which Thou hast given me." (John 17:9).[335]

Saint Irenaeus of Lyons, writing some seventy years before the rise of the Novatianists and one hundred and thirty years

---

333. Apostolic Canon 46.

334. This phrase, used often by St. Ignatius to refer to the Eucharistic Synaxis, can be translated roughly as "in one place, gathered or come together." It is also used in the New Testament with a similar meaning. See 1 Cor 11:20, Acts 2:1.

335. Romanides, "Ecclesiology of St. Ignatius of Antioch."

before the rise of the Donatists, expressed the Church's mind on the matter with great lucidity. As in St. Ignatius' epistles, it was taken for granted that schismatics and heretics were to be shunned by the faithful, and they were to "cleave to those who keep the Apostles' doctrine."[336] Saint Irenaeus would have considered the mysteries performed by a bishop who had been justly defrocked and excommunicated on account of schism or heresy to be inauthentic and void of any spiritual content. It was inconceivable in the early church to think of a bishop apart from his church and flock.[337] As Saint Irenaeus held in common with all of the early Fathers that "the Church was the sole fountain of grace, and that outside it none can be assured of salvation or of sacramental grace, he would have ruled out as entirely worthless the sacraments of schismatics."[338]

According to St. Irenaeus, it is in the Church alone that the Holy Spirit acts mysteriologically:

> For in the Church God hath set apostles, prophets, teachers and all the other means through which the Spirit works; of which all those are not partakers who do not join themselves to the Church, but defraud themselves of life through their perverse opinions and infamous behavior. For where the Church is, there is the Spirit of God; and where the Spirit of God is, there is the Church, and every kind of grace; but the Spirit is truth.

The last phrase is supposed by some today to mean that the Church is coterminus with the Holy Spirit and, since the Holy Spirit acts throughout creation, therefore the boundaries

336. Ireneaus, *Against Heresies*, 4:26.2–5; PG 7.1052–1056.
337. Willis, 145.
338. Ibid.

of the Church cannot be determined with any certainty. They also say that "We know where the Church is; it is not for us to judge and say where the Church is not."[339] Orthodox friendly theologians at Vatican II, such as Bishop Christopher Butler from England, cited this sentiment of P. Evdokimov as influential in the formation of the new ecclesiology of Vatican II.[340] But such an interpretation actually is the very opposite of the Saint's meaning. It ignores both the context of the phrase and the content of the treatise. Moreover, it stands in contradiction to the mind of the early Church Fathers on the question, of which Saint Irenaeus was both a preserver and bearer and an exceptional expositor. In the passage in question he begins with the Church and Her identity and location, which is certain, and places the Holy Spirit within Her. In this, he is following the order of the day of Pentecost, when the assembly of those being saved, the Church, was gathered together and the Holy Spirit descended. For, as Fr. Georges Florovsky has written, "the Body of Christ was created and formed already by the Incarnation."[341] Or, as St. John Chrysostom famously said on the eve of his exile, at the Incarnation Christ "took to himself the flesh of the Church."[342]

There is no identity crisis in St. Irenaeus' thought, no uncertainty as to character or confusion as to boundaries. "The ultimate identity of the Church is grounded in her sacramental structure, in the organic continuity of the body."[343] Of all the

339. P. Evdokimov, *L'Orthodoxie* (Neuchatel: Delachaux et Niestlé, 1959), 343.

340. See chapter 14 for more discussion of this idea.

341. Georges Florovsky, *Vol. 14 of the Collected Works of Georges Florovsky* (Vaduz, Europa: Büchervertriebsanstalt, 1989), 35.

342. Homily before the exile, 2, PG 52:429.

343. Florovsky, *Collected Works*, 14:36.

early fathers, St. Irenaeus stressed this the most. He knows where the Church is and it is within Her that the Holy Spirit, Who is truth, dwells, and, furthermore, as he already stated, all those are not partakers of the Holy Spirit who do not join themselves to the Church whose boundaries are clearly marked by the company of apostles, prophets, and teachers.

Vatican II had an answer to this obvious problem created for contemporary ecumenism by the traditional view of the Church and the Holy Spirit's presence within it. Rather than recognizing the mysteries of schismatics and heretics as actions of the Holy Spirit (such that the Holy Spirit must be said to work outside the Church), the council, on the basis of Baptism, extended the Church to include the schismatics and heretics themselves. In this way the Holy Spirit can be said to be at work mysteriologically only within the Church. Schismatic and heretical Baptism is now seen as fruitful because it is the one Baptism of and into the one Body, which is the work of the Holy Spirit.[344]

In this way, however, an inversion of the patristic vision of the Church and understanding of schism and heresy was brought about. To say that heretical Baptism is the one Baptism means that the criteria employed for recognizing the Church have changed. The Church as a mysteriological unity is no longer to be found in an identity based upon unity in faith, apostolic succession, the episcopate, and the mysteries.[345] The marks of the Church confessed in the Symbol of Faith, that it is one, holy, catholic, and apostolic, do not correspond to this

344. See UR 3b, Fr. Jorge A Scampini, O.P., "*We acknowledge one Baptism.*"

345. See chapter 11 herein, section on "The Twofold Unity of, and Membership in, The Body of Christ."

new vision of the church—a church that is divided, mingled with error, lacking wholeness, and inclusive of teachings not of apostolic origin. This new church can be identified in elements, in parts of the whole, establishing communion but incompletely so, semi-autonomously and ambiguously. If, however, the Church as essential and undivided unity has been replaced by a church marked by incompleteness and imperfection, and, as Blessed Augustine has famously written, to be is to be in unity, has not the very meaning of "church" been changed at Vatican II? Has not the very meaning of the Church as unity ceased to exist?

10

DISCERNMENT OF THE SPIRIT
IN *UNITATIS REDINTEGRATIO*

To recognize an efficacious Baptism among schismatics and heretics is of necessity to recognize the presence and activity of the Holy Spirit in such Baptism. Therefore, in references to the action of the Holy Spirit among the "separated brethren" in both *Unitatis Redintegratio*[346] and *Lumen Gentium*,[347] no distinctions are made between the activity of the Holy Spirit within and outside the Roman Catholic Church. Indeed, it is clear that the authors of these documents believe that the same salvific and sanctifying activity of the Holy Spirit they see at work among those "fully incorporated"[348] is also at work among those in "imperfect communion."[349] This indiscriminate referencing of the Holy Spirit's work within and outside the Roman Catholic Church is indicative of both a crucial deficiency underlying the new ecclesiology and the drawing of new, indiscernible boundaries around the Body of Christ.

As we have seen, the new ecclesiology was drafted precisely for the purpose of moving away from the sharp, exclusivist distinctions drawn in *Mystici Corporis*, which placed the "separated brethren" "outside of the life of the Divine Spirit." The views

346. See UR 3b, 3d, and 4i.
347. See LG 15.
348. LG 14. See also UR 3a.
349. UR 3a.

of the theologians who were instrumental in drafting *Unitatis Redintegratio* (Congar, Bea, Ratzinger, et al.) had converged, and the consensus they reached concerning the status of the "separated brethren" was one based on a common experience. Their experience convinced them, in the words of Joseph Ratzinger, that, contrary to past understanding, "there manifestly existed in reality intermediate degrees of belonging."[350] They had come to believe that the Holy Spirit was at work in the separated brethren as He was in their own communion: sanctifying and saving souls. Those in schism and heresy belonged in the Church, albeit in a diminished way. Even so, their "ecclesiological insufficiency" existed on an institutional rather than necessarily an experiential level.[351] As participants in the "life of the Divine Spirit" and incorporated into Christ, it necessarily followed that they shared a common spiritual foundation and an identity of experience in the Holy Spirit.

When explanation is given of this essential aspect of the new ecclesiology, seeing that it is claimed that *Unitatis Redintegratio* was a return to the sources, one would expect to encounter here the patristic teaching concerning the activity of the Holy Spirit within and outside the Church, which flows from the teaching on the Divine Essence and Energies of God. On the contrary, this teaching is totally absent from both *Lumen Gentium* and *Unitatis Redintegratio*.

In the tradition of the Church a distinction is made between God's essence and His energies. And, although the two are

---

350. Joseph Ratzinger, "The Ecclesiology of Vatican II," a talk given at the Pastoral Congress of the Diocese of Aversa, Italy, September 15, 2001.

351. Gregory Baum, "The Ecclesial Reality of the Other Churches," in *The Church and Ecumenism* (New York: Paulist Press, 1965), 82.

often contrasted, it is understood that the energy is the natural energy of the essence, or an essential energy. This natural energy is utterly simple, even as God's essence is utterly simple. Nevertheless, one finds in the works of the Holy Fathers, such as St. Gregory the Theologian, St. John of Damascus, and St. Gregory Palamas, that this simple energy "μερίζεται ἀμερίστως ἐν μεριστοῖς" ("is indivisibly divided among individual creatures").[352] This means that it is one and yet has many consequences, many resultant energies, and this energy of God is present throughout creation. This one energy exists in each thing as one energy, and within each of these energies, all of God is present.[353]

In spite of this energy being simple, differences can be perceived between God's creative or providential energies and His purifying, illuminating, and deifying energies. "These distinct forms of the one selfsame energy of God are not identical. If they were identical, then all creation would partake, for example, of God's glorifying energy."[354] We know, from the Church's experience of the grace of God, that there is a difference between the illuminating grace of God and the deifying grace of God. We know this because not all have reached theosis.[355]

352. See, for example Ἁγίου Ἰωάννη Δαμασκηνού, Ἔκδοσις ἀκριβὴς τῆς ὀρθοδόξου πίστεως [St. John Damascene, Exact Exposition of the Orthodox Faith] (Θεσσαλονίκη: Πουναρά, 1983), 94 (14.22).

353. Protopresbyter John S. Romanides, *Patristic Theology* (Thessaloniki, Greece: Uncut Mountain Press, 2008), 159.

354. Ibid.

355. Ibid. The illuminating grace of God referred to here, which has as a prerequisite the purifying energy of the grace of God given in the Holy Mysteries of initiation, should not be confused with the general enlightenment that God gives to all men who come into the world, nor with the enlightenment that God sheds upon all those seeking the Truth.

The distinction of energies is also apparent in the Church's preeminent prayer to the Holy Spirit, in which we call on Him "Who is everywhere present and fillest all things" to "come and abide in us and cleanse us. . . ." If He was already present in creation in the same way that He makes His abode in us, to cleanse, illumine, and deify us, there would be no reason to call on Him to come and dwell in us. Hence, there is a great difference between His creative and providential energies, which pervade all creation, and His illuminating and deifying energies, which only dwell in those who have been purified and illumined in Baptism and chrismation and persevere in the unity of the Body, exchanging the kiss of peace and communing of the Immaculate Body and Blood of Christ.[356]

Fr. John Romanides explains this point further:

> The distinctions between the spiritual stages are the grounds for including among the divine energies the energies of theosis, illumination, and purification, which is the energy associated with those being instructed in the faith. . . . You have to be an Orthodox Christian in order to participate in these energies and every Orthodox Christian does not do so, but only those who are properly prepared, spiritually speaking.[357]

St. Maximus the Confessor, in his *Questions to Thalassius*,[358]

---

356. Fr. Georges Florovsky distinguishes between the "special presence" and "providential presence" of God: "In all the sacraments forming the real core of Church life, God is present in creation, really and effectively—by the special presence of grace, distinct from the providential presence everywhere" (Florovsky, *Collected Works*, 13:63.)

357. Ibid., 178.

358. *Πρὸς Θαλάσσιον τον ὁσιώτατον πρεσβύτερον καὶ ἡγούμενον, Περὶ Διαφόρων ἀπόρων τῆς θείας Γραφῆς, ἐρώτησις* ΙΕ´ [Question 15], PG 90 297.

explains that while the Holy Spirit is present in all creation generally, preserving, providing, and enlivening, He is present in a particular way in those who have, by their faith, gained the name of Christian—"the divine and indeed divinizing name of Christ" (ibid.). He is present in them "not only as guarding and foreknowingly enlivening and moving natural reason and showing the transgression or the keeping of the commands and announcing things foretold about Christ, but also as creative of the adoption, which was granted according to grace through faith" (ibid.). This is the threshold the believer passes in Baptism.

But, there is, furthermore, an even more particular way in which the Holy Spirit dwells in Christians who are spiritually worthy: "For the Holy Spirit becomes as generating wisdom only in those who have been cleansed in soul and body through the precise exercise of all of the commandments, speaking to them as relatives, and forming their mind according to the holy perceptions of the ineffable things, in order to divinize them" (ibid.).

All men, then, of whatever background or belief, participate in the creative, sustaining, and providential energies of God, without which the world would cease to be. In this sense, and only in this sense, there is a differentiated participation for schismatics and heretics, not in the life of the Church, as Congar and his colleagues supposed,[359] but in those divine energies common to all creation—the creative, sustaining, and providential energies of God. This participation, however, does not make them members of the Church, for they, not having fulfilled the necessary presuppositions for such participation, are not participating in the purifying, illuminating, and deify-

359. See chapter 1, pages 22–30.

ing energies of God. This grace of the Holy Spirit is imparted only in the Body of Christ, the Church, in the "economy of grace," in the "body" of grace. For, as Hieromonk (now retired Bishop) Athanasius Yevtich has written:

> Grace is given by Christ, as Head and Savior of the Body of the Church, while union in one body and life "in Christ" take place only "in the Holy Spirit." This is why the Apostle [Paul] says emphatically, "if any man have not the Spirit of Christ, he is none of his." (Rom. 8:9). How is it possible for one to have the Spirit of Christ who is not in the body of Christ, the Church, and is not a member of Christ?[360]

Without these distinctions regarding the divine energies of the Holy Spirit, participation in the life of the Church in order to receive the grace that heals and saves would be pointless, for why is the Church needed if grace is identified with the general presence of the Holy Spirit in the world, of which all men partake?[361]

The extent to which this singular identification could be taken is apparent in the theological thought of an influential

---

360. Ἱερομονάχου Ἀθανασίου Μ. Γιέβτιτς. [Hieromonk Athanasius M. Yevtich], Ἡ ἐκκλησιολογία τοῦ ἀποστόλου Παύλου κατὰ τὸν ἱερὸ Χρυσόστομο [The Ecclesiology of the Apostle Paul According to Blessed Chrysostom] (Athens: Gigori Publications, 1984), 198–99.

361. This is the case in Cardinal Kasper's noteworthy essay, "Ecclesiological and Ecumenical Implications of Baptism." See part II, section 2, where Kasper makes no distinction between the actions or energies of the Holy Spirit in the Church and in creation. He justifies the possibility of salvation for those who've never heard the Gospel (apparently referring to Rom. 2:10–16), by identifying the enlightening of every man by the Logos (Jn. 1:9) as salvific, that is, as identical with the enlightenment that comes to the believer in the Church through the mysteries.

Vatican II ecclesiologist, Cardinal Charles Journet.[362] As with Congar and Bea, Journet held that since the "separated brethren" are rightly considered to be "invincibly ignorant"—that is, unable to know Jesus Christ and/or the Roman Catholic Church as the One Church—they are therefore not guilty of the sin of schism or heresy. Furthermore, the ecclesiastical bodies in which they live out their Christian life are not to be considered heretical.[363] As Joseph Ratzinger phrased the new understand-

362. Charles Cardinal Journet (1891–1975) was a well-respected Swiss theologian who was elevated to Cardinal in 1965. His most famous work is considered to be *The Church of the Word Incarnate*, published in French as *L'Église du Verbe incarné* (Paris: Desclée de Brouwer, 1951) and in English as *The Church of the Word Incarnate* (Sheed and Ward, 1955); it is available in English online at www.ewtn.com/library/THEOLOGY/CHWORDIN.htm. Although he attended only the last session of the Second Vatican Council in 1965, Journet was nevertheless a rather influential figure at the council and in the post-conciliar period. Today, his work is being revisited in the more conservative circles of Roman Catholic theology.

363. This peculiar Latin teaching is unknown to the Fathers. St. Ignatius of Antioch lays out the same result for both the leaders into schism and those following them: "Do not err, my brethren. If any man follows him that makes a schism in the Church, he shall not inherit the kingdom of God" (Ign. Phil. 3). Likewise, he is unequivocal that all those outside the unity of the Eucharist are deprived of the benefits that accompany it: "Let no man deceive himself: if any one be not within the altar, he is deprived of the bread of God" (Ign. Eph. 5). Blessed Augustine also rejected this idea, as is apparent in section 1.5.6 of his work *On Baptism, Against the Donatists*. Neither the passage of time nor the lack of guilt of those in apostasy can change the reality of separation and therefore the consequences that accompany it. To hold to the contrary can only lead to a magical conception of salvation that negates freedom. God, of course, can save whomever He pleases, however, it won't be because they magically became participants in the mysteries of the Church even though they either knew nothing of them or rejected them without knowing it.

ing in 1966, shortly after the council: "Something that was once rightly condemned as heresy cannot later simply become true, but *it can gradually develop its own positive ecclesial nature* which the individual is presented with as his church, and in which he lives as a believer, not a heretic."[364] Consequently, according to their righteousness and participation in some sacraments, chief of which is Baptism, those who do not belong to the Roman Catholic Church still belong to the One Church in a variety of ways, according to a system of concentric circles.[365] At the center of the circle is, of course, the Roman Catholic Church as the concrete historical expression of the Church. Immediately outside this core, however, are the Orthodox, "the Greeks and Russians," followed by non-Chalcedonians, Anglicans, Lutherans, and other Protestants.

Fr. Charles Morerod succinctly explains Journet's views, which are said to be in harmony with the new ecclesiology: "Where God 'touches' someone, where the Holy Spirit leads a person towards a future conversion, *the Church is already present. . . .* [T]he sacraments given outside the Roman Catholic Church . . . 'have a natural tendency to invest some corporeal appearances.'[366] This means that *every action of the Spirit is part of the process of building the Body of the Church,* which is thus always visible though we do not always recognize it. . . . [T]he

364. Joseph Ratzinger, *The Open Circle: The Meaning of Christian Brotherhood,* trans. W. A. Glen Doeple (New York: Sheed and Ward, 1966), 125 (emphasis added).

365. Fr. Charles Morerod, O.P. (based on the theology of Cardinal Charles Journet), taken from "A Roman Catholic Point of View about the Limits of the Church," *The Greek Orthodox Theological Review* 42: 3–4 (1997).

366. Charles Journet, *L'Église du Verbe incarné,* 2:953.

frontier of the Church crosses our heart: *everyone is a member of the Church in the measure that he receives divine grace.*"[367]

Accordingly, it is not surprising that the concentric circles of the Church extend to every human being, even to the righteous among the unbaptized, insomuch as they receive grace that is "a beginning of the Body of Christ" (ibid.). According to Fr. Morerod, for Cardinal Journet "the Body of Christ is always visible [although not always recognizable as such], and non-Catholics belong to it in various degrees" (ibid.).

We observe several sharp diversions from the patristic vision of the Church in Journet's idea of the Church. The Body of Christ and the one, holy, catholic, and apostolic Church as an institution, with the Mysteries marking Her boundaries, are not identical. The Body of Christ is said to be visible but not always recognizable. Membership in the Body of Christ, "what it means to belong to the Church," is somehow extended to those who are not yet initiated, since they are recipients of divine grace. All three of these notions are incompatible with the Orthodox patristic vision of the Church. They all share the same erroneous supposition: that all grace initiates into the life of the Church; that all God's energies in the world are purifying, illuminating, or deifying. From this error the claim is then put forth that the new ecclesiology has not, in fact, done away with the patristic maxim that there is no grace given by the Holy Spirit outside the Church, since "every grace bestowed by the Holy Spirit serves to build up the visible Body" (ibid.). Grace on the outer reaches of the "circle," among the unbaptized, is "touching someone" and thus the Church is present and the Holy Spirit is said to not be outside the boundaries of the Church. Such an idea of the Church can only be countenanced

367. Morerod, "A Roman Catholic Point of View" (emphasis added).

by disregarding, not only the distinctions of divine energies, but unity of faith, apostolic succession and faith, and the life of unity centered in the Eucharist.

The failure to discern the energies of God is quite likely also behind the Papal condemnation of the Jansenists' proposition that "outside the Church, no grace is given." As we saw in chapters 4–6, the Pope and Latin theologians of the seventeenth and eighteenth centuries reacted against this claim, which was, in fact, held by none other than Blessed Augustine, and insisted that grace is given outside the Church. Then, the grace and activity of the Holy Spirit were separated from the visible Body, and said to work outside. Now, again in apparent ignorance of the patristic distinction of divine energies, the Body is again said to be inseparable from the grace and action of the Holy Spirit, but now the Body is separated from the institutional Church, the Roman Catholic communion, and said to be built up by "every action of the Spirit," even among the unbaptized.

According to the Orthodox patristic teaching, however, the Body of Christ is built up, not with "every action of the Spirit," but when, "by the Spirit of our God" (1 Cor. 6:11), man participates in the human nature of the incarnate Son of God through Baptism: "For by one Spirit are we all baptized into one body . . . and have been all made to drink into one Spirit" (1 Cor. 12:13). What makes one a member of the Body and connects the members one to another is the oneness of their nature—the human nature of the incarnate Son of God. In Baptism each member "puts on" (Gal. 3:27) his own human nature free from sin, and thus enlightened by the Holy Spirit he becomes a son of God by adoption and is led into the likeness of God and immortality. Baptism is a repeat of the event of Pentecost in the baptized one, who is made spiritual (Gal. 6:1) and born again "of water and of the Spirit" (John 3:3–6). Only in this fundamental change effected in Baptism is one made a member of the Body of Christ, the Church, in which all distinctions cease and where "all are one in Christ Jesus" (Gal. 3:28). And if it is in Baptism alone that all distinctions disappear, then membership cannot be had "by degrees," nor can there be a beginning of the Church with every action of the Spirit.

There can be no doubt, of course, that, as St. Athanasius the Great states, "the Savior is working mightily among men, every day He is invisibly persuading numbers of people all over the world . . . to accept His faith and be obedient to His teaching."[368] It is likewise undoubted that, with the initiation of the seeker into the catechumenate, or, rather, even long before he is formally enrolled as a catechumen, the Holy Spirit is at work bringing his soul to Christ. There is, however, a difference between the work of the Holy Spirit in bringing a soul to the Church and the work of the Spirit in forming the Church. Only in and upon emerging from the baptismal font can we speak of the purifying, illuminating, and deifying energies of God being at work. Beginning with Holy Baptism, the entire institution of the Church is established by the Holy Spirit: "The Holy Spirit provides everything. . . . [He] forms the entire institution of the Church."[369] He is, according to Saint Basil the Great, "the master-builder of the Church."[370] Before Baptism, however, the activity of the Holy Spirit is restricted to drawing the soul towards Christ. After Baptism, in which the whole man has "put on" Christ (Gal. 3:27), the Holy Spirit works to form Christ within (Gal. 4:19, Eph. 3:16–17).

368. PG 25 148.
369. See *The Pentecostarion*, the Sunday of Pentecost, Great Vespers.
370. *In Isaiam*, chap. III; PG 30, 289D.

This is the patristic teaching, which Saint Diadochos of Photiki explains thus: "Before Holy Baptism, grace encourages the soul towards good from the outside, while Satan lurks in its depths trying to block the intellect's (*nous*) way of approach to the divine. But from the moment that we are reborn through Baptism the demon is outside, grace within."[371] Clearly, then, a threshold exists that one must cross to enter into the Church, and that is when one begins to be purified from within in the waters of Baptism. For, only when man has passed through the waters of purification can he begin to receive the grace of God, which is to say, the illuminating and deifying energies of God. Up until this moment we can speak of man receiving the grace of God only in the sense that all creation is sustained and governed by God's grace, such as in the words of the Evangelist John: [He is] the true Light, which lighteneth every man that cometh into the world (John 1:9).[372] Every man receiving the grace of this light is not, however, a member of the Body of Christ. Likewise, according to the Apostle Paul, "the grace of God that bringeth salvation hath appeared to all men" (Tit. 2:11). This revealing of grace cannot be identified with the building up of the Body of the Church, which is not without presuppositions.

The Spirit does indeed blow where He wills (John 3:8), but as He is the Spirit of Truth, "we know that He wills to blow in the direction of Christ (John 16:14),"[373] which can only mean He leads them to "the pillar and ground of the truth" (1 Tim. 3:15), which is the Church. He is "the Spirit of communion,

371. "On Spiritual Knowledge and Discrimination: One Hundred Texts," 76, *Philokalia* (London: Faber and Faber, 1979), 1:279.
372. See chapter 10, notes 355, 356, and 361.
373. J. D. Zizioulas, "The Pneumatological Dimension of the Church," *International Catholic Review* 2:2 (1973).

and wherever He blows He does not create good individual Christians but a community (cf. Acts 2)" (ibid.), and this community is the One Church—holy, catholic, and apostolic. The "one Spirit" that dwells in and constantly builds up the "one Body" (Eph. 4:4) cannot be at work creating "incomplete communion," much less parasynagogues, for, as the Lord has said, "if a kingdom be divided against itself, that kingdom cannot stand" (Mark 3:25). The spirit behind such fragmentation is not the Spirit of Truth. That which is not "of the Truth" cannot be in the communion of the Church for "the Spirit of Truth is also that of sanctification and communion" (ibid.).

The discernment of spirits and of the activity of the evil one is closely linked to the discernment of the energies of the Holy Spirit; if one kind of discernment is missing, the other will also be absent. This is because Orthodox soteriology has both a positive and a negative aspect. In its positive aspect, there is communion with the Source of Life through the flesh of Christ in the Eucharist in the assembly of the faithful. In its negative aspect, there is the war against the divisive powers of the devil, carried out as selfless love in this same Eucharistic way of life.

That is why it is quite significant that, in addition to lacking the distinctions of the energies of the Holy Spirit, the conciliar texts also lack any reference to the machinations of the evil one before and after Baptism. More generally, both *Unitatis Redintegratio* and *Lumen Gentium* lack a developed demonology. In *Lumen Gentium* the devil is referred to only four times, whereas in *Unitatis Redintegratio* he is not even mentioned once. What is more, the significance of the unity of faith and assembly of the faithful *epi to auto* (in one place, in the Divine Eucharist) for the destruction of the powers of Satan is nowhere mentioned.[374]

---

374. It is noteworthy that this is likewise the case in the *Catechism of*

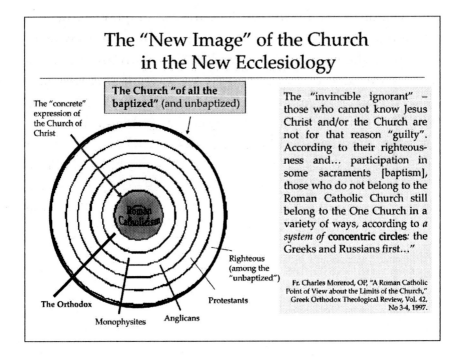

The "New Image" of the Church in the New Ecclesiology

The "concrete" expression of the Church of Christ

The Church "of all the baptized" (and unbaptized)

Roman Catholicism

The Orthodox

Monophysites   Anglicans

Protestants

Righteous (among the "unbaptized")

The "invincible ignorant" – those who cannot know Jesus Christ and/or the Church are not for that reason "guilty". According to their righteousness and... participation in some sacraments [baptism], those who do not belong to the Roman Catholic Church still belong to the One Church in a variety of ways, according to *a system of* **concentric circles**: the Greeks and Russians first..."

Fr. Charles Morerod, OP, "A Roman Catholic Point of View about the Limits of the Church," Greek Orthodox Theological Review, Vol. 42, No 3-4, 1997.

Discernment of the methods of the fallen spirits, or demonology, is a requirement in the formation of Christology and Ecclesiology.[375] Its absence from the conciliar texts is especially significant. Without an adequate understanding of the work and methods of the demons, Christology and Ecclesiology are incomprehensible. As the Evangelist John writes, "For this purpose the Son of God was manifested, that he might destroy the works of the devil" (1 John 3:8).

The war against sin and corruption has never ceased to be waged by the Church, often directed against the sin of its own members, and among its clergy. Yet, in every age the Church

the Catholic Church (New York: Doubleday, 1997).

375. See J. S. Romanides, "The Ecclesiology of St. Ignatius of Antioch," *The Greek Orthodox Theological Review* 7:1 and 2 (1961–62), 53–77.

has been able to recognize the enemy and employ the appropriate remedies. This discernment of spirits is characteristic of the Church alone, and that which most clearly distinguishes it as of divine origin and nature, over and against heresy.[376] "The Church exists in the truth not because all its members are without sin, but because the sacramental life is always present in Her and against Her the Devil is defenceless."[377] "When you often assemble in one place (*epi to auto*), the power of Satan is destroyed."[378] Outside this synaxis there is no Church; "there is the rest of humanity being carried to and fro by the prince of this world" and "only God can know if there is any salvation."[379]

376. See Hieromonk Damascene, *Fr. Seraphim Rose: His Life and Works* (Platina, CA: St. Herman Brotherhood, 2003), 688.

377. John S. Romanides, "Life in Christ" (originally appeared as "La Vie dans Christ"), SYNAXE 21, pp 26–28, and 22, pp.23–26.

378. St. Ignatius of Antioch, Letter to the Ephesians, 13.

379. Romanides, "The Ecclesiology of St. Ignatius of Antioch."

11

COMMUNIO: THE NEW ECUMENICAL
INSIGHT AND GUIDING CONCEPT

his Christocentric, Eucharist-centered ecclesiology of St.
Ignatius of Antioch is the perennial self-understanding
of the Orthodox Church, and not a twentieth-century
discovery of certain academic theologians of Western Europe.
For historians of Vatican II, however, much credit is given to
Orthodox theologians for a discovery of a Eucharistic ecclesiology at Vatican II. For Roman Catholicism, there is no doubt
that the ecclesiology of Vatican II represented a break with its
immediate past and the ecclesiology of Pius XII. Did it, however, mean a return to the patristic vision of the Church of St.
Ignatius? Is the "communio" ecclesiology of Vatican II essentially identical with the Eucharist ecclesiology of St. Ignatius
and the Orthodox?

Throughout the post-Reformation history of Catholicism
there existed on the one hand a theology that extended membership de facto beyond the strict confines of "the Holy Roman Church,"[380] and on the other hand, a Church hierarchy
that spoke and often acted in a manner much more Augustinian and absolute. All dissidents were considered baptized and
subjects of the Pope, albeit in rebellion. Yet the policy of the
Vatican regarding *communicatio in sacris* was that any participa-

---

380. See our analysis of the history of this development in part 1.

tion in liturgical actions would constitute a sign of unity with those who are not in union with the Church. Such joint prayer would, therefore, manifest a sign of disunity from the Church, an occasion of scandal, and confirm schismatics and heretics in their errors.

The theoretical basis for this policy was the "firm conviction of the Catholic Church that it is the one and only true Church of Christ, and that it alone has the right to offer legitimate public worship to God."[381] This understanding of the Church, well grounded in history and tradition, came to an end with Vatican II.

Today, the Second Vatican Council, and in particular the principles of ecumenism laid out in chapter one of *Unitatis Redintegratio*, are celebrated by Roman Catholic apologists as providing a new basis for ecclesiology: the ecclesiology of "communio"—"the guiding concept" of Roman Catholic ecumenical theology.[382] Only by understanding the concept of communio can we properly understand the place and importance of the recognition of a common Baptism in *Unitatis Redintegratio*. Moreover, in understanding the place of Baptism in the new ecclesiology, the difference between the communio ecclesiology and Orthodox Eucharistic ecclesiology is also brought into clear focus.

Whereas in the Orthodox Eucharistic ecclesiology the boundaries of Church unity are clearly drawn along "blood lines," that is, including all those who share in the common cup of His Blood, in the Roman Catholic concept of communio,

381. Wilhelm de Vries, S.J., "Communicatio in Sacris," *The Church and Ecumenism*, vol. 4 (New York: Paulist Press, 1965), 39.

382. Cardinal Walter Kasper, "Communio: The Guiding Concept of Catholic Ecumenical Theology," in *That They May All Be One: The Call to Unity Today* (London/New York: Burns and Oates, 2004), 50.

boundaries are first drawn in the water of Baptism. As Cardinal Kasper writes: "among the baptized there already exists a fundamental unity or communio, so that the distinction is not between full unity and no communio at all, but between full and incomplete communio" (UR 3; ibid. 51). And, whereas in Orthodoxy the mysteriological basis for communion is not one or the other mystery, but all the mysteries together, united in a common life and a common cup, for the new ecclesiology of Vatican II "the sacramental basis of communio is the communio in the one Baptism" with participation in the Eucharist being but "the summit" of communio reserved for those in full communion (ibid. 55). Immediately it becomes clear that between Orthodox ecclesiology and the Roman Catholic concept of communio there exists a different understanding of Baptism and its connection to the Eucharist.

The roots of this basic divergence reach back centuries. As we have already seen in chapter 3, theological and liturgical developments in the West led Roman Catholicism to an understanding of Christian initiation very different from that of the Orthodox Church. From the Orthodox understanding and practice of Christian initiation as Baptism, chrismation, and communion celebrated together, as one unit, one Rite of Initiation, the West progressively stripped initiation down to Baptism alone, with chrismation and communion being separated both theologically and chronologically.

Such legalistic reductionism was not, however, limited only to dissolving the unity of the mysteries. The Mystery of Baptism itself was also reduced to a shell of its original meaning. As we saw in chapters 5 and 6, in the West the understanding of the nature of the mystery itself underwent transformation from that of Blessed Augustine to that of Thomas Aquinas and Scholastic and neo-Scholastic theologians. The result was that by the nineteenth century what made one a member of the Church and imparted to him the gifts inherent in Baptism was simply "validity," the existence of "the proper form and matter" that imparts the "baptismal character."

Already, then, from the Middle Ages in the West there existed the idea, albeit apparently neglected, that all those "validly baptized" share in certain common benefits that "Baptism" imparts to them. Neither the idea of a "common Baptism" nor the acceptance of common benefits flowing from it is entirely new for Western Christians. Yet, there is something new—a "new and ecumenical insight" celebrated by such apologists for the communio ecclesiology as Cardinal Walter Kasper.[383]

Ecumenists, among them even some Orthodox hierarchs and theologians, broadly hold that a *"fundamental," albeit incomplete, unity or communion is derived from "our common Baptism."*[384] The "rediscovered brotherhood" touted by Pope John Paul II (UUS 41f), it is explained, is not a "good will" gesture, but is in fact theologically grounded in the one common Baptism and the

383. Ibid., 51.
384. Emphasis added. For Cardinal Kasper's examination of this idea, see his "Ecclesiological and Ecumenical Implications of Baptism," *The Ecumenical Review* (Geneva: WCC, 2000). For a Protestant and ecumenical adoption of this idea, see Thomas F. Best and Dagmar Heller, eds., *Becoming a Christian: The Ecumenical Implications of Our Common Baptism*, Faith and Order Paper 184 (Geneva: WCC, 1999); and Michael and Risto Saarinen, eds., *Baptism and the Unity of the Church* (Grand Rapids and Geneva, Eerdmans and WCC, 1998). For Orthodox hierarchs expressing this idea, see, for example, *Episkepsis* 520 (July 31, 1995), 20 [in Greek]; *Episkepsis* 370 (January 15, 1987), 8–13 [in Greek]. For an Orthodox theologian who accepts the idea of Baptism delineating the boundaries of the Church, see John D. Zizioulas (present-day Metropolitan of Pergamon, Ecumenical Patriarchate), "Orthodox Ecclesiology and the Ecumenical Movement," *Sourozh Diocesan Magazine* (UK) 21 (August 1985), 16–27.

new communio ecclesiology of Rome. Thus a once obscure, hidden reality of unity and communion has surfaced in the twentieth century, discovered and expounded at the Second Vatican Council.

In fact, what is being hailed here as "the new and basic ecumenical insight" is an ecumenically motivated extension of the implications of the Thomistic idea of baptismal character.[385] The original Scholastic extension of certain kinds of efficacy to every valid Baptism was the post-schism origin of a development of doctrine that led to seeing every valid Baptism as Church-initiating and thus Church-defining.

Proponents of ecumenism at Vatican II sought to develop an ecclesiology that would be consistent with Aquinas' baptismal theory and inclusive of the separated brethren.[386] Their aim was to make real the implications of every Baptism being the one Baptism: Baptism delineates the boundaries of the Church and establishes the basis for a communio of all baptized in the One Church, so that every "valid Baptism" is one more point on the great boundary line of the Church. Wherever a valid Baptism, there is the Church of Christ.[387]

385. As noted earlier, the Secretariat for Promoting Christian Unity, under the leadership of Augustin Cardinal Bea, drew directly from Aquinas' text on baptismal character and from Canon 87 of the 1917 Code of Canon Law, ultimately based on Aquinas' theology. The Secretariat and Cardinal Bea led the way in shaping the council's ecumenical theology. See Jerome-Michael Vereb, *"Because He Was a German": Cardinal Bea and the Origins of Roman Catholic Engagement in the Ecumenical Movement* (Grand Rapids, MI: Eerdmans, 2006), 236–37.

386. See our examination of the theology of Yves Congar and Cardinal Bea as examples of this in chapters 7 and 8.

387. See LG 11, 15; UR 22; *Acta Synodalia*, III/2, 335. Cardinal Kasper explains it this way: "Baptism . . . is the sacrament of faith, whereby those who have been baptized belong to the one body of Christ which

In order to accomplish this reorientation, the "exclusivity" of *Mystici Corporis* had to be set aside and the criteria for participation in the One Church broadened. This meant that the criteria for both participation in the Church and the nature of the Church had to be redefined—first and foremost as concerning the "separated brethren."

With the new communio ecclesiology there was an epiphany of sorts, such that theologians started connecting the theological dots jotted down from the thirteenth through the twentieth centuries, until finally a new image of the Church emerged.[388] The claim, however, of apologists for the new ecclesiology is that, far from being a development of post-schism doctrine or an innovation, the new ecclesiology is a return to the sources

is the church. Non-Catholic Christians are therefore not outside of the one church, they already belong to it in a most fundamental way. On the basis of the one common Baptism ecumenism . . . has an ontological foundation and an ontological depth. It is an event of the Spirit." Walter Kasper, "The Decree on Ecumenism—Read Anew After Forty Years," Pontifical Council for Promoting Christian Unity, Conference on the 40th Anniversary of the Promulgation of the Conciliar Decree "Unitatis Redintegratio," Rocca di Papa, Mondo Migliore, November 11, 12 and 13, 2004, sec. 4, par. 3.

388. It is helpful to recall here what Jerome-Michael Vereb states in the conclusion of his study on the origins of Roman Catholic ecumenism: through the efforts of such influential figures as Cardinal Bea and Yves Congar, "a new and irreversible image of the Church Universal" emerged at Vatican II. This new image appeared not as a result of a return to the Fathers but by a selective reading and "harmonization of texts" such as Canon 87 of the 1917 Code of Canon Law and Pius XII's two encyclicals on the Church. See Vereb, *"Because He Was a German,"* 236–37, 245–46, and 290–91. What Vereb neglects to point out is that the "harmonization of texts" he cites is a harmonization of selected texts and selected verses from those texts. One could have just as easily chosen other texts or even other passages from the same texts and stressed other aspects of past teaching to come to the opposite conclusion.

and a patristic renewal. The fact that a few Orthodox theologians have reacted positively toward *Unitatis Redintegratio*[389] and have even declared their agreement with the common Baptism theory might seem to lend credence to this claim.[390] However,

389. John D. Zizioulas, "Unitatis Redintegratio: An Orthodox Reflection," in *Searching for Christian Unity* (New York: New City Press, 2007), 37–54.

390. See the following examples: Athenagoras Kokkinakis, *The Thyateira Confession* (London: The Faith Press, 1975), 62. John D. Zizioulas, (present-day Metropolitan of Pergamon, Ecumenical Patriarchate) "Orthodox Ecclesiology and the Ecumenical Movement," *Sourozh Diocesan Magazine* (UK) 21 (August 1985), 23: "If we take into consideration the canons of the early Church, then we can speak of the limits of the Church on the basis, I would suggest, of baptismal unity. By this I mean that baptism is such a decisive point in our existence that it automatically creates a limit between the pre-baptismal and post-baptismal situation: if you are baptized you immediately cease to be what you were. You die, as St. Paul says, with regard to the past and there is therefore a new situation. Baptism does create a limit to the Church. Now with this baptismal limit it is conceivable that there may be division, but any division within these limits is not the same as the division between the Church and those outside of the baptismal limit. . . . I think we must take seriously the baptismal limits of the Church and accept that outside of baptism there is no Church. Within baptism, even if there is a break, a division, a schism, you can still speak of the Church. Even if you take the Eucharistic model as your basis, you will see that this applies to every Christian. Let us take the Liturgy of the early Church as an example: up to the point of the reading of the Scriptures, or, as we still have in the Liturgy today, up to the kiss of peace which is the sign of unity in love and the Creed, which is the sign of unity in faith—up to this point it was conceivable that someone could take part in the Liturgy and then not be allowed to continue for various reasons (as a penance, for instance, or if he was a catechumen). He would then leave before the Sacrament. Now this suggests that we may understand divisions with the Church as taking place precisely at these points: either at the kiss of peace, or at the Creed. If we are not in a position to love one another and to confess the same faith, then there is a break in communion. But

from the evidence presented in part 1 of this study concerning

this break does not mean that one falls outside the realm of the Church. The Orthodox, in my understanding at least, participate in the ecumenical movement as a movement of baptized Christians, who are in a state of division because they cannot express the same faith together. In the past this happened because of a lack of love which is now, thank God, disappearing."

Επίσκεψις, τ. 520 (31 Ιουλίου 1995), σελ. 20, *Κοινή διακήρυξις του Πάπα Ιωάννου Παύλου II και Πατριάρχου Βαρθολομαίου* [Common Declaration of Pope John Paul II and Patriarch Bartholomew] "Call to Unity," 29 Ιουνίου 1995, section 4: "We urge our faithful, Catholics and Orthodox, to reinforce the spirit of brotherhood which stems from the one baptism and from participation in the sacramental life."

The Declaration of the Seventh Plenary Session of the Joint International Commission for Theological Dialogue Between the Catholic Church and the Orthodox Church: "Uniatism, Method of Union of the Past, and the Present Search for Full Communion" (Balamand, Lebanon, 1993), section 13: " . . . since the Pan-Orthodox Conferences and the Second Vatican Council, the rediscovery and the giving again of proper value to the Church as communion, both on the part of Orthodox and of Catholics, has radically altered perspectives and thus attitudes. On each side it is recognized that what Christ has entrusted to His Church—profession of apostolic faith, participation in *the same sacraments*, above all the one priesthood celebrating the one sacrifice of Christ, the apostolic succession of bishops—cannot be considered the exclusive property of one of our Churches. In this context it is clear that rebaptism must be avoided."

Baptism and Sacramental Economy, An Agreed Statement of The North American Orthodox-Catholic Theological Consultation, St. Vladimir's Orthodox Seminary, Crestwood, New York, June 3, 1999: "The Orthodox and Catholic members of our Consultation acknowledge, in both of our traditions, a common teaching and a common faith in one baptism, despite some variations in practice which, we believe, do not affect the substance of the mystery. We are therefore moved to declare that *we also recognize each other's baptism as one and the same*. This recognition has obvious *ecclesiological consequences. The Church is* itself both the milieu and *the effect of baptism*, and is not of our making. *This recognition requires each side of our dialogue to acknowledge an ecclesial reality in the other. . . . *. In our common reality of baptism, we discover the foundation of our

the history of the question, it is apparent that pre-schism Western sources, Augustine and his legacy, have not been reclaimed

dialogue, as well as the force and urgency of the Lord Jesus' prayer 'that all may be one.' *Here, finally, is the certain basis for the modern use of the phrase, 'sister churches.'*"

"Austalian Churches Covenanting Together," "Covenanting Document" of the National Council of Churches of Australia which the Australian dioceses of the Patriarchates of Constantinople, Antioch, Romania, and Serbia signed, by which they recognize the Sacrament of Baptism that is performed in heterodox communities (Roman Catholic, Anti-Chalcedonian, Anglican, Lutheran, Uniate, and Congregationalist) and agree to promote the use of one baptismal certificate. For the entire document, see http://www.ncca.org.au/files/Departments/Faith_and_Unity/Covenanting/2010_July_Australian_Churches_Covenanting_Together.pdf.

In October 2004 the representative of the Ecumenical Patriarchate in Germany, Metropolitan Augustine, signed a declaration with the Evangelical Church in Germany recognizing a common Baptism and vowing not to baptize converts. See http://www.goarch.org /news/goa.news1213.

In 2007, the Commission of the Orthodox Church in Germany (KOKiD), headed by Metropolitan Augustine, joined eleven German denominations in signing a common Baptism declaration. This, the first national agreement on a common Baptism in Germany, was initially proposed by Cardinal Walter Kasper in 2002. It reads, in part: "Deshalb erkennen wir jede nach dem Auftrag Jesu im Namen des Vaters und des Sohnes und des Heiligen Geistes mit der Zeichenhandlung des Untertauchens im Wasser bzw. des Übergießens mit Wasser vollzogene Taufe an und freuen uns über jeden Menschen, der getauft wird. Diese wechselseitige Anerkennung der Taufe ist Ausdruck des in Jesus Christus gründenden Bandes der Einheit (Epheser 4,4–6). Die so vollzogene Taufe ist einmalig und unwiederholbar." For the official document in German, see www.ekd.de/presse/pm86_2007_ wechselseitige_taufanerkennung.html. On August 8, 2007, the Patriarchate of Moscow distanced itself from this declaration, claiming that it only expressed the personal opinion of its representative in Germany, Archbishop Longinos of Kliv, not the position of the Russian Orthodox Church. For the Russian text, see http://www.mospat.ru /index.php?page=36165.

by reformers such as Congar, Bea, and Ratzinger. Rather, a "new and unique image of the church" was sought and fashioned—an image unknown to the Holy Fathers.

However, what of communio ecclesiology in the conciliar text itself? How is the unity of the Church understood in the Decree?

The Twofold Unity of, and Membership in, the Body of Christ

The theological starting point and foundation of *Unitatis Redintegratio* is laid down in article two, which is preceded by the title "Catholic Principles on Ecumenism." The picture of the Church and its unity as set forth in this article is considered by Fr. Francis Sullivan to be "the best description to be found anywhere in the documents of the Council of the kind of unity that Christ gave to his Church."[391]

Fr. Sullivan was the Professor of Ecclesiology at the Gregorian University in Rome from 1956 until 1992 and has written extensively on the subject. He writes that the Church described here is "intended to be visibly united in the profession of the same faith, the celebration of the same sacraments, in the fraternal concord of one people of God."[392] That this might come

---

391. Francis A. Sullivan, S.J., "The Significance of the Vatican II Declaration that the Church of Christ 'Subsists in' the Roman Catholic Church," in René Latourelle, ed., *Vatican II: Assessment and Perspectives, Twenty-five Years After (1962–1987)* (New York: Paulist Press, 1989), 2:277. Fr. Sullivan is the author of numerous articles and books on the ecclesiology of the Second Vatican Council, including *The Church We Believe In* (Dublin: Gill and Macmillan, 1988). See also his important work *Salvation Outside the Church?: Tracing the History of the Catholic Response* (New York: Paulist Press, 1992; Eugene, OR: Wipf and Stock, 2002).

392. Sullivan, 277.

about, Christ imparted to His Church a threefold ministry of word, sacrament, and leadership, and entrusted this ministry to the apostles "with Peter at their head" (UR 2d) "and then continued in the college of bishops under the Pope."[393] This is the unity envisioned later in UR 4c, which is said to be inalienable and permanent and to "subsist" in the Roman Catholic Church alone: "We believe that the unity with which Christ from the beginning endowed his Church is something it cannot lose; it subsists in the Catholic Church."[394]

While article two is meant to be a description of the unity Christ has given to Roman Catholics and their church, it was also designed to set the stage for the redefining, in theological terms, of the relationship between Roman Catholicism and non–Roman Catholics in the next article.[395]

At first, it would seem that the two purposes should be at odds with one another. If the unity of the Church refers to the Roman Church and this unity is "a given" and immutable, how could it set the stage for a redefinition of the relationship of the "dissidents" to the church? If we have in article two the finest description of what Vatican II means by the unity of the Church—a threefold, visible unity in common sacraments, faith, and episcopacy—presumably, then, we should, on this basis, determine the relationship of the "separated brethren" to the Church. That is not, however, the path followed.

Let us turn to Johannes Feiner's commentary to determine how article two provides us with the traditional basis for the unity of the Church and the basis for redefinition in relation

393. Ibid.
394. Ibid. See also UR 4c.
395. Johannes Feiner, "Commentary on the Decree," in *Commentary on the Documents of Vatican II*, vol. 2 (London: Burns and Oates Limited, 1968), 69.

to the non–Roman Catholics. First, Feiner points to the text's emphasis on the role of the Holy Spirit in gathering together the assembly of the Church "into a unity of faith, hope and love." Feiner claims that this provides, "in association with the one Baptism, which is referred to [in the text], the basis for the recognition [given later] of the reality of non-Catholic communities as Churches, and for the statement concerning individual members of these Churches, that in them the Church (from this more fundamental point of view) is more fully realized than in individual members of the Catholic Church, in so far as faith, hope, and love are more lively in the former than the latter."[396]

Gregory Baum concurs with Feiner. He states that the Roman Catholic Church is the institutionally perfect realization of the Church of Christ, while other churches, not in communion with Rome, are institutionally imperfect realizations of the same Church. This allows us to say that "concretely and actually the Church of Christ may be realized less, equally, or even more in a Church separated from Rome than in a Church in communion with Rome . . . [because,] seen from the viewpoint of God's merciful and sovereign action, which uses institutional elements but is *never dependent on or limited by them*, a Christian community is more truly Church when it is more transformed into the People of God, into his family, into a spiritual brotherhood of faith and charity."[397]

Second, Feiner notes that the Church of Christ and Roman Catholicism "are not simply identified here," and "the 'Catholic Church' is not simply used in place of 'the Church of Christ.'

---

396. Feiner, 66.
397. Gregory Baum, O.S.A, "The Ecclesial Reality of the Other Churches," in *The Church and Ecumenism* (New York: Paulist Press, 1965), 82 (emphasis added).

Thus the question (which is answered later in the text) remains open, whether *the Church of Christ is not also present in some way in other Christian communities.*"[398] The Decree will answer this positively in article three.

Third, "the doctrine of the Church underlying the whole account can be described as a communio ecclesiology. . . . This means an ecclesiology which defines the Church as an organic whole composed of spiritual bonds (faith, hope, and charity), and of visible structural forms (the profession of faith, the sacramental economy, and pastoral ministry), and which *culminates in the eucharistic mystery,* the source and expression of the unity of the Church. . . ."[399] Here, clearly described, is the unity said to subsist in the Roman Catholic Church alone.

Yet, at the same time, because the Church is seen as a "communio," or a "complex reality in the form of a communion, the unity of which has been brought about by numerous and various factors, the possibility remains open that *the constituent elements* of the Church may be present even in Christian communities outside the Catholic Church, and *may give these communities the nature of a Church.* Thus, the one Church of Christ can also be present outside the Catholic Church, and it is present, and also, indeed, visible, in so far as factors and elements which create unity and therefore the Church are here."[400]

Feiner's interpretation is consistent with the official explanation, or Relatio, which refers to the "ecclesial communities" in the West in this way: "[they] are not merely a sum or collection of individual Christians, but they are constituted by

398. Feiner, 68 (emphasis added).
399. Ibid., 64 (emphasis added).
400. Ibid., 68–69 (emphasis added). The "elements ecclesiology" put forth by Congar but initially drawn from Calvin, is apparent here.

social ecclesiastical elements . . . which confer on them *a truly ecclesial character.* In these communities the one sole Church of Christ is present, albeit imperfectly. . . ."[401] *Unitatis Redintegratio* states this point thus: "some and even very many of the significant elements and endowments which together go to build up and give life to the Church itself, can exist outside the visible boundaries of the Catholic Church: the written word of God; the life of grace; . . . interior gifts of the Holy Spirit, and visible elements too" (UR 3b).

Thus, what emerges is a twofold, two-tiered, unity of the Church: one tier of union complete, as intended and ordained by God; and one incomplete, unintended but allowed by God. This view of the Church and her "elements" could only have developed within the context of a Latin sacramental theology that determines sacramental authenticity on the basis of proper form and matter (validity)—irrespective of whether there is catholic agreement in faith and practice. From the moment that the outward sign alone was sufficient to be indicative of an inward reality and the mysteries were detached from the context of the visible Mystery of the Body of Christ, the path was cleared for what is essentially a Latin version of the Protestant invisible church theory. For, in this view, factors or elements (first of which is Baptism) independent of the visible,

---

401. *Acta Synodalia*, III/2, 335 (emphasis added). As Douglas M. Koskela notes, one of the most striking changes to take place with Vatican II is that, prior to the council, more progressive Roman Catholic theologians were only willing "to speak in terms of non-Catholic *individual* Christians being imperfect members in the church of Christ." After Vatican II, theologians began to speak "in terms of the imperfect presence of the church of Christ in non-Catholic *communities*." Douglas M. Koskela, *Ecclesiality and Ecumenism: Yves Congar and the Road to Unity* (Milwaukee: Marquette University Press, 2008), 59.

true Church, are supposed to impart to autonomous, heterodox bodies the character of the Church.

Gradation of Membership in the Body

In order better to grasp this new two-tiered nature of the Church's unity, let us turn to the theology of Pope Benedict, writing at the time of the council as a young Fr. Joseph Ratzinger. As we have seen, on the eve of *Unitatis Redintegratio* a consensus existed among Catholic theologians, in favor of a theology of the differentiated participation of the non-Roman communions in the treasure of the single Church. The future Pope Benedict XVI was one of the leading voices before and at the council calling for recognition of Church membership for the "separated brethren," although in a limited, diminished way.

Before the council's commencement, and as early as 1961, Ratzinger had already affirmed "the constitutive Church membership of all those baptized outside the Catholic Church," as well as the "existence of ecclesial elements" and "a certain presence of the reality of the Church" in Protestantism."[402]

In a later article, written after Vatican II had adopted this view, Ratzinger noted that, owing to the threefold requirement of (1) Baptism, (2) orthodoxy, and (3) unity under the episcopacy, the pre–Vatican II official teaching "completely excluded

---

402. J. Ratzinger, "Protestantismus: III. Beurteilung vom Standpunkt des Katholizismus" [Protestantism: III. Assessment from the Catholic point of view], in *Religion in Geschichte und Gegenwart* (third edition, 1961), 5:663–66, cited in Joseph Ratzinger, *Pilgrim Fellowship of Faith: The Church as Communion*, trans. Henry Taylor, ed. Stephan Otto Horn and Vinzenz Pfnur (San Francisco: Ignatius Press, 2005 [German 2002]), 14–15.

non-Catholics from membership of the Church." He then re-joined, following in the footsteps of Cardinal Bea:

> According to the Church's legal tradition[403] . . . Baptism provided an unlosable form of constitutive membership of the Church. This approach made it clear that in certain circumstances a legal approach can offer more flexibility and openness than a "mystical" one. It was asked whether the image of the mystical body was not too narrow . . . to be able to define the multitude of different forms of Church membership that now existed thanks to the confusion of human history. For membership, the image of the body can only offer the idea of member in the sense of limb: one is either a limb or not, and there are no intermediary stages. . . . [Yet] quite clearly there are intermediary stages.[404]

As we have noted,[405] the older idea of unity, the threefold, visible unity in common sacraments, faith, and episcopacy, was one of those concepts which Ratzinger had ruled out as a "Scholastic formula" unsuitable for the new ecumenical con-

---

403. He is referring to the oft-quoted Canon 87 of the 1917 Code of Canon Law, which follows theological tradition arising out of the Aquinian sacramental theology, which we examined in chapter 5.

404. Joseph Ratzinger, *Church, Ecumenism, and Politics, New Endeavors in Ecclesiology* (San Francisco: Ignatius Press, 2008), 15. See also Pope Benedict XVI, *Joseph Ratzinger in communio: Vol. I—The Unity of the Church* (Grand Rapids, MI: Eerdmans, 2010), 73 (emphasis added).

405. See the introductory text to part 2 at n. 269, where we cite Cardinal Ratzinger's (later Pope Benedict's) listing of older concepts supplanted because of their unsuitability in the new ecumenical context; the full quotation follows in the text at that location. They are referenced to *Theological Highlights of Vatican II* (New York: Paulist Press, 2009), 102–104.

text. There is, however, no essential difference between the ideal description of unity in article two of *Unitatis Redintegratio* and the abandoned Scholastic formula. From time immemorial, to be united to the Church, to be a participant in its unity, one had to share the same sacraments, same faith, and submit to the local bishop of the one, holy, catholic, and apostolic church. This is not an idea that began with the Scholastics, but with the Apostles.

So, was Ratzinger mistaken, then, when he said that the older view was discarded for a more ecumenically acceptable vision of unity? Well, no, not exactly. Strangely enough, the former was kept and the latter was adopted: the first was retained for Roman Catholics alone, while the second was adopted for non–Roman Catholic Christians.[406] In the case of the "separated brethren" the old, Scholastic formula was replaced by the newly recognized unity, that unity or communion enjoyed by the "separated brethren." Only for them is the old, traditional threefold unity not applicable, nor immediately necessary, in order to be incorporated into Christ, to be in communion with the Church, to enjoy the life of grace (UR 3a, b). The bar of communion, even if labeled "partial," has been lowered. The irony is, however, that even as Vatican II has been hailed as the council of a return to primary sources, it discarded the threefold criterion for membership outlined in *Mystici Corpo-*

---

406. It is not without reason, then, that many speak of a double standard and a two-faced stance on the part of Roman Catholicism. It may not be an accident that the Second Vatican Council, especially in the texts of *Lumen Gentium* and *Unitatis Redintegratio*, is the source for both those who advance an "exclusive" ecclesiology and those who advance an "inclusive" ecclesiology. "They use the same sources, but come to entirely different conclusions." Τσομπανίδης, Ἡ Διακήρυξη *Dominus Iesus*, 82.

ris—three criteria that more closely resemble the patristic and Orthodox view than that of the new communio ecclesiology.

Ratzinger's rationalization of the council's departure from the traditional threefold criterion for membership is striking. Just as with the problematic article 22 of *Mystici Corporis*, which Cardinal Bea bypassed without confronting, here the traditional, threefold criterion of membership in the Church is not rejected outright, but simply side-stepped as no longer relevant to the question of the status of non–Roman Catholic Christians. The call for some form of Church membership to be extended to the "separated brethren" is seen as necessary in order to cover the anomaly of "intermediary stages" of belonging to the Church created throughout history. Ratzinger thus supposes that the nature of belonging to the Body of Christ is changeable, even that St. Paul's God-inspired ecclesiology is outdated and inadequate. This is believed to be the result of the tumult of history, which can affect the Church to such a degree as to change her inner constitution and criteria for membership.

Can it be, though, that the "confusion of human history" forces new forms of membership on the Church? Can the scriptural imagery of the Body of Christ, with the baptized becoming "members one of another" (Rom 12:5) in the Eucharist, become inadequate to describe the Mystery of the Church? Is it possible that St. Paul missed what Vatican II grasped two millennia later: that there are, in fact, "intermediary stages" of membership in the Body of Christ, and this irrespective of the unity of the faith?

Two Kinds of Baptism

The dual nature of the Church in the new ecclesiology is also viewed by some interpreters of Vatican II with respect to the meaning of Baptism and incorporation into the Church. In the first paragraph of article 3 of *Unitatis Redintegratio*, the "separated brethren" are said to be incorporated into Christ (Christo incorporantur) through Baptism. Having in mind *Lumen Gentium*'s restriction of the phrase "full incorporation" to members of the Roman Catholic Church, the following question is raised: are we to understand this incorporation into Christ to signify something else than becoming a member of the Body of Christ? Most theologians agree,[407] as Johannes Feiner points out in his commentary on the Decree, that "the concept of the body [is] retained in the verb (incorporantur). The translation [of the Latin] 'they are incorporated into the body of Christ' is as much in accord with the meaning as the rendering 'they are incorporated into Christ.'"[408]

What, however, does it now mean to "be incorporated into the Body of Christ," to be a member of the Church? What does Baptism signify for a non–Roman Catholic Christian post–Vatican II? Nearly fifty years after the council this remains a disputed point among Roman Catholic theologians.

The historical development of the understanding of Baptism as an element of the Church present among the dissidents, connecting them and their community to the Church, even as an expression of the Church, and the process by which it came

407. George May, *Die Okumenismusfalle* (Stuttgart: Sarto Verlag, 2004) is an exception. He differentiates incorporation into Christ from incorporation into the Church: "UR par. 3 does not maintain that Baptism makes non-Catholics part of the Body of Christ, as the German translation has it, but that they are rather 'incorporated into Christ.'" Fr. George May, ordained in 1951, was professor of canon and ecclesiastical law and history of canon law at the University of Mainz (1960–1994). He is a leading voice of the traditionalist movement in Germany and author of many critical essays on the post-conciliar Church.

408. Johannes Feiner, "Commentary on the Decree," in *Commentary on the Documents of Vatican II* (London: Burns and Oates Limited, 1968), 73.

to be a cornerstone of Roman Catholic thinking on the nature and extent of the Church have already been touched upon. In Blessed Augustine's response to the Donatists we find the origin of the idea. Baptism as a sacrament validly exists among the dissidents, but to no use or benefit because of their continuation in schism.

Augustine's sacramental theology became the patristic sacramental theology for the West, with every new exposition continuing to base itself on his distinctions. The reduction to essentials, the minimalism, already present in Blessed Augustine's thought, however, blossomed and spread from the twelfth century onward as a result of practical problems combined with Scholastic interpretations. The unity of the mysteries, once a given in Roman practice, was finally shattered, first in practice and then in theory, such that Baptism became synonymous with initiation. Whereas in the Orthodox Church initiation continued to mean Baptism, Chrismation, and Communion together, in the West this unity was lost, and children were baptized *quamprimum* (as soon as possible) but communed and confirmed years later.

The significance of this disunity in the development of the vision of the Church and the view of what constitutes initiation into Her have not been given proper attention among historians of dogma and ecclesiologists. Although it cannot be reduced to this alone, it should be recognized that only when it becomes normal to think of Christian initiation as Baptism alone can one then consider a child baptized in a schismatic or heretical community as being "truly incorporate in Christ and in the Church—the True Church," as Yves Congar remarks in *Divided Christendom*.[409] If the unity of the mysteries had been

---

409. Yves Congar, *Divided Christendom, A Catholic Study of the Problem of Reunion* [*Chrétiens désunis: principes d'un oecuménisme catholique*], trans.

maintained in the West, such that every child baptized was also chrismated and communed straightaway, as is the case in the Orthodox Church, it would be impossible to speak of initiation into the Church for those lacking Chrismation and the Eucharist.

The documents of Vatican II present a confused picture on this question of initiation. There is, as we have seen, evidence of two opposing movements—one for the reinstitution of the unity of the mysteries, and the other for maintaining the minimalistic status quo. Moreover, there appears to be a double standard: one for the believer who has been initiated into the Church as a Roman Catholic and one for the believer who has been initiated into the Church as a member of a dissident community.

Karl Becker, who moves within the same theological milieu as Pope Benedict XVI, insists that there are different kinds of Baptism—one of a Catholic and another of a non-Catholic. Only the Baptism of a Catholic incorporates one into the Catholic Church, he says: "If someone does not receive this Baptism, he is not a member of it."[410] For Christians outside the Catholic Church, "the administration [of Baptism] can have had its effect only in a diminished form, and the reception can likewise not express the full Catholic profession of faith."[411] He gives no explanation as to what he means by "a diminished form," nor what UR 3a intends when it declares "all who have been justified by faith in Baptism are incorporated into Christ."

M. A. Bousfield (London: Geoffrey Bles: The Centenary Press, 1939 [Paris: Cerf, 1937]), 230.

410. Karl Becker, "The Teaching of Vatican II on Baptism: A Stimulus for Theology," in René Latourelle, ed., *Vatican II: Assessment and Perspectives, Twenty-five Years After (1962–1987)* (New York: Paulist Press, 1989), 2:72.

411. Ibid.

Becker's perspective appears to be unique, but it does illustrate the degree to which post-conciliar theology is twisting and turning in order to make sense of apparently contradictory theological stances in Vatican II documents on this issue. For, there is no precedent to speak of one mystery producing two different results, initiation into two different tiers of the One Church, or of a Baptism that does not initiate one into the Church. Becker's view raises many questions (which we've touched on elsewhere), such as: can one be incorporated into Christ without being a member of the Catholic Church? If so, to which Church does he belong? If another, are there then two Churches? Is the non-Catholic fully incorporated into Christ? If so, how is it that he is not fully a member of His Body, since Christ and His Body are one? Or, can one be incorporated into Christ without simultaneously being in communion with His entire Body?

This view of initiation and the Church as somehow happening on two levels is not only incompatible with the patristic understanding of unity and the mysteries; it is reflective of the degree of fragmentation and disunity characteristic of the new ecclesiology. The unity of the vertical and horizontal dimensions of the One Body of Christ, effected on the Cross, appears to have disintegrated.

Intended and Unintended Unity

In order better to understand why the council saw a need for this innovation recognizing shades of communion-membership—this change from, as it were, that which Christ instituted (full) to that which He did not institute (incomplete)—it is worthwhile again to quote the eyewitness and *peritus* of the council Father Ratzinger, at length:

The first schema [on the Church] of 1962 still clung to
the traditional scholastic formula which saw membership in the Church as dependent on the joint presence of
three prerequisites: Baptism, profession of the same faith
and acceptance of the hierarchy headed by the bishop
of Rome. Only those who met these three requirements
could be called members of the Church. Obviously this
was *a very narrow formulation*. Other formulations were
not necessarily excluded, yet the result was that the notion of "member of the Church" could be applied only
to Catholics. With such an answer to the question of
Church membership, it became very difficult to describe
the Christian dignity of the non-Catholic Christian. His
association with the Church was expressed only in the
questionable concept of the *votum Ecclesiae*, meaning that
non-Catholic Christians belonged to the Church by virtue
of their "desire" to be a part of it. Since "Church" here
obviously meant the Roman Catholic Church, it can easily
be seen that such a description was insufficient. . . . Accordingly modifications were made in the text submitted
in 1963 to the Council Fathers.

*The new text avoided the expression "member of the
Church," hallowed by long usage in Catholic theology.* Use
of this expression would have immediately aroused the
scholastic theologians who saw this notion as necessarily including the three above-mentioned prerequisites. In
view of these difficulties, the decision was taken to avoid
this controversial term. *The new text describes the relationship between the Church and non-Catholic Christians without
speaking of "membership." By shedding this terminological armor, the text acquired much wider scope.* This made possible
a much more positive presentation of the way Christians

are related to the Church as well as a positive Christian status for Christians separated from Rome. The text submitted to the fathers in the fall of 1963 states therefore that *multiple internal ties* existed among Christians. Baptism was one such tie, as was . . . faith in Christ . . . common possession of other sacraments . . . an inner hidden unity in the Holy Spirit . . . [and] as another bond of unity the common possession of sacred scripture.[412]

Ratzinger's description reveals a group of theologians confronting the "problem of schism" by weighing, on the right, concern for reactionary Scholastics and, on the left, ecumenical expectations, in order to produce a new ecclesiastical status for schismatics and heretics. The aim is to "solve" this problem with a new consideration—not to return to the patristic view, which could not provide a new solution. Behind this attempt there lies a conviction that the problem is not a falling away *from* the Church, not a division in faith that appeared through separation from the *Church,* but rather our own *perception of division* and the limits of an older, "narrow" ecclesiological formulation. At the heart of this approach is an attitude toward the fact of division that is very different from that of the Holy

412. Ratzinger, *Theological Highlights of Vatican II* (New York: Paulist Press, 2009), 102–104 (emphasis added). Gregory Baum echoes Ratzinger's comments in his article "The Ecclesial Reality of the Other Churches," written shortly after the council. While noting that the Theological Commission to the Council held that "all the baptized are in some way incorporated in the Church," he also notes that "the word 'member' and the notion of 'membership' have been avoided in the Constitution . . . for it was believed that this theological concept, variously understood in different theological systems, does not really help us in giving an account of the ways in which Christians participate in the mystery of the Church." Baum, "Ecclesial Reality," 71.

Fathers, for whom "elements" outside the fullness of Tradition and the Truth of Orthodoxy have no ecclesiological significance.[413] For the Fathers, the marks of the church are unrecognizable outside genuine unity in faith.[414]

These changes in understanding of the church and the place of the schismatics and heretics in it were bound to provoke theological reflection in search of a total solution. Indeed, much has been made about the "reception" of the council by the church, by which is meant, in part, a further working out and

413. Fr. Alexander Schmemann's astute observations from twelve years before Vatican II are quite illuminating on this point: "The attitude of the majority of contemporary theologians to the fact of division is very different from the attitude of the Eastern Church at the time of the Ecumenical Councils and in Byzantium. It may be said that contemporary theologians seek above all to discover the meaning of division and wish paradoxically to determine what might be called the theological status of division. How is division possible, what happens to the Sacraments in a Church or a community separated from what is supposed to be the true Church, what is the validity of their orders—these are the questions raised today. It seems to me that all these questions, which 'a theology of schism' attempts to answer, are fundamentally connected with the Roman conception of the Church as one universal organism and can arise only out of Roman presuppositions. A theology of schism is a product of the desire of theologians to find a place for the Church where, according to their own presuppositions, there should be no place for her. But the whole trouble is that, from the Orthodox point of view, these questions are unanswerable, because the whole problem is falsely posited, and formulated in the wrong terms. This may best be proved by the fact that neither the early Church nor the Church of the period of the Ecumenical Councils ever raised these questions, and in contemporary Orthodox theology they are a product of Roman and, generally, Western influence." Fr. Alexander Schmemann, "Unity, Division, Reunion in the Light of Orthodox Ecclesiology," address given at the Annual Conference of the Fellowship of St. Alban and St. Sergius at Abingdon, England, in August 1950 (Θεολογία, KB), 243–54.

414. See Schmemann, "Unity, Division, Reunion."

development of the conciliar theology. Joseph Ratzinger was quick to respond to this invitation with his own unique reinterpretation of the Body of Christ, what Maximilian Heim calls a "pneumatic understanding."[415] A brief look at his theory will aid us in better understanding the new view of membership in the Church in *Lumen Gentium* and *Unitatis Redintegratio*.

Ratzinger maintains that the biblical accounts of the institution of the Eucharist presuppose that "Jesus, because he was crucified and is risen, no longer exists in the form of σάρξ, but has left this historical form of existence behind"[416] and meets man in a totally new openness. Speaking of the pierced side of Christ (John 19:34), Ratzinger writes:

> Jesus' side is opened, and from it come forth blood and water, that is, the two fundamental sacraments of Baptism and Eucharist, and therein the Church. From this open side comes the fact that Jesus now exists as otherwise only spirit can exist, namely, as the one who is opened, the one who at all times can be there and is there for everyone. And that means, in biblical terminology, that the σῶμα of Jesus, that is, his form of corporeality, is πνεῦμα.[417]

Accordingly, the "pneumatic understanding" of the Body of Christ concept "is no longer faced with the exclusive alterna-

415. Maximilian Heinrich Heim, *Joseph Ratzinger: Life in the Church and Living Theology: Fundamentals of Ecclesiology with Reference to Lumen Gentium*, trans. Michael J. Miller (San Francisco: Ignatius Press, 2007), 241.

416. Ibid. Heim is quoting from "Kirche als Tempel des Heiligen Geistes," an abridged and slightly revised version of the lecture "Aspekte der Kirche" given on September 19, 1967, in Salzburg.

417. Ibid., 152, quoting "Kirche als Tempel."

tive, "member or non-member," belonging to the Body or not belonging to it; instead, a completely different pair of concepts emerges, namely, belonging in a supportive and productive way or belonging in a supported and derivative way.[418]

Here, the idea of a two-tiered membership is quite evident. Ratzinger's solution, like the ecclesiology of Vatican II itself, was born out of an effort to reconcile the traditional conception of the Church as the Body of Christ, "with the concerns of the ecumenical movement, for which a corporate interpretation of Corpus Christi was problematic."[419]

By "opening up" the Body of Christ concept, Ratzinger demonstrates that, according to Maximilian H. Heim,

> there are many layers to the Church as Body of Christ . . . [and this understanding] overcomes the corporate rigidity of [the older] image of the Church [Body of Christ = Catholic Church] and proposes in contrast to it a concept of the Body of Christ *with multiple shadings of meaning.* This multivalence characterizes *both the eucharistic Body given by the Lord and also the ecclesial communion founded by him,* with the result that new light is thereby shed on the relationship between the Church and the world and a completely new horizon emerges for the question of membership in the Church.[420]

As novel as Ratzinger's views will seem to an Orthodox observer, they are nothing more than a working out of the ecumenical character of *Lumen Gentium* 8 and the new conception of the Church of Christ as inclusive of more than simply the Roman Catholic Church. In this context, in particular, exclusiv-

---

418. Ibid., 242, quoting "Kirche als Tempel."
419. Ibid., 141.
420. See Schmemann, "Unity, Division, Reunion," 242–43 (emphasis added).

ity gives way to a transformed and broadened communio that has been "opened up to a great variety,"[421] so that "a gradation of Church membership becomes conceivable."[422] While Ratzinger's theological speculations and opening up of new horizons for the question of membership may be consistent with the conciliar texts on the church and on ecumenism, they are unknown to the patristic tradition—even a radical departure from it.

Communion at Various Degrees of Fullness

Surveying the ground we've covered so far, while *Lumen Gentium* established new criteria for participation in the Church, even a new view of the Church itself, it did not discard the traditional view of the unity of the Church either; it simply no longer applies it to non–Roman Catholics. In *Lumen Gentium*, the two views follow one after another. Full participation in the unity of the Church, for Roman Catholics, is described in article 14 of *Lumen Gentium*.[423] Unity in Christ and the Holy Spirit,

421. H. Fries, "Das Konzil: Grund ökumenischer Hoffnung," in König, *Bleiblende Bedeutung*, 107–21, citation at 113, quoted in Heim, *Joseph Ratzinger*, 75.

422. B. Korner, "*Extra ecclesiam nulla salus*: Sinn und Problematik dieses Satzes in einer sich wandelnden fundamentaltheologishchen Ekklesiologie," *ZKTh* 114 (1992): 274–92, citation at 280, quoted in Heim, *Joseph Ratzinger*, 75.

423. "This Sacred Council wishes to turn its attention firstly to the Catholic faithful. . . . They are fully incorporated in the society of the Church who, possessing the Spirit of Christ accept her entire system and all the means of salvation given to her, and are united with her as part of her visible bodily structure and through her with Christ, who rules her through the Supreme Pontiff and the bishops. The bonds which bind men to the Church in a visible way are profession of faith, the sacraments, and ecclesiastical government and communion."

and the mysteries of the Church—the "multiple internal links" that establish the separated brethren in an incomplete communion—are described in article 15.[424] While *Lumen Gentium* does not explicitly say that they are members of the Church, *Unitatis Redintegratio* states plainly that they are incorporated into Christ (Christo incorporantur) (UR 3a). The unity of the Church for non–Roman Catholics—participation-membership not based on a common faith and episcopacy, but only on a common Baptism and other "elements"—is not the unity of the Roman Catholic Church. Or, rather, more accurately, it exists for that portion of the Church of Christ that isn't the Roman Catholic Church.

In accord with this twofold unity, Rome continues to view itself as the only "concrete manifestation" of the Church—the Church willed by Christ—while non–Roman Catholic churches are churches only in a diminished way (see UR 3d and e). However, strangely, no matter how "weakened" or "wounded"[425]

---

424. "The Church recognizes that in many ways she is linked with those who, being baptized, are honored with the name of Christian, though they do not profess the faith in its entirety or do not preserve unity of communion with the successor of Peter. For there are many who honor Sacred Scripture, taking it as a norm of belief and a pattern of life, and who show a sincere zeal. They lovingly believe in God the Father Almighty and in Christ, the Son of God and Savior. They are consecrated by Baptism, in which they are united with Christ. They also recognize and accept other sacraments within their own Churches or ecclesiastical communities. Many of them rejoice in the episcopate, celebrate the Holy Eucharist and cultivate devotion toward the Virgin Mother of God. They also share with us in prayer and other spiritual benefits. Likewise we can say that in some real way they are joined with us in the Holy Spirit, for to them too He gives His gifts and graces whereby He is operative among them with His sanctifying power."

425. See the declaration by the Congregation for the Doctrine of the Faith, *Dominus Iesus*.

they are supposed to be, these churches are said to have fully legitimate mysteries.[426] Fully united with Christ, their unity with and in the Church is, nonetheless, imperfect. Such a state, hitherto unheard of, is stated but left unexplained. Whatever may be lacking, they are a part of the Church. Schismatics and heretics can be united to Christ and become members of the Body of Christ without, however, being members of the Roman Catholic Church. Roman Catholics, Protestants, and Orthodox are all a part of the One Church, even if at varying degrees of fullness.

As Fr. Francis Sullivan writes, summing up the image of the universal Church of Christ created by the new ecclesiology:

> one can think of the universal Church as a communion, at various levels of fullness, of bodies that are *more or less fully churches*. . . . It is a real communion, realized at various degrees of density or fullness, of bodies, all of which, though some more fully than others, have *a truly ecclesial character*.[427]

It is not surprising, then, that this understanding of Baptism and the Church in the communio ecclesiology has become a

---

426. This is apparent, for example, in UR 15a: "through the celebration of the Holy Eucharist in each of these [Orthodox] Churches, the Church of God is built up and grows in stature."

427. Sullivan, "The Significance of the Vatican II Declaration that the Church of Christ 'Subsists in' the Roman Catholic Church," 283 (emphasis added). Likewise, according to I. Spiteri, "[from a reading of the encyclical UUS] a new image of the Church emerges, a Church which is constituted by a communion of Churches, in which, in some way, all Christian Churches belong." Ἰ. Σπιτέρης, "Ἡ Καθολικὴ Ἐκκλησία καὶ οἱ ἄλλες χριστιανικές Ἐκκλησίες" [The Catholic Church and the other Christian Churches], Θ. Κοντίδης (ἐπιμ.), (Ὁ Καθολικισμος, Ἀθήνα 2000), 246.

real point of convergence between Roman Catholics and Protestants in the World Council of Churches.[428] This was, after all, the thrust of the communio ecclesiology, with its emphasis on the elements of the Church as the ecclesiological bridge to the "separated brethren." This is clearly stated by the theological commission of the council in its explanation of a key element of the new ecclesiology.

The official explanation given to explain the change from the Church of Christ "is" the Catholic Church, as was stated in *Mystici Corporis*, to the Church of Christ "subsists in" the Catholic Church was "so that the expression might better agree with the affirmation about the ecclesial elements which are found elsewhere."[429] These "elements" are what transform and broaden communio beyond that of the institutional limits of the Roman communion and thus make the inclusion of the separated brethren within the mystery of the Church possible. Without the recognition of these elements—first of all which is Baptism—as "ecclesial," and thus the inclusion of the separated brethren in the mystery of the Church, the communio ecclesiology loses its *raison d'être*. It would mean that the new ecclesiology differed little from the pre–Vatican II "exclusivist" conception, and would signify the end of ecumenism as Rome knows it.

If, however, the traditional criteria are retained as necessary for "full" communion, for those subject to the Pope, while the

428. See "Ecclesiological and Ecumenical Implications of a Common Baptism, A Joint Working Group Study," *Information Service of The Pontifical Council for Promoting Christian Unity*, No. 117 (Vatican City: 2004/ IV), 188–204.

429. The phrase is from LG 8. The theological commission's explanation can be found in the *Acta Synodalia* III/1, 177.

new criteria are used to determine an "incomplete" communion for the "separated brethren," then the advantages of both are realized. The aim of the new ecclesiology is thus achieved: a broadened Church in which schismatics and heretics are members, albeit in an incomplete, diminished state, with the Roman Church alone possessing "fullness" and concrete "subsistence."

These two standards are everywhere present in the texts and commentaries: one for the Church that Christ founded and another for a church that emerged out of historical circumstances. There are, as it were, two different realms of ecclesial possibilities, two different classes of the baptized, two kinds of unity, Baptism, communion, and church. Such a state of "disunitedness," however, cannot but be totally at odds with the patristic view of the Church.

12

FULLNESS, UNITY, AND THE IDENTITY
OF THE CHURCH

From the foregoing it should be clear now that essential to the new ecclesiology is the distinction of *plene* (full) and *non plene* (incomplete) or *non perfecta* (imperfect) *communione*. The addition of the adjective "full" may seem minor, but, in fact, it represents a sharp and extremely important departure not only from *Mystici Corporis* and previous Latin ecclesiology but even from the original schema *De Ecclesia* presented to the council in its opening session of 1962, which still spoke simply of a separation "from the communion of the Catholic Church."

The introduction of a differentiation between full and incomplete communion is closely tied to the introduction of a differentiated relation between Jesus Christ and the Church, and between the Church of Jesus Christ and the Roman Catholic Church. The implications of these new distinctions are momentous.[430]

According to Cardinal Kasper, both Jesus Christ and the Church, and the Church of Jesus Christ and the Roman Catholic Church "*cannot be identified with each other* or confused, but neither can they be separated from, or simply placed alongside, each other. The very essence of the Church has to be seen as *analogous, not identical, to the incarnation.* Still, it is maintained

---

430. It is beyond the scope of this study to fully address the implications of this differentiation between Jesus Christ and the Church.

that the divine and human dimensions are neither to be confused nor separated (LG 8). Nevertheless, *the Church is not the continuation of the incarnation,* not the *Christus prolongatus,* the prolonged Christ, but Jesus Christ through and within the Spirit is sacramentally present and at work in the Church as his body and as the temple of the Spirit."[431]

The Orthodox, however, stress the very point Kasper says Rome no longer accepts—*Christus prolongatus*—even if, perhaps, from a different perspective, history, and context. Kasper is basing himself, in part, on *Lumen Gentium* 8, which states that "the divine and human element" that coalesces to form "one complex reality," which is the Church, is only to be "*compared* to the mystery of the incarnate Word." For the Fathers and for the Orthodox, the phrase of the Apostle Paul, "body of Christ," means that we cannot speak of this as a simple "analogy" but rather as an ontological identification.

St. Nicholas Cabasilas, when speaking of the theanthropic reality of the Church, says this regarding the Church and the Holy Eucharist:

> The Church is known in the mysteries, not as symbols but as the limbs are present in the heart, as the twigs are present in the root, and, as our Lord has said, the branches are present in the vine (John 15:1–5). For here is no mere sharing (κοινωνία) of a name or a likeness of analogy, but *an identity* (ταυτότης) of reality. For these

---

431. Cardinal Walter Kasper, *That They May All Be One: The Call to Unity Today* (London/New York: Burns and Oates, 2004), 50–74, especially p. 70 (emphasis added). For the views of Cardinal Joseph Ratzinger (by this time Pope Benedict XVI), see Maximilian Heinrich Heim, *Joseph Ratzinger: Life in the Church and Living Theology: Fundamentals of Ecclesiology with Reference to Lumen Gentium,* trans. Michael J. Miller (San Francisco: Ignatius Press, 2007), 300–330.

mysteries are the Body and Blood of Christ, which are the Church's true food and drink. When it partakes of them, it does not transform them into the human body ... but *is itself changed into the Body and Blood of Christ.* ... And if one could see the Church of Christ insofar as it is united to Him and shares His sacred Body, one would see nothing other than the Body of the Lord.[432]

As Christos Voulgaris has written: "Christ's perfect humanity forms the nature, as well as the entity of the Church which in this way constitutes the perpetual continuation of His incarnation extending beyond time. Hence, any thought of an ontological separation between Christ and Church rules out both the fact of Christ's incarnation and the reality of the Church."[433] Likewise, Hieromonk Athanasius Yevtich (now the retired bishop of Herzegovina) provides the patristic understanding, especially that of St. John Chrysostom, thus: "For, in the mystery of the Incarnation God appeared in the flesh, became body and made the Church His body, and the Church is the continuation, extension, prolongation and completion of the Mystery of the Incarnation."[434] Professor Ioannis Karmiris wrote in the same vein: "Christ and the Church are connected one to the other ontologically and exist in an absolute, indivisible and eternal union"[435] And St. Justin Popovich states un-

432. Nicholas Cabasilas, *A Commentary on the Divine Liturgy*, 38; PG 150: 452C–453A (emphasis added).

433. Christos Sp. Voulgaris, *The Church, the Body of Christ*, http://www.myriobiblos.gr/texts/english/voulgaris_churchbody.html.

434. Ἱερομονάχου Ἀθανασίου Μ. Γιέβτιτς [Athanasius M. Yevtich], Ἡ ἐκκλησιολογία τοῦ ἀποστόλου Παύλου κατὰ τὸν ἱερὸ Χρυσόστομο [*The Ecclesiology of the Apostle Paul According to Blessed Chrysostom*] (Athens: Gigori Publications, 1984), 94.

435. Ἡ Ἐκκλησιολογία τῶν Τριῶν Ἱεραρχῶν (Athens, 1962), 57–58.

equivocally: "The Church is Christ the Theanthropos extending through all ages and all eternity."[436]

These expressions (and many more of equal strength could be cited) are far removed from the comparison referred to as "no weak analogy" in *Lumen Gentium* 8. For the Orthodox, to deny that the Church is the continuation of the incarnation is nothing less than to depart from the miracle of Chalcedon— "the mystical and unutterable union of the two natures in the Person of the Theanthropos Christ"[437]—which is the essence of the Mystery of the Church.

The differentiation of the Church of Jesus Christ from the Roman Catholic Church was, in fact, the aim of the introduction of the expression *subsistit in* to replace the earlier formula *est*, which expressed a strict identity between the two. The new expression is meant to say that, while the Church of Christ is really present or concretely real and is to be found in the Roman Catholic Church, it is not to be strictly identified with it. Rather, there are not only elements of sanctification and truth and an "ecclesial reality" outside the Roman Church, but even—in the case of Christians of the East—genuine particular churches. What this recognition ultimately implies for the self-understanding of the Roman Catholic Church is, however, still disputed among Roman Catholic theologians even today, fifty years after Vatican II.[438]

---

436. Ἀρχιμ. Ἰουστίνος Πόποβιτς [St. Justin Popovich], *Ἑρμηνεία τῆς Ἐπιστολῆς τοῦ Ἀποστόλου Παύλου πρὸς Ἐφεσίους* [Interpretation of the Epistle of the Apostle Paul to the Ephesians]. (Thessaloniki: ἐκδ. Β. Ρηγοπούλου, 1989), 64.

437. Ἡ ἐκκλησιολογία τοῦ ἀποστόλου Παύλου, 94.

438. See, for example: Karl Joseph Becker, "An Examination of Subsistit in: A Profound Theological Perspective," *L'Osservatore Romano*, Weekly English Edition, December 14, 2005, 11; Karl J. Becker, "The

Dominus Iesus: Full Realization of the Church Requires Communion with the Pope

In an attempt to clarify the meaning of *subsistit in*, the Congregation for the Doctrine of the Faith issued the document *Dominus Iesus* in the year 2000.[439] It asserted that the Church of Jesus Christ is fully realized only in the Roman Catholic Church.[440] According to Cardinal Kasper, this means that, al-

Church and Vatican II's 'Subsistit in' Terminology," *Origins* 35 (2006): 514–22; Francis A. Sullivan, "Response to Karl Becker, S.J., on the Meaning of Subsistit in," *Theological Studies* 67:2 (June 2006), 395–409; The Congregation for the Doctrine of the Faith, "Responses to Some Questions Regarding Certain Aspects of the Doctrine on the Church" (June 29, 2007); Francis A. Sullivan, "Quaestio disputata. The Meaning of *Subsistit in* as Explained by the Congregation for the Doctrine of Faith," *Theological Studies* 69:1 (2008), 116–24. "The interpretation of [subsistit in] amounts to 'Disiderat' (Kasper) and includes amphoteric elements which accept twofold interpretations; it is at once inclusive and exclusive" (Τσομπανίδης, Ἡ Διακήρυξη *Dominus Iesus*, 122–23).

439. The declaration by the Congregation for the Doctrine of the Faith, *Dominus Iesus*, was approved in a plenary meeting of the Congregation, and bears the signature of its then Prefect, Cardinal Joseph Ratzinger, later Pope Benedict XVI. The declaration was approved by Pope John Paul II and was published on August 6, 2000. It is subtitled "On the Unicity and Salvific Universality of Jesus Christ and the Church." It is most widely known for its recapitulation of the Catholic dogma that the Catholic Church is the sole true Church of Christ.

440. *Dominus Iesus*, in its answer to the Second Question, states: "It is possible, according to Catholic doctrine, to affirm correctly that the Church of Christ is present and operative in the churches and ecclesial Communities not yet fully in communion with the Catholic Church, on account of the elements of sanctification and truth that are present in them (cf. John Paul II, Encyclical Letter *Ut Unum Sint*, 11.3: *AAS* 87 [1995-II] 928). Nevertheless, the word "subsist" can only be attributed to the Catholic Church alone precisely because it refers to the mark of unity that we profess in the symbols of the faith (I believe . . . in the

though there is no full realization of the Church of Jesus Christ outside the Catholic Church, there still is an imperfect realization.[441]

This begs the question: What constitutes *fullness* for contemporary Roman Catholicism? Cardinal Kasper echoes the views of Feiner and Baum presented in the previous chapter:

> [T]he Council texts show that this fullness does not concern salvation, or its subjective realization. . . . The reality and fullness of what is Catholic does not refer to subjective holiness but to *the sacramental and institutional means of salvation*, the sacraments and ministries (UR 3). . . . Both Catholic fullness and the *defectus* of the others are . . . not existential or even moral in nature; they are on the level of signs and instruments of grace, not on the level of the *res*, the grace of salvation itself.[442]

What, then, in particular, do the Orthodox lack in order to have, according to the new ecclesiology, a "perfect realization" of the Church? In UR 15a the Orthodox Church is recognized as possessing valid orders and a valid Eucharist, through which "the Church of God is built up and grows in stature." The "summit" of communio, then, according to Kasper's own characterization of the Eucharist (and not only "the basis" of communio, which is Baptism) is not absent from Orthodoxy. If

---

"one" Church); and this "one" Church subsists in the Catholic Church (cf. *LG*, 8.2.)."

441. Walter Kasper, "Communio: The Guiding Concept of Catholic Ecumenical Theology," in *That They May All Be One: The Call to Unity Today* (London/New York: Burns and Oates, 2004), 66. See also Τσομπανίδης, Ἡ Διακήρυξη *Dominus Iesus* καὶ ἡ Οἰκουμενικὴ Σημασία τῆς (Θεσσαλονίκη: Πουρναρά, 2003), 61–63.

442. Ibid. (emphasis added).

the "summit" of communio is present, what else could be lacking? Beyond the Eucharist, the very Presence and Fullness of God, is it possible for something else to be necessary for a local church to be the Church, the Body of Christ?

According to the *Dominus Iesus* document, "fullness" requires something else above and beyond the Lord Himself in the Eucharist. That which is lacking for the Orthodox Church to be a "full realization" of the Church of Christ is nothing but the recognition of the primacy of the pope of Rome and communion with him. The Eucharist—the Lord come in the Flesh, by which we are all made members of His Body—is not enough to constitute the full, unmitigated Church of Christ *epi to auto*. This is because outside communion with the head of the college of bishops, the Pope, an individual bishop cannot exercise his authority and thus the local church is "wounded" and cannot be "fully realized" as a particular church.

On this very important point for our understanding of fullness in the new ecclesiology, Fernando Ocáriz, vicar general of Opus Dei and one of the primary authors of *Dominus Iesus*, writes:

> It is easy to see that where Christ is made present in the Eucharistic sacrifice of his Body and his Blood, there the Church is present as the Body of Christ, through which Christ effects salvation in history. However, *not any and every form of the Church's operative presence constitutes a particular Church, but only this presence with all its essential elements.* Therefore, for a Christian community to be truly a particular Church, "there must be present in it, as a proper element, the supreme authority of the Church: the Episcopal College 'together with its head, the Supreme

Pontiff, and never apart from him'"[443] (LG, n. 22).[444]

Ocáriz assists us in understanding that, for Rome today, in the hierarchy of elements that make the Church the Body of Christ in a particular location (a particular Church), that "essential" element above all other elements—even the "element" of the Lord Himself in the Eucharist—is the Supreme Pontiff.[445] While the Eucharist is seen as sufficient to manifest the Church as the Body of Christ, it is insufficient to make that local synaxis, the faithful together with their bishop, into a particular Church. This view of the Church appears to totally justify Fr. John Romanides' judgment that the Church of Rome does not

443. Here Ocáriz cites the Congregation for the Doctrine of the Faith, Letter *Communionis Notio* (May 28, 1992, n. 13). Professor J. Karmiris comments on this point in LG 22 thus: "in spite of the attempted harmonization of the two powers, in the end the danger of *diarchia* in the Roman Catholic Church has not been avoided." ('Ιωάννου Καρμίρη, "Τὸ Δογματικόν Σύνταγμα Περί Ἐκκλησίας, τῆς Β' Βατικανῆς Συνόδου" [The Dogmatic Constitution on the Church of the Second Vatican Council] [Ἀθήνα: 1969], 15). According to N. Arseniev: "So that a certain duality came to be stated in the structure of the Church—duality in unity!—the Pope and the Bishops, both as detainers of the supreme power in the Church, but the Bishops only as long as they are in union with the Pope. It is not stated, however, that the Pope retains supreme power only in union with the body of the Bishops. So that the duality turns again to be rather a unity: a unity in the Pope." (N. Arseniev, "The Second Vatican Council's 'Constitutio de Ecclesia,'" *St. Vladimir's Seminary Quarterly* 9 [1965], 21).

444. Fernando Ocáriz, "Christ's Church Subsists in the Catholic Church," *L'Osservatore Romano*, Weekly Edition in English, December 21, 2005, p. 9 (emphasis added).

445. It is apparent that, as Stylianos Tsombanidis has written, "the objective goal of the document is to stress that canonical communion with the bishop of Rome is not only necessary for complete ecclesiastical communion, but is also the sine qua non for the ecclesiastical authenticity of a local Church" (Τσομπανίδης, Ἡ Διακήρυξη *Dominus Iesus*, 213).

understand "the Eucharist as an end in itself" but rather views "the office of the bishop [as] something in itself."[446]

This theological schism between the power of jurisdiction and the presence of Christ in the Holy Mysteries, which Vatican II somewhat attempted to overcome, is still quite apparent.[447] This is so because, even though power of jurisdiction is

446. Romanides, "The Ecclesiology of St. Ignatius of Antioch." Romanides came to this conclusion on the basis of the historical evidence presented by Dom Gregory Dix in his seminal work *The Shape of the Liturgy*. Romanides writes: "Whereas in the city of Alexandria liturgical centers at first had each a bishop (P. Trembelas, *Taxeis Cheirothesion kai Cheirotonian* [Athens, 1949], 26–29), in Rome not only were presbyters appointed to the different liturgical centers, but they were originally not given permission to administer the Eucharist. Rather, a portion of the already consecrated elements was sent from the bishop's liturgy to the faithful gathered together at the lesser centers. When finally the presbyters did receive permission to celebrate the liturgy, the bishop of Rome continued to send a portion of the consecrated elements from his own liturgy to be put into the chalices of the lesser eucharistic centers. This practice continued in Rome until the fourteenth century and did not completely disappear until 1870 (Dom G. Dix, *The Shape of the Liturgy*, 21)." Thus, Romanides concludes, "the Churches in Rome very early lost the meaning of the Eucharist as an end in itself and vividly introduced the idea that the office of the bishop is rather something in itself and that somehow the elements consecrated at the bishop's liturgy were somewhat superior to those consecrated at the liturgy of the presbyters."

447. In the third chapter of LG (21f) the council attempted to do away with the traditional Latin distinction between the powers of consecration and jurisdiction in order to draw closer to the Orthodox and the ancient practice. The traditional Latin teaching states that the power to teach and to rule is the power of jurisdiction; the power to sanctify is the power of orders. (The power to sanctify sometimes requires jurisdiction, as in the sacrament of Penance.) The bishops of the Church are the successors of the apostles because they have received their power of orders by valid consecration through an unbroken line of successors of the apostles, and have received their power of jurisdiction through their

now seen to be given with ordination and no longer directly from the Pope, exercising this authority is still predicated upon "communio hierarchica" with the Pope.[448] If, however, the Eucharist is recognized as existing in a local church, as Rome does in the case of Orthodox Local Churches, then there is likewise a local manifestation of the Body of Christ. In this Eucharistic Synaxis the fullness of Christ dwells in the faithful who gather together in the life of Christ *epi to auto,* and the episcopate is an inseparable part of this life. In this unity in Christ, does not the bishop rightfully exercise his authority unencumbered and unmitigated? For, "as all other things pertaining to the Church, the clergy also exists for the sole purpose of preserving and increasing the life of unity and love *epi to auto* in the flesh and blood of Christ. . . . [T]he authority of the clergy is founded exclusively upon the mysteries of unity in Christ and not at all upon any imagined personal power or magic."[449] And, moreover, "each community having the fullness of Eucharistic life is related to other communities not by a common participation in something greater than the local life in the Eucharist, but by an

union with the Pope, the successor of Saint Peter. According to Cardinal Walter Kasper, this theory "arises out of the Western universalist, centralist and pyramidal concept of the Church in the Latin West in the second millennium." Kasper, "Communio," 84.

448. See LG 21f, which reads: "Episcopal consecration, together with the office of sanctifying, also confers the office of teaching and of governing, which, however, of its very nature, can be exercised only in hierarchical communion with the head and the members of the college." This seems to be contradicted by UR 16, which recognizes the eastern churches (including the Orthodox Church) as true churches that "have the power to govern themselves according to the disciplines proper to them." The Local Orthodox Churches, which do not have communion with the Pope, are recognized both as celebrating the Eucharist and as self-governing.

449. Romanides, "The Ecclesiology of St. Ignatius of Antioch."

identity of existence in Christ: 'wherever Jesus Christ is there is the Catholic Church' (Ign. Smyr. 8)" (ibid.).

The differences between the understanding of the fullness, unity, and identity of the Church as presented in *Lumen Gentium, Unitatis Redintegratio,* and later in *Dominus Iesus,* and the Orthodox, patristic understanding of these matters are here brought into stark contrast. In the Orthodox view, the Church is present and active in the Eucharist, in and by which the Body of Christ is formed, such that any and all "essential elements" not only cannot be divided from the Eucharist, but rather spring from it. Where the Eucharist is, there is the whole Christ: priest, king, and prophet. He is the "supreme authority" of the Church, present and abiding in His Body in and through the Eucharist. There can be nothing higher than this that, if absent, makes His presence insufficient.[450]

Interestingly, *Dominus Iesus,* following the Letter *Communionis Notio* of 1992, did, in fact, attribute the title "particular churches" to the Local Orthodox Churches. Ocáriz's explanation of what this attribution means shows even more clearly the divergence that exists between the two views of the Church. He claims that this attribution is based not upon the real, Eucharistic presence of Christ but upon "the real presence of the

---

450. See Fr. John Meyendorff, *Byzantine Theology: Historical Trends and Doctrinal Themes* (New York: Fordham University Press, 1970), 210, who writes: "The Eucharist is, indeed, the *ultimate* manifestation of God in Christ; and there cannot be, therefore, any ministry higher or more decisive than that which presides over the Eucharist. The centrality of the Eucharist, the awareness that the fullness of Christ's Body abides in it and that the Episcopal function is the highest in the Church will be the principal foundation of the Byzantine opposition to any theological interpretation of supra-episcopal primacies: there cannot be, according to them, any authority 'by divine right' over the Eucharist and the bishop who heads the Episcopal assembly."

Petrine Primacy (and of the Episcopal College) in non-Catholic Churches, based on the unity of the 'one and undivided' episcopate—a unity that cannot exist without the Bishop of Rome." Further, he writes:

> Where, on account of apostolic succession, a valid episcopate exists, the Episcopal College with its Head is objectively present as supreme authority (*even if, in fact, that authority is not recognized*). Furthermore, in every valid celebration of the Eucharist, there is *an objective reference* to the universal communion with the Successor of Peter and with the entire Church, independent of subjective convictions.[451]

As the supreme and final criterion of full ecclesiality the Pope is seen not only to supplant the Eucharistic Presence of the Lord Himself, but to be present as "supreme authority" in the Eucharistic Synaxis of those not in communion with him, *even if this is against their will*. Whereas, for the Orthodox, the ever-present and existential reality manifested by the Holy Spirit at every Eucharistic gathering is *dogmatic truth* and a unity in truth freely espoused, for the Latins it is the "objective reference to the universal communion" with the Pope "independent of subjective convictions."

Latin theologians are forced into this contorted position of negating the freedom in Christ of the members of the Body by, on the one hand, their recognition of the Eucharist (on the strength of apostolic succession) and, on the other, their denial of all this entails, namely, the fullness and identity of the One

---

451. Fernando Ocáriz, "Christ's Church Subsists in the Catholic Church," *L'Osservatore Romano*, Weekly Edition in English, December 21, 2005, p. 9 (emphasis added).

Church *epi to auto*. The recognition of the former and the denial of the latter both stem from a fragmented, legalistic view of the Church in which unity of faith together with participation in the Eucharist is not seen as the decisive criterion for the recognition of authentic mysteries.

The Criterion for the Recognition of Authentic Mysteries

For the Roman Catholic Church it is possible to recognize mysteries, even the Eucharist, as existing outside the unity of faith and the episcopate on the strength of an historical apostolic succession.[452] If apostolic succession is recognized, a valid episcopate exists and thus a valid celebration of the Eucharist.[453]

---

452. It is interesting to note that, although Vatican II conceded Baptism, on the strength of the rite alone, to Protestants generally and even ceased to "conditionally" baptize them, the same was not the case with the Eucharist. "According to Catholic teaching, it is not sufficient at the celebration of the Eucharist for bread and wine to be used, and the words of the institution to be spoken; rather, the ordained minister, who, *personam Christi gerens*, carries out the actions, also belongs to the full sacramental sign" (Johannes Feiner, "Commentary on the Decree," in *Commentary on the Documents of Vatican II* [London: Burns and Oates Limited, 1968], 2:154). That is to say, this refusal is based on the non-recognition of apostolic succession among the Protestants. But, this begs the question: the same apostles who were given the power to baptize, were they not also given the power to offer the sacrifice? This power is not an autonomous power, but resides *in the apostolic church*, whether it be for the carrying out of the one or the other mystery. Whether one is empowered to baptize or to offer the sacrifice, he is empowered *by the Church*. If the Protestants do not have apostolic succession, and thus are not the apostolic church, by what power are they baptizing? And into what are they initiating those baptized?

453. See UR 15c and no. 1399 of *The Catechism of the Catholic Church* (New York: Doubleday, 1997): "The Eastern churches that are not in full communion with the Catholic Church celebrate the Eucharist with great love. 'These Churches, although separated from us, yet possess true

For the Orthodox Church, apostolic succession does not mean simply the tracing of ordinations back to the Apostles. Together with this historical inheritance must be combined a spiritual and dogmatic inheritance, namely, the Orthodox Faith. This Faith is the παρακαταθήκη or deposit (2 Tim. 1:14) that has been alone guarded by the One Church. "Where there is no Orthodox dogma, the Church is not in a place to speak of the existence of mysteries."[454] Moreover, "according to the Fathers of the Church, the Orthodox dogma is never separated from spirituality. Where there is erroneous dogma, there also exists an erroneous spirituality and vice versa."[455] Maintaining the entirety of the authentic Christian faith and practice is, however, possible only within the boundaries of the One Church.

Therefore, for the Orthodox Church, authenticity hinges upon both the expressing of Orthodox dogma and the fact that the mystery lies within the boundaries; that is, it is of the Church.[456] The Orthodox insist that "the home of authentic grace is that body which alone has . . . obediently and faithfully adhered to Christ's original and unadulterated institutions of faith and practice. . . . The Orthodox see no justifiable

sacraments, above all—*by apostolic succession*—the priesthood and the Eucharist, whereby they are still joined to us in closest intimacy' (UR 15c). A certain *communio in sacris*, and *so in the Eucharist*, 'given suitable circumstances and the approval of Church authority, is not merely possible but is encouraged'" (UR 15c; cf. CIC, canon 844 § 3) (emphasis added). See also sections 77, 1209, 1576, and 833 of the *Catechism of the Catholic Church* for treatment of apostolic succession.

454. John S. Romanides, *An Outline of Orthodox Patristic Dogmatics* (Rollinsford, NH: Orthodox Research Institute, 2004), 80–81.

455. Romanides, *An Outline of Orthodox Patristic Dogmatics*, 80–81.

456. As Fr. Georges Florovsky has written: "it is impossible to speak in a strict sense of the retention of 'apostolic succession' beyond the limits of canonical communality" (Florovsky, *Collected Works*, 13:44).

grounds for the fragmentation that insists only on the intention of a given sacramental act, apart from the intention to maintain the entirety of authentic Christian faith and practice."[457]

In lacking the distinction of exactness and economy that is so basic to Orthodox mysteriological theology, this theology of the Latins "places excessive emphasis on the external form of the mystery at the expense of the right Faith that endows it with life, of which this form must always be the practical expression, and runs the risk of lending a kind of magical efficacy to the formal celebration of the mystery."[458] The fatal error, then, committed here on the basis of the legalism characteristic of Latin theology, is the jarring loose of the form and practice from the right faith and confession, as if the former has, in and of itself, value when separated from the latter.

If that which is authentic is that which is acceptable within the Body of Christ, an historical apostolic succession cannot make a Christian body authentic. Rather, it is the Church, the Body of Christ, in which alone the Orthodox Faith is both confessed and lived, that makes orders ("a valid episcopate") authentic. "Divided ministries[459] cannot produce authenticity or unity; only the one authentic Church can authenticate the divided ministries, and then only within her own unity."[460]

457. Bailey, Charles-James N., "Validity and Authenticity: The Difference Between Western and Orthodox Views on Orders," *St. Vladimir's Seminary Quarterly*, 8 (1964), 86–92 (87).

458. P. Trembelas, *Dogmatic Theology of the Orthodox Catholic Church* [in Greek] (Athens, 1961), 3:48.

459. The phrase "divided ministries" means those ministerial actions of schismatic or heretical groups. Strictly speaking the priesthood is indivisible from the Church, such that when ordained ministers depart from the Church their ministry in the Church ceases.

460. Charles-James N. Bailey, "Validity and Authenticity: The Difference Between Western and Orthodox Views on Orders," *St. Vladimir's Seminary Quarterly* 8 (1964), 88.

For communities that have fallen away from catholic agreement in faith, "the Orthodox Church cannot raise the problem as to their 'validity' as Churches, because outside the fullness of Tradition, outside the manifested truth which is Orthodoxy, we can not 'know,' 'acknowledge' or recognize . . . validity.... [O]utside this Tradition we simply know nothing of 'validity' or 'invalidity.'"[461]

Therefore, the Orthodox Church does not recognize "valid Eucharists" on the strength of "valid episcopates" separate from the entire Christ, which means outside the unity of faith manifested in full catholic agreement in which the One Catholic Church is known and recognized as one and the same in every Eucharistic Synaxis *epi to auto*. Mysteries are unrecognizable apart from the Mystery of the Church, which is only made known to those within, according to the word of the Lord: "Unto you it is given to know the mystery of the kingdom of God: but unto them that are without, all these things are done in parables" (Mark 4:11). For the kingdom is nothing but the Lord Himself.[462] Where there is not the full catholic agreement in faith, the Christ of the Mysteries remains unrecognizable, for the identity of Christ is not ascertained using superficial, external, and legalistic criteria but within the unity and mind of Christ, Who is the Truth (1 Cor. 2:16, John 14:6).

---

461. Fr. Alexander Schmemann, "Unity, Division, Reunion in the Light of Orthodox Ecclesiology," address given at the Annual Conference of the Fellowship of St. Alban and St. Sergius at Abingdon, England, in August 1950 (Θεολογία, ΚΒ), 243–54.

462. With His incarnation the kingdom of God became a present reality in the world. As St. John Chrysostom says, speaking on behalf of Christ: "Τί ἐστιν, Ἡ βασιλεία; Ἡ παρουσία ἡ ἐμή." ("What is 'The Kingdom'? My presence.") (Ματθ. ομ. 41.2. PG 57.447.)

Christ of the Mysteries, Christ of Dogmatic Truth

In the new ecclesiology a critical rupture between Christ in the Mysteries and Christ in dogmatic truth is apparent. In an essay written shortly after the council, Fr. John Meyendorff addresses this essential disunity.[463] On the one hand, he notes, in *Unitatis Redintegratio* it is claimed that, since every "valid" mystery is the property of the Church (UR 3b), it is possible to accept a limited practice of sacramental communion (communicatio in sacris)[464] with separated Christians. *Unitatis Redintegratio* states that intercommunion between Roman Catholics and Orthodox is possible because the Orthodox, "although separated from us, yet possess true sacraments and above all, by apostolic succession, the priesthood and the Eucharist, whereby they are linked with us in closest intimacy" (UR 15c). In other words, as Bishop Kallistos Ware has written, "intercommunion is seen from one point of view as the expression of a unity that already exists. But at the same time the Council recognizes that this existing unity is still gravely incomplete and therefore the practice of *communicatio in sacris* is definitely intended as a means for securing fuller unity."[465] The Decree on the Eastern Catholic Churches goes even further to state that intercommunion is permitted "in order more and more to promote union with the Eastern Churches separated from us."[466] Thus, in spite of the

---

463. It was entitled, "A Turning Point in the Ecumenism of the Roman Church" [Μία καμπή εἰς τὸν Οἰκουμενισμὸν τῆς Ρωμαϊκῆς Ἐκκλησίας] in the volume, Ὀρθόδοξος Θεώρησις τῆς Β´ Συνόδου τοῦ Βατικανοῦ, ἐπιμέλεια Μαρίας Δ. Σπυροπούλου (Athens, 1967), 77–80.

464. *Communicatio in sacris* (sharing in the sacraments) is to be distinguished from *communicatio in spiritualibus* (sharing in common prayer).

465. Bp. Kallistos (Ware), "Intercommunion: The Decisions of Vatican II and the Orthodox Standpoint," *Sobernost*, ser. 5, no. 4 (1966), 262.

466. Decree on the Eastern Catholic Churches, section 26.

state of separation, and even though dogmatic differences are acknowledged as existing,[467] in multiple documents Vatican II nonetheless promoted intercommunion.

On the other hand, writes Fr. Meyendorff, those bishops that do not have communion with the throne of Rome have no dogmatic authority whatsoever, as is specified in *Lumen Gentium* (III, 22): "But the college or body of bishops has no authority unless it is understood together with the Roman Pontiff, the successor of Peter as its head. . . . The order of bishops, which succeeds to the college of apostles and gives this apostolic body continued existence, is also the subject of supreme and full power over the universal Church, provided we understand this body together with its head the Roman Pontiff and never without this head. This power can be exercised only with the consent of the Roman Pontiff."

Taking these two ideas together, Fr. Meyendorff rightly sees behind the idea of partial or incomplete communion as put forth in UR (1c, 2h) "a legalistic notion of the Church, which sees it as a worldwide institute of control and dogmatic security, separating the Christ of the mysteries from dogmatic Truth." Accordingly, there exists "a theological schism between the sacramental presence of Christ and His revelation as unique Truth" and, thus, "the authority of expressing dogmatic teaching is separated from the reality of the mysteries." Consequently, there is no essential obstacle to communion in the mysteries

---

467. Bishop Kallistos in his article in *Sobernost* shortly after the council quoted Msgr. Neophytos Edelby, Archbishop of Edessa, a leading spokesman then for the Uniates, in this regard: "As for the partial communion which the Council allowed between the two Churches, it certainly does not exclude dogmatic differences, but it can contribute towards preparing the rapprochement. . . ." See *Eastern Churches Review*, 1:1 (1966), 22.

in "those cases in which the 'validity' of the sacrament in the community of another dogma is recognized."[468]

As Fr. Meyendorff rightly points out, this idea is not new, but has been the reigning one in the Protestant world for centuries, which only confirms, and remarkably so, the famous claim by Alexis Khomiakov: "Romanism was protestant right from its birth."[469] Indeed, one cannot but ask: how is the new ecclesiology essentially different from the dominant Protestant conception in which each confession, while recognizing other confessions as a part of the Church, retains a conviction that it has best maintained the fullness of the Gospel and will of the Lord for His people?[470]

468. Fr. John Meyendorff, "Μία Κάμπη εἰς τὸν Οἰκουμενισμὸν τῆς Ρωμαϊκῆς Ἐκκλησίας" [A Turning-point in the Ecumenism of the Roman Church] στο τόμο Ὀρθόδοξος Θεώρησις τῆς Β΄ Συνόδου τοῦ Βατικανοῦ, ἐπιμέλεια Μαρίας Δ. Σπυροπούλου (Athens, 1967), 79–80. Hereafter cited as "A Turning-point."

469. Ibid. Post-Vatican II commentators take it for granted that the visible and invisible Church are not to be identified, for outside the Roman Catholic Church "any validly ordained priest, including priests of the Orthodox Church, can administer Baptism and consecrate the Eucharist, thus making their communicants members of the One Body" (Francesca Aran Murphy, "De Lubac, Ratzinger and von Balthasar: A Communal Adventure in Ecclesiology," in *Ecumenism Today: The Universal Church in the Twenty-first Century*, ed. Francesca Aran Murphy and Chris Asprey [Hampshire, UK: Ashgate, 2008], 47). This amounts to a nuanced version of the "invisible church" theory of the Protestants because the boundaries are indeterminate and do not coincide with the canonical boundaries of the Church, which is another way of saying, with unity in the Eucharist and in faith.

470. In his important treatise *Τὸ Βάπτισμα τῶν Αἱρετικῶν* [The Baptism of Heretics], Archimandrite Dimitrios Georgiadis points out that the invisible church theory is not unique to Protestants, but is, in fact, the predominant Latin interpretation of Blessed Augustine's writings on our subject (ἀρχιμ Δημήτριος Γεωργιάδης, Νέα Σιὼν 19 (1924),

The refusal of the Orthodox to admit any level of intercommunion and the acceptance of a limited intercommunion at Vatican II together point to a deeper rift with regard to the understanding of fullness and the mysteries. The Orthodox reject every kind of intercommunion because they utterly refuse to accept any division of Christ. Given that such division is a fact within the various heterodox communities, since in one way or another they shatter the fullness of truth, the Orthodox are forbidden to enter into communion with them, as that would mean the segmentation of the Body of Christ.[471] "The catholicity of the Church implies that every division between the members of the Body is likewise a division of Christ. Consequently, Christian unity is essentially a living unity in Him and with Him. This is exactly what the Orthodox express when they refuse to separate dogmatic truth from the mysteries."[472]

The catholicity of the Church likewise means that "its invisible essence is verily present and incarnate in its visible nature and its visible structure; these are not mere symbols, for the visible Church is verily the Body of Christ."[473] There is, then, an integral connection of all aspects of the Body. "The unity of the Church, the unity of the Church hierarchy, the unity of grace, the unity of the Spirit—all these are connected insepa-

73–83, 97–112, 165–81, 253–60). No lesser man than the great ecclesiastical historian K. J. Hefele (pp. 117-132) in the first volume of his *History of the Councils* (*Conciliengeschichte*) includes (wrongly) Augustine, along with Aquinas and Bonaventure, as a source for the teaching that the Baptism of heretics necessarily imparts sanctification *and* regeneration (*sanctificatio et renovatio interioris hominis*).

471. Meyendorff, "A Turning-point," 80.
472. Ibid.
473. Schmemann, "Unity, Division, Reunion in the Light of Orthodox Ecclesiology."

rably from each other."[474] Deviation from any one of these is a deviation from the Holy Spirit, from Christ Himself.

The insistence of the Orthodox that ecclesiastical communion can only be full arises out of their experience of it as organic unity. Truth as a Person, Christ Himself, is only accessible within the corporate and organic union in Christ. Convergence in theological opinion, similarity in baptismal rite, or use of the same scriptural canon cannot be considered a basis for establishing ecclesiastical unity of any kind, full or "incomplete." This is so because all such unity in the realm of ideas, history, and tradition remains fragmented unless it flows from unity in the Person of Christ in the Eucharist, which is an organic unity in the flesh and blood of the God-Man.[475] Therefore, whether the basis proposed for ecclesiastical unity is Baptism, the Scriptures, or a supreme pontiff, every attempt to establish ecclesiastical unity in anything else besides Christ in the Eucharist reveals an individualistic attitude that ultimately leads into error. All attempts to unify that are not anchored in the Eucharist remain but purely human and fragmented. A Christian communion that is not whole, but fragmented, is necessarily heretical. That is why "the loss of the moral principle of organic unity can lead only to heresy," and also why "the flesh of Christ Itself is the foundation of dogma."[476]

---

474. Florovsky, *Collected Works*, 13:67.

475. Similarly, there is no repentance in Hades because, the soul having been separated from the body, there man is in a fragmented state. For a man to make a return to the "image and likeness" he must be whole—soul and body. So, too, in ecclesiastical life, fullness, unity, is impossible outside the wholeness of the Body, outside the flesh and blood of the Body of Christ. "Unity" outside the Eucharist is chimerical, resembling a soul without a body, the state of being dead.

476. John S. Romanides, "Orthodox Ecclesiology According to Alexis Khomiakov," *The Greek Orthodox Theological Review* 2:1 (1956), 57–73.

At Vatican II the Roman Church introduced the idea that an ecclesiastical unity can be established that is not organic. A "real, but incomplete" ecclesiastical unity in a "duly administered Baptism" was accepted without that "Baptism" initiating one into the Eucharist, the professed "summit of communion." For the Orthodox, such fragmented "unity" cannot be organic, and thus neither can it be ecclesiastical. Likewise, neither can a "Baptism" that does not initiate into the organic unity of the Church in the Eucharist rightly be called ecclesiastical.

The idea of full and partial communion, so central to the new ecclesiology, is inconsistent with this understanding of the organic unity of the Church. Once again, in this regard as well, Vatican II was not a return to the patristic vision of the Church, but rather a further step away from it. As Metropolitan Kallistos Ware has written: "The Bible, the Fathers or the Canons know of only two possibilities: communion and non-communion. It is all or nothing. They do not envisage any third alternative such as 'partial intercommunion.'"[477] Father Georges

According to Khomiakov, the loss of organic unity predates the schism and is the root cause of it, as is apparent in the case of the Filioque. The underlying sin that made and makes reconciliation impossible is an individualistic pride that justifies autonomy and belittles conciliarity. Such fragmentation was transferred from the level of church governance to that of theology and the mysteries, only to later bring forth the fruit of extreme disintegration in the Reformation. As Fr. John Romanides writes, "Khomiakov does not see in Romanism and Protestantism two contrary extremes, but rather two sides of the same coin. Both Latin unity and Protestant freedom are of a purely external nature deprived of the bond of the inner organic communion of love. Both pretend to be able to fashion the theology of the Church by applying ordinary rules of logic and reason borrowed from an analysis of material phenomena."

477. Archimandrite Kallistos Ware, *Communion and Intercommunion: A Study of Communion and Intercommunion Based on the Theology and Practice of the Eastern Church* (Minneapolis: Light and Life, 1980), 16.

Florovsky likewise points out that in the patristic view of the Church "there was simply the question of 'full communion,' that is, of membership in the Church. And there were identical terms of this membership for all."[478]

The identification of "full membership" with "membership

---

478. Fr. Georges Florovsky, "Terms of Communion in the Undivided Church," in *Intercommunion. The Report of the Theological Commission Appointed by the Continuation Committee of the World Conference on Faith and Order together with a Selection from the Material Presented to the Commission*, ed. D. Baillie and John Marsh (London, 1952), 50, as quoted in Ware, *Communion and Intercommunion*, 16–17. Professor George Galitis is also quoted by Ware in the same vein, that in the ancient Church "there is only communion and non-communion" (G. Galitis, *The Problem of Intercommunion with the Heterodox from an Orthodox Point of View: A Biblical and Ecclesiological Study* [in Greek] [Athens, 1966], 24–25.) It is important to note that Fr. Georges Florovsky, whose views are often cited in support of versions of theories of baptismal theology-ecclesiology, quite early on explicitly qualified his scholarly musings on the views of St. Augustine and stated that the Saint's views were "no more than a *'theologoumenon,'* a doctrine set forth by a single Father." Likewise, he urged the Orthodox to take it into account, not for its own sake or on its own terms, and certainly not as it has been played out within Latin theology, but simply as one view that can aid in the formation of a "true ecumenical synthesis." Indeed, Fr. Florovsky lamented that the Orthodox have too often expounded upon the doctrine of the sacraments using the Roman model, without any creative or transforming adoption of St. Augustine's conception. On the contrary, Fr. Florovsky formally and firmly rejected the theory of primordial unity in a common Baptism as is stressed by Roman Catholicism, explaining that it, like the Protestant branch theory, glosses over and minimizes the scandal of "dis-union," which for him was to be faced forthrightly and explained in terms of "the true [Orthodox] Church and secessions." Florovsky stressed the unity of the mysteries, especially the first three, and hence thought less in terms of regeneration linked to Baptism than of incorporation into the common Body of Christ in the Eucharist. See Andrew Blane, *Georges Florovksy, Russian Intellectual and Orthodox Churchman* (Crestwood, NY: St. Vladimir's Seminary Press, 1997), 311–17.

in the Church"—a membership based on identical terms for all—could not come into more direct opposition to the heart of the new ecclesiology, which is based upon the possibility of there being degrees of membership in the Body of Christ. This idea stems from the acceptance of a division of the mysteries from each other and from the Mystery of the Church as a whole. They suppose that Baptism can exist outside the unity of the Church and the other mysteries, mechanically, as it were, imparting membership to those who receive it in separation.

However, just as the Eucharist "is indissolubly bound to the whole content of faith, and likewise to the visible structure of the Church,"[479] so too is Baptism. And, just as "those who advocate intercommunion on the basis of 'Eucharistic ecclesiology'" treat the Eucharist "too much in isolation (ibid.)," those who advocate a partial communion on the basis of a "common Baptism" likewise consider Baptism too much in isolation. While putting forth Baptism as a point of unity, they fail to realize that, apart from unity in faith and unity in the bishop, unity in a "common Baptism" is impossible. Just as communing together in the Holy Eucharist cannot compensate for, let alone create, unity in faith (ibid.), so too sharing the *typos* of Baptism (if it is actually shared)[480] cannot create ecclesiastical unity or even a so-called "partial" unity.

Moreover, just as the Eucharist is celebrated and received locally and visibly, such that the separation of the heterodox from participation in the Eucharist is likewise visible and local, so too is Baptism performed in the local Eucharistic Synaxis, from which the heterodox are necessarily excluded. The One Church does not exist as an abstract idea, but is manifested

479. Ware, *Communion and Intercommunion*, 20.

480. See chapter 2 where the divergence of Rome from the apostolic τύπος of Baptism is discussed.

visibly in time and space as the local Church. "One cannot be baptized into the Catholic Church without belonging at the same time to a local Church,"[481] for the local Church, "as an 'organism,' a sacramental body, is not a 'part' or a 'member' of a wider universal organism. It is the very Church itself."[482] Likewise, one cannot be baptized into the "Catholic Church" of Christ without being in communion with all of the members of the Body, for Christ, the Head of the Church, is inseparable from all of His members. "Why," asks St. John Chrysostom, "letting go the Head, dost thou cling to the members? If thou art fallen off from it, thou art lost."[483] Whether one falls from the Head or from the Body, the result is the same: he has lost both the one and the other.

There is, therefore, no basis to suppose, as proponents of *Unitatis Redintegratio* and the new ecclesiology do, that "despite divisions and mutual condemnations all communities of the baptized . . . are in communion,"[484] even if only partially. Com-

481. Ware, *Communion and Intercommunion*, 23.

482. Schmemann, "Unity, Division, Reunion."

483. PG 62.344.36: Τί τοίνυν τὴν κεφαλὴν ἀφείς, ἔχει τῶν μελῶν; ἐὰν ἐκεῖθεν ἐκπέσῃς, ἀπόλωτας.

484. Jorge A. Scampini, "*We acknowledge one Baptism for the forgiveness of sins*," address given at the Faith and Order Plenary Commission in Kuala, Malaysia, July 28–August 6, 2004. It is significant to note that Pope John Paul II, in his encyclical *Ut Unum Sint* (par. 42), linked this idea of deep communion in spite of division to "baptismal character," thus following faithfully the precedent established by Congar, Bea, and Vatican II: "The very expression separated brethren tends to be replaced today by expressions which more readily evoke *the deep communion— linked to the Baptismal character—which the Spirit fosters in spite of historical and canonical divisions*. Today we speak of "other Christians," "others who have received Baptism," and "Christians of other Communities." . . . This broadening of vocabulary is indicative of a significant change in attitudes. There is an increased awareness that we all belong to Christ."

munion is one both vertical and horizontal, both with God and among men, both between the Head and His Body, and it is full and only full: "being complete here and complete there also."[485] The Lord shows no partiality, but distributes the gifts to all alike within the Body. Once united, all become a single house, all are related and brothers in Christ. Just as there can be no partial Christ, there can be no partial communion in Christ, for the Body of communion, "which is his body, [is] the fulness of him that filleth all in all" (Eph. 1:23). From the moment one is a member, the communion he enjoys in Christ is full, for Christ only gives Himself fully. Whether or not he fully actualizes this self-offering of Christ is not an institutional but an individual issue, and that within the Body.

Whether we speak of one mystery or another, of Baptism or the Eucharist, one and the same Christ is offering Himself to man, uniting man to Himself. This unity with God is accomplished in the mysteries, all of which have certain presuppositions, first of all, and common to all, unity in faith. That is why what Fr. Dimitru Staniloae insists upon, and warns against, with regard to the Eucharist and "intercommunion" is equally true of Baptism and "partial communion":

> Ecclesiastical unity, unity in faith, and unity in the Holy Eucharist are all three inseparable and interdependent for the total communion and life in Christ. Consequently, the Orthodox Church cannot accept "intercommunion," which separates communion in the Holy Eucharist from unity in faith and ecclesiastical unity. More correctly, "intercommunion" is a danger which threatens to destroy

485. PG 63.131.39, Saint John Chrysostom, *Homily on the Epistle to the Hebrews*, 17.6.

the Church, break up the unity of faith and [communion in] the Holy Eucharist [among the Orthodox]."[486]

So, too, the Orthodox Church cannot accept "partial" or "incomplete" communion in a "common Baptism," for there can be no division between the mysteries and the Mystery and between Christ in the mysteries and Christ in whom we believe and trust, whom we confess, and in whom we have our being, our unity. Therefore, the acceptance of an "incomplete communion" between the Church and the heterodox is, like intercommunion in the Eucharist, a grave danger to the unity of the body of Christ. The body of the Church is joined together with the Lord such that, as St. John Chrysostom has written, even the slightest division, the slightest "imperfection" or "incompleteness," would eventually bring the dissolution of the entire body.

The Church Is the Fullness of Christ

In his commentary on 1 Corinthians 3:9, St. John Chrysostom stresses that there can be no intervals whatsoever between the members of the Body and the Head, and hence, between themselves, since through the Head they are made one. After relating all the various images by which He brings us into union—body–head, vine–branches, foundation–building, bridegroom–bride, shepherd–sheep, the Way–those who walk therein, the temple–He Who indwells, the First-begotten–the brethren, the Heir–those heirs together with Him, the Life–the living, the Resurrection–those who rise with Him, the Light–the enlightened—the Saint says emphatically: "All these things indicate

---

486. Dimitru Staniloae, Γιὰ ἔναν Ὀρθόδοξο Οἰκουμενισμὸ [Toward an Orthodox Ecumenism] (Athens, 1976), 29.

unity; and they allow no void interval, not even the smallest. For he that removes but to a little distance will go on till he has become very far distant."[487]

All Christians grow up in all things in the Head, Who is Christ, such that there is not the slightest break in the Body. According to the enduring words of the Apostle Paul:

> Speaking the truth in love, [we] may grow up into him in all things, which is the head, even Christ: From whom the whole body fitly joined together and compacted by that which every joint supplieth, according to the effectual working in the measure of every part, maketh increase of the body unto the edifying of itself in love.[488]

Far from allowing room for a partial communion or gradation of membership, in his commentary on this passage St. John Chrysostom states plainly that it is all or nothing when it comes to communion. If a member of the body be separated, "the spirit which proceeds from the brain seeks the limb, and if it finds it not, does not leap forth from the body, and fly about and go to the hand, but if it finds it not in its place, does not touch it."[489] Moreover, not only is wholeness necessary for membership, but also order and one's proper place within the

---

487. PG 61.73. "πάντα ἔνωσιν ἐμφαίνει, καὶ οὐδὲν μέσον κενὸν ἀφίησιν εἶναι, οὐδὲ τὸ μικρότατον. Ὁ γὰρ μικρὸν ἀποστάς, καὶ πολὺ προϊὼν ἀποστήσεται."

488. Ephesians 4:15–16: "ἀληθεύοντες δὲ ἐν ἀγάπη αὐξήσωμεν εἰς αὐτὸν τὰ πάντα, ὅς ἐστιν ἡ κεφαλή, Χριστός, ἐξ οὗ πᾶν τὸ σῶμα συναρμολογούμενον καὶ συμβιβαζόμενον διὰ πάσης ἁφῆς τῆς ἐπιχορηγίας κατ᾽ ἐνέργειαν ἐν μέτρῳ ἑνὸς ἑκάστου μέρους τὴν αὔξησιν τοῦ σώματος ποιεῖται εἰς οἰκοδομὴν ἑαυτοῦ ἐν ἀγάπη."

489. Homily 11 on Ephesians, PG 62.84.28.

Body, such that it is put together "with exceeding art and nicety, since if it gets out of place, it is no longer."[490]

For St. John there is a clear lesson from this passage: "If we desire to have the benefit of that Spirit which is from the Head, let us cleave one to another."[491] Whether one's love grows cold or he commits acts unworthy of the Body, the result is the same: "we cut ourselves off from the fullness of Christ."[492] We see here that for St. John the fullness of Christ is synonymous with the Church, such that one can only be a full member. That is also why in ecclesiastical language τὸ πλήρωμα is synonymous with the entire Body:[493] He gave him to be the head over all things to the church, "which is his body, the fulness of him that filleth all in all" (Eph. 1:23).

St. John Chrysostom, in his commentary on this passage, states:

> The fullness of Christ is the Church. And rightly, for the complement of the head is the body, and the complement of the body is the head. Mark what great arrangement Paul observes, how he spares not a single word, that he may represent the glory of God. The fullness, he says, that is, the head, is, as it were, filled up by the body, because the body is composed and made up of all its several parts, and he introduces Him as having need of each single one and not only of all in common and

490. Ibid., PG 62.84.38.
491. Ibid., PG 62.85.20.
492. Ibid., PG 62.85.25.
493. In the Divine Liturgy of Saint John Chrysostom, in the prayer behind the Ambo, the faithful are called "τὸ πλήρωμα" (the fullness): "protect the fullness of your Church," that is, the whole body of Christ's Church.

together; for unless we be many, and one be the hand, and another the foot, and another some other member, the whole body is not filled up. It is by all then that His body is filled up. Then is the head filled up, then is the body rendered perfect, when we are all knit together and united.[494]

In commenting on the Apostle Paul's statement in his epistle to the Colossians, "For it pleased the Father that in him should all fullness dwell" (Col. 1:19), Saint John Chrysostom writes: "He spoke of 'fullness' with reference to the Godhead, as John said, 'Of His fullness have all we received.' That is, whatever was the Son, the whole Son dwelt there, not a sort of energy, but a Substance."[495] St. Paul writes further down in the same epistle, "and you are complete [or made full] in Him" (Col. 2:10), which St. John interprets as meaning, "That ye have nothing less than He. As it dwelt in Him, so also in you."[496]

---

494. Eph. Hom. 3.2, PG 62.26: "Τὸ πλήρωμα τοῦ Χριστοῦ ἡ Ἐκκλησία. Καὶ γὰρ πλήρωμα κεφαλῆς σῶμα, καὶ πλήρωμα σώματος κεφαλή. Ὅρα πόσῃ τάξει κέχρηται Παῦλος, πῶς οὐδενὸς φείδεται ῥήματος, ὥστε παραστῆσαι τοῦ Θεοῦ τὴν δόξαν. Πλήρωμα, φησί· τουτέστιν, οἷον κεφαλὴ πληροῦται παρὰ τοῦ σώματος· διὰ γὰρ πάντων μερῶν τὸ σῶμα συνέστηκε, καὶ ἑνὸς ἑκάστου χρῄζει. Ὅρα πῶς αὐτὸν κοινῇ πάντων χρῄζοντα εἰσάγει. Ἂν γὰρ μὴ ὦμεν πολλοί, καὶ ὁ μὲν χεὶρ, ὁ δὲ πούς, ὁ δὲ ἄλλο τι μέρος, οὐ πληροῦται ὅλον τὸ σῶμα. Διὰ πάντων οὖν πληροῦται τὸ σῶμα αὐτοῦ. Τότε πληροῦται ἡ κεφαλή, τότε τέλειον σῶμα γίνεται, ὅταν ὁμοῦ πάντες ὦμεν συνημμένοι καὶ συγκεκολλημένοι."

495. PG 62.320.56: "Τὸ πλήρωμα περὶ τῆς θεότητος εἴρηκε, καθάπερ ὁ Ἰωάννης ἔλεγεν· Ἐκ τοῦ πληρώματος αὐτοῦ ἡμεῖς πάντες ἐλάβομεν. Τουτέστιν, εἴτε ἦν ὁ Υἱὸς, εἴτε ὁ Λόγος, ἐκεῖ ᾤκησεν οὐχὶ ἐνέργειά τις, ἀλλ᾽ οὐσία."

496. PG 62.339.43: "Ὅτι οὐδὲν ἔλαττον ἔχετε αὐτοῦ· ὥσπερ ἐν ἐκείνῳ ᾤκησεν, οὕτω καὶ ἐν ὑμῖν."

If we are in Christ, we are "of his fullness." St. John leaves no room for an "incomplete" life in Christ, an incomplete communion with the Church. The fullness of divinity dwells in Christ bodily (Col. 2:9), Who is Himself our salvation and in Whom there can be no division, nor separation. Furthermore, Christ our salvation is given freely as a gift to all the members of the Body without discrimination at the time of their Baptism. It is inconceivable that the perfect gift of salvation could be imparted incompletely, imperfectly, or that upon receiving it the recipient could still be lacking full communion with the Body of Christ.

According to Clement of Alexandria, fullness is attained in every baptized person. All gifts—especially Baptism—coming down from the father of lights are perfect and lack nothing:

> Straightway, on our regeneration, we attained that perfection after which we aspired. For we were illuminated, which is to know God. He is not then imperfect who knows what is perfect. . . . Being baptized, we are illuminated; illuminated, we become sons; being made sons, we are made perfect; being made perfect, we are made immortal. . . . Now we call that perfect which wants nothing. For what is yet wanting to him who knows God? For it were truly monstrous that that which is not complete should be called a gift (or act) of God's grace. Being perfect, He consequently bestows perfect gifts.[497]

---

497. *Paedagogus*, 1.6.25.1 and 1.6.26.2–3, PG 8.280B and 281A. "ἀναγεννηθέντες γοῦν εὐθέως τὸ τέλειον ἀπειλήφαμεν, οὗ ἕνεκεν ἐσπεύδομεν. Ἐφωτίσθημεν γάρ· τὸ δὲ ἔστιν ἐπιγνῶναι τὸν θεόν. Οὔκουν ἀτελὴς ὁ ἐγνωκὼς τὸ τέλειον . . . βαπτιζόμενοι φωτιζόμεθα, φωτιζόμενοι υἱοποιούμεθα, υἱοποιούμενοι τελειούμεθα, τελειούμενοι ἀπαθανατιζόμεθα . . . τέλειον δὲ τὸ ἀπροσδεές φαμεν. Τί γὰρ ἔτι λείπεται τῷ θεὸν

The Church is complete, and into this fullness is every Christian born at Baptism. As St. Justin Popovich has written:

> Every Christian, after having become a member of the Church through holy Baptism, becomes also an integral part of fullness "of Him that filleth all in all" (Eph. 1:23), himself fulfilling "all the fullness of God" (Eph. 3:19). And in this way he arrives at the "complete fullness" of his human existence, his human personality. Each Christian arrives at this fullness through the holy mysteries and holy virtues, according to the "measure" of his faith and his life "in grace" within the church. This is in effect for all Christian in all ages. All are fulfilled with the fullness "of Him that filleth all in all."[498]

The kingdom of God, which is the Body of Christ gathered in the Eucharist *epi to auto,* is perfect and lacks nothing, such that the catholicity or unity of the Church could never be impaired. "Incompleteness" "belongs only to the individual appropriation of the given fullness by the members, who are

ἐγνωκότι; Καὶ γὰρ ἄτοπον ὡς ἀληθῶς χάρισμα κεκλῆσθαι θεοῦ τὸ μὴ πεπληρωμένον· τέλειος δὲ ὢν τέλεια χαριεῖται δήπουθεν

498. Πόποβιτς, Ἑρμηνεία τῆς Ἐπιστολῆς τοῦ ἀποστόλου Παύλου πρὸς Ἐφεσίους, 65: "Κάθε χριστιανός, ἀφοῦ γίνει μέ τό ἅγιο Βάπτισμα μέλος τῆς Ἐκκλησίας, γίνεται καί ἀναπόσπαστο μέρος τοῦ πληρώματος 'τοῦ τά πάντα ἐν πᾶσιν πληρουμένου' (Ἐφ. 1,23), πληρούμενος καί «ὁ ἴδιος 'εἰς πᾶν τό πλήρωμα τοῦ θεοῦ' (Ἐφ. 3,19). Καί μέ τόν τρόπο αὐτό φτάνει στήν 'παντέλεια πληρότητα' τῆς ἀνθρωπίνης ὑπάρξεώς του, τῆς ἀνθρωπίνης προσωπικότητάς του. Σέ αὐτή τήν πληρότητα φτάνει κάθε χριστιανός μέ τά ἅγια μυστήρια καί τίς ἅγιες ἀρετές, σύμφωνα μέ τό μέτρο τῆς 'πίστεώς' του καί τήν 'ἐν χάριτι' ζωή του μέσα στήν Ἐκκλησία. Αὐτό ἰσχύει γιά ὅλους τούς χριστιανούς ὅλων τῶν ἐποχῶν. Ὅλοι εἶναι 'πεπληρωμένοι' μέ τό πλήρωμα 'τοῦ τά πάντα ἐν πᾶσιν πληρουμένου.'"

limited by belonging to the "old Adam"; it does not exist in the Body of Christ, indivisible, divine, glorious."[499] The gifts of God are always given "fully, abundantly, and overwhelmingly." God "does not give the Spirit by measure" (John 3:34), and "of His fullness we have all received, and grace for grace" (John 1:16). Now it must be appropriated, truly received, made ours. And this is the goal of Christian life."[500]

Fullness Understood as Identity

Insisting that communion can only be full and that there is no "partial communion" in the Church, does not necessarily imply a legalistic conception of the Church. Yet, in the debate on the floor of the council, those opposed to the introduction of this distinction in communion were rejected on these grounds. According to Johannes Feiner, the objections of the more conservative bishops were swept aside as belonging to an older, legalistic view of the Church not in accord with the new communio ecclesiology:

> Anyone who conceives of the Church only in terms of the normal canonical and juridical concept of communio cannot speak of a greater or lesser degree of communion with the Catholic Church: either one is in communion with the Church or one is not in communion with it. A few of the Council Fathers in fact put forward, on the basis of a purely juridical concept of communion, the view that one could not be *plene* or *non plene* in communion with the Church. [However], on the basis of its dogmatic

499. Fr. John Meyendorff, *Byzantine Theology, Historical Trends and Doctrinal Themes* (New York: Fordham University Press, 1970), 209.

500. Fr. Alexander Schmemann, *Of Water and the Spirit* (Crestwood, NY: St. Vladimir's Seminary Press, 1974), 107.

concept of communio the decree affirms the possibility of an incomplete communion.[501]

There is another, non-legalistic, way to understand fullness that connects it to identity. The fullness of divinity or of Christ or of the Church has no counterpart—an incomplete divinity, Christ, or Church. Fullness here refers to Christ, who cannot be anything else but full. Just as there is not a partially true or salvific Christ, there cannot be a partially true or salvific Church, for Christ is the Church. Therefore, as Fr. Alexander Schmemann has written, "if that which is given is the fullness, always identical with itself, the eschatological fullness of the Church, even Christ Himself, it is yet impossible to abstract this fullness from its incarnation and manifestation in history."[502]

This means that the fullness of Christ is identified with the Body of Christ, which is, like Christ when He walked on earth as Theanthropos, visible and marked by divine-human characteristics. In His Body, the Church, the fullness of divinity and the fullness of salvation are granted to men. A "church" or "ecclesiastical community" that cannot be identified with this fullness cannot be the Body of Christ or a body in which His presence is actualized mysteriologically, for in every manifestation of the Body there is fullness.[503] "From the point of view of *Heilsgeschichte* (salvation history) the Church has no history, it is already *in statu patriae*, and is always the actualization of the fullness of salvation accomplished by Christ ἐφάπαξ—once for all."[504]

---

501. Feiner, "Commentary on the Decree," 70.

502. Schmemann, "Unity, Division, Reunion."

503. Saint John Chrysostom, *Homily on the Epistle to the Hebrews*, 17.6.

504. Schmemann, "Unity, Division, Reunion." This point is summed up well in Protestant scholar Daniel Clendenin's work *Eastern Orthodox*

In the Orthodox, patristic understanding, that which is recognized as the Church is recognizable as one and the same in
each place, identical, as in a mirror. In Christ, "there is no and
can be no partial Christianity."[505] The local churches are not
"parts" of the whole. The unity of the churches is "ontologically expressed in terms of identity. . . . [E]ach Church, as a
church, as a sacramental unity, is the same church, manifested
in a given place. This identity is based on the identity of sacramental structure of every church: on the apostolic succession,
on the episcopate, and on the sacraments."[506] The unity of
the Church is an established fact, an ontological given, made
certain by Christ through the constant presence of the Holy
Spirit. This unity is expressed institutionally in a triple union
of faith, worship, and administration. These are interdepen-
dent and indivisible forms of the one complete unity of the
Church.[507] Christ, and His Body, is manifested in each time and

Theology (Grand Rapids, MI: Baker Academic, 2003), thus: "The church
as a whole is a means of grace, the sacrament of the kingdom. Therefore
its structure—hierarchical, sacramental, liturgical—has no other function but of making the church ever capable of fulfilling itself as the body
of Christ, as the temple of the Holy Spirit, to actualize its very nature as
grace. For the God-given fullness of the Church, or rather the church
as fullness—and this is an essential aspect of Orthodox ecclesiology—
cannot be manifested outside these ecclesiastical structures. There is no
separation, no division, between the church invisible (in *statu patriae*)
and the visible church (in *statu viae*), the latter being the expression
and the actualization of the former, the sacramental sign of its reality.
Hence the unique, the central ecclesiological significance of the Eucharist, which is the all-embracing sacrament of the church" (198).

505. Florovsky, "The House of the Father," in *Ecumenism I: A Doctrinal Approach, Collected Works*, vol. 13, 79.

506. Schmemann, "Unity, Division, Reunion."

507. Βλ. Δημητρίου Τσελεγγίδης, Ἡ λειτουργία τῆς ἑνότητας τῆς
Ἐκκλησίας καὶ οἱ ἐσφαλμένες θεολογικὲς προϋποθέσεις τοῦ Παπικοῦ

place as the same Christ, "yesterday, today, and forever" (Heb. 13:8). Wherever there is Christ, there is fullness: "Christ is one everywhere, being complete here and complete there also, one Body."[508]

Fundamental to both Catholicism and Protestantism, but absent from Orthodoxy, is the view of the Church as a universal organism anterior to its different parts—parts that are united to the Church in and through the whole. Previously, in the "closed" and exclusive system of Pius XII, this universal organism had a visible head that united the visible Church— the entire Church militant. At Vatican II the Roman Catholic Church is distinguished from the *ecclesia universalis*, the Church as such. One can now participate in the Body of Christ without being a member of the Papal Church, a belief that, if it were applied to the Orthodox Church, would be impossible for the Orthodox to accept. "In contrast to such views, the Orthodox Church stresses the visible aspect of the Church and teaches that outside the Church, there is no salvation. The Church as the Body of Christ is the dwelling place of the uncreated glory of God. We cannot separate Christ from the Church, nor the Church from Christ."[509]

Spiritual participation in this Church, in divinity through the human nature of Christ, is visible and dynamic but it is

πρωτείου [The Function of the Unity of the Church and the Fallacious Theological Presuppositions of Papal Primacy], speech given at the conference "Primacy, Collegiality and the Unity of the Church," sponsored by the Diocese of Peiraeus of the Church of Greece.

508. Saint John Chrysostom, *Homily on the Epistle to the Hebrews,* 17.6: "εἰς πανταχοῦ ὁ Χριστός, καὶ ἐνταῦθα πλήρης ὢν, καὶ ἐκεῖ πλήρης, ἓν σῶμα."

509. J. S. Romanides, *An Outline of Orthodox Patristic Dogmatics* [Ἐπίτομος Ὀρθόδοξος Πατερικὴ Δογματική] (Rollinsford, NH: Orthodox Research Institute, 2004), 77.

not divisible or quantifiable, because it is not apprehended by the rational organ of man but by the heart. The inner life in Christ, the kingdom of God, is not subject to apprehension on the level of the quantifiable or divisible. "The kingdom of God does not come with observation; nor will they say, 'See here!' or 'See there!' For indeed, the kingdom of God is within you." (Luke 17:20). The internal action of the grace of the Holy Spirit is indivisible and immeasurable, for it is "indivisibly divided among individual creatures."[510] This indivisible division of the grace of the Holy Spirit points not only to the unity of the divine energies with the divine essence but also to the unity of the mysteries with the Mystery of the Church. The many mysteries are one mystery distributed to each believer without being divided, for in each of them is Christ, "He Who is divided but not disunited," "Who offers and is offered, and Who accepts and distributes."[511] "Christ is all and in all" (Col. 3:11), such that in each mystery the fullness of Christ is present— "indivisibly divided among individual creatures." The Church is the extension and the "fullness" of the Incarnation, or rather of the Incarnate life of the Son,[512] "with all that for our sakes was brought to pass, the Cross and tomb, the Resurrection on the third day, the Ascension into Heaven, the sitting on the right hand."[513]

---

510. Ἁγίου Ἰωάννου Δαμασκηνοῦ, Ἔκδοσις Ἀκριβὴς Ὀρθοδόξου Πίστεως, ἔκδ. Πουρναρᾶς, Θεσσαλονίκη), 94 (14.22): "μερίζεται ἀμερίστως ἐν μεριστοῖς."

511. Divine Liturgy of Saint John Chyrsostom, prayer said during the cherubic hymn: "ὁ μελιζόμενος καὶ μὴ διαιρούμενος," "ὁ προσφέρων καὶ προσφερόμενος, καὶ προσδεχόμενος, καὶ διαδιδόμενος . . ."

512. Georges Florovsky, *L'Église: sa nature et sa tache*, in *L'Église universelle dans le Dessein de Dieu* (Neuchatel-Paris, 1949), 1:70. English translation: "The Church: Her Nature and Task," in Georges Florovsky, *Collected Works*, vol. 1 (Belmont, MA: Nordland, 1972–1979).

513. Divine Liturgy of St. John Chrysostom, Prayer of Consecration.

At once, the unity, fullness, and identity of the Church is Christ, the fullness of Whom we live in the mysteries, in which the unity of the Church is realized. In this *communio in sacris* we seal our organic unity both vertically and horizontally—with Christ and with one another—and we thus constitute the "one Christ."[514] The catholicity of the Church, then, which is her very identity, is her fullness—the fullness of Christ Himself: "the whole Christ, Head and body."[515]

To this patristic vision of the Church Vatican II, the celebrated council of reform and *ressourcement*, did not return. Rather, reacting against an earlier reactionary and legalistic counter-Reformation ecclesiology, the council moved away from the patristic vision once again, this time toward Calvin and the Reformers.[516]

Identity of Baptism: Initiation into the Church in the Eucharist

> This is a fundamental identity: the Church in the Eucharist and the Eucharist in the Church. Where the God-man is not, the Church is not, and where the Church is not, there is no Eucharist. Everything outside this is heresy, non-church, anti-church, and psuedo-church.
>
> *St. Justin Popovich*[517]

514. Schmemann, "Unity, Division, Reunion."

515. St. Augustine, *On the Epistle of John*, 1.2: "*totus Christus, Caput et Corpus.*"

516. See chapter 9, section on "Ecclesiastical Unity through Elements," for a discussion of the central importance of Congar's development of Calvin's doctrine of "*vestigia ecclesiae.*"

517. Archimandrite Justin Popovich, *The Orthodox Church and Ecumenism*, trans. Benjamin Emmanuel Stanley (Birmingham: Lazarica Press, 2000), 69.

The identification of the Body applies to the Body as a whole and to each of its aspects simultaneously. Each manifestation of the Body contains within it the fullness of the Body. "Each mystery constitutes a particular aspect or manifestation of a united reality,"[518] of the one mystery of Christ (Eph. 3:4), "which hath been hid from ages and from generations, but now is made manifest to his saints" (Col. 1:26). We recognize a mystery, such as holy Baptism, only when it is a reflection of the One Church. "No mystery can be conceived of per se, but only in relation to the Mystery, which recapitulates the entire 'mystery of Christ,' that is, the Divine Eucharist."[519]

The Baptism of the Church is not simply form, matter, and intention. It is first of all initiation. That Baptism that we recognize as the one Baptism brings one into the life of the Church, the heart of which is the Eucharist. As Fr. George Florovsky has written: "The entire meaning and strength of the sacrament of Holy Baptism is that the baptized enters into the one Church, 'the one Church of angels and men,'[520] taking root and growing into the one Body of Christ, and becomes a 'fellow citizen of the saints and friend of God' [Eph. 2:19], for 'we are all one Spirit baptized into one body' [1 Cor. 12:13]. Holy Baptism is a mysterious initiation into the Church, as into the kingdom of grace."[521]

---

518. John Zizioulas (Metropolitan of Pergamon), "Holy Baptism and Divine Liturgy," in *Holy Baptism: Our Incorporation into the Church of Christ* [in Greek: "Άγιον Βάπτισμα καὶ Θεία Λειτουργία" στό *Τό Άγιο Βάπτισμα: Ἡ ἔνταξή μας στήν Ἐκκλησία τοῦ Χριστοῦ* (Athens: Apostoliki Diakonia, 2002), 11].

519. Zizioulas, ibid., 12.

520. *Paraklitiki* (Divine service book), Tone 1, Wednesday morning, *aposticha*.

521. Florovsky, "House of the Father," 79.

Hence, if one is not initiated into the Church, if one does not enter into the one Church, into a particular local church through his parish community,[522] and become a member of the Body by partaking of the Eucharist, it would be impossible for the Orthodox to recognize that he has been truly baptized. Such a Baptism is not the Baptism of and into the Church. Such a Baptism, "a Baptism disconnected from the Holy Eucharist," "is a death without resurrection."[523]

How does Baptism integrate us into the Church? Precisely by opening us up to the gift of the Holy Spirit, which then gives us access to the Eucharist. The one presupposes the other, for they all belong together, with the Eucharist being the "self-evident fulfillment" of the others.[524] There is a "sacramental interdependence" such that it is impossible to speak

522. "The fact that the newly illumined one must immediately gather *epi to auto*, and not simply commune of the Mysteries, means that with Baptism and Chrismation he is inscribed into a particular local church through his parish community, and is under a particular bishop, who presides at the Eucharist. Just as there are no absolute ordinations, neither can there exist absolute Baptisms." (Zizioulas, "Holy Baptism and Divine Liturgy," 24).

523. Ibid., 20.

524. The patristic witness to this unity of the Mysteries of Baptism and the Eucharist is ancient. See, for example: Saint Justin the Philosopher, First Apology, LXV; Psuedo-Clement, 100, 141; Hippolytus of Rome, *Apostolic Tradition*, 21; Canons of Hippolytus, 21, § 142–143; Saint Ambrose of Milan, *On the Mysteries*, 8; Saint John Chrysostom, *Catechetical Homily* II.2 and IV.6; Saint Basil the Great, *Concerning Baptism*, 1.3. See the brief treatment of these sources and their witness in John (Zizioulas), Metropolitan of Pergamon ("Holy Baptism and Divine Liturgy," 13–15. For a more extensive treatment of these sources see I. Yazigi (Hani), Hierodeacon, Ἡ τελετή τοῦ ἁγίου βαπτίσματος, (Ἱστορική, θεολογική καί τελετουργική θεώρησις) [The service of holy Baptism: Historic, theological and liturgical consideration], doctoral thesis, Thessaloniki, 1982).

of one without the other two, impossible to speak of someone being baptized without approaching Christ's table in His Kingdom. In the words of Father Alexander Schmemann, for the Fathers the Eucharist is "the 'focus,' the source and the fulfillment of the entire—and not merely the liturgical—life of the Church, the sacrament of the Church's self-manifestation and edification."[525]

Baptism as integration, as entry, presupposes communion in the common cup of the Eucharist. For, "if the Church's ultimate being and essence are revealed in and through the Eucharist, if Eucharist is truly the sacrament of the Church and not only one of the Church's sacraments, then of necessity to enter the Church is to enter into the Eucharist, then Eucharist is indeed the fulfillment of Baptism."[526] No mystery is an end in itself—except for the Eucharist. All other mysteries must be placed in the context of the Eucharist. Therefore, the faithful are baptized "*so that* having died with Christ they might partake of His Risen Life, and it is this Risen Life that the Eucharist manifests and communicates in the Church, making her members into witnesses of the things to come."[527]

Having this in mind, when we turn to the text of *Unitatis Redintegratio* 3a, which recognizes those among the "separated brethren" who are not in "full communion" with the Roman Catholic Church as being "truly baptized" and "incorporated into Christ," members of Christ's Church, one is at a loss to know what this could mean. What kind of Baptism is this that incorporates into Christ without leading to the fulfillment of Baptism in the Eucharist? Or, what kind of "incorporation"

---

525. Schmemann, *Of Water and the Spirit,* 117.
526. Ibid., 117–18.
527. Ibid., p. 119 (emphasis added).

is this that is effected without the Eucharist, since becoming one with the Body of Christ takes place in the Eucharist?[528] For what else could "incomplete communion" mean here except that they have not reached the "summit" of communion, according to Cardinal Kasper's description of the Eucharist? Certainly, as it pertains to most Protestants who do not have a "valid" Eucharist, this must be what is meant. Thus, it is evident that what the mysteries, Baptism and the Eucharist, are understood to mean by the Orthodox does not coincide with the meaning found in *Unitatis Redintegratio* and *Lumen Gentium*.

The implications for ecclesiology are immense, for the members of the Church are constituted as the Church first and foremost through these mysteries. The separation and independence of Baptism from the Eucharist, on both a theoretical as well as a practical level, is not only unchallenged in *Unitatis Redintegratio*, it is an important pillar of the new ecclesiology developed therein.[529] This independence of Baptism from the Eucharist signifies much more than simply a liturgical diversion from traditional practice. It touches upon the faith itself and signals "a deep perversion of the identity of the Church with wide-ranging and serious consequences."[530]

One cannot be incorporated into Christ and become His member in Baptism alone.[531] The Church is not created in the

---

528. Stressing that the Divine Eucharist is the perfection of all the mysteries and the image of the Kingdom of God, Met. John (Zizioulas) of Pergamon asks rhetorically: "What benefit is Baptism, when the baptized does not immediately join the Eucharistic synaxis *epi to auto*? Can he become a son of the Kingdom without this?" ("Holy Baptism and Divine Liturgy," 23).

529. See UR 3 and 22.

530. Zizioulas, "Holy Baptism and Divine Liturgy," 27.

531. One cannot stress this point enough. For Orthodox Christians it

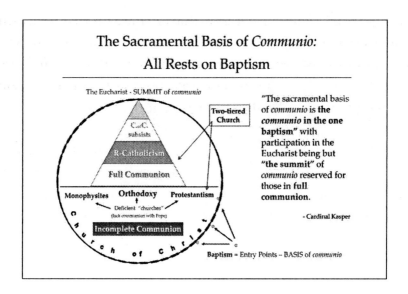

The Sacramental Basis of *Communio:*
All Rests on Baptism

"The sacramental basis of *communio* is **the *communio* in the one baptism"** with participation in the Eucharist being but **"the summit"** of *communio* reserved for those in full communion.

- Cardinal Kasper

waters of Baptism alone, but, rather, was born from the side of Christ when "forthwith came there out blood and water" (John 19:34); neither blood alone, nor water alone, but both together.[532] Those born have to be nourished; those baptized partake straightaway of divine food. That is why, for the Orthodox, "every Eucharistic assembly is an assembly of the en-

is an heretical idea to believe, as Fr. John Romanides has written, that "all baptized Christians are members of the body of Christ even though they hardly go to Church to commune and have not the slightest desire to struggle for selfless love and fight against the devil *epi to auto* as they solemnly swore at Baptism" ("The Ecclesiology of St. Ignatius of Antioch," *The Greek Orthodox Theological Review* 7:1 and 2 [1961–62]). "[G]race is never given absolutely, but always in the synaxis and in the Church" (Zizioulas, "Holy Baptism and Divine Liturgy," 26).

532. See St. Cyril of Alexandria, *On John*, 12, PG 74.677B, and St. John Chrysostom, *On John*, 85.3, PG 59.463. "Let it not be forgotten that not only does the Eucharist give meaning to Baptism, but that Baptism constitutes an inexorable presupposition for the Eucharist" (Zizioulas, "Holy Baptism and Divine Liturgy," 26).

tire Church,"[533] τὸ πλήρωμα, "the flesh of the Church"[534] which Christ assumed. Those not incorporated into this assembly[535] are not of the fullness, which means they have not been made members of Christ's Body. For, we know of no such Baptism that is not fulfilled in the Eucharist.

533. Hieromonk Gregorios, *The Divine Liturgy: A Commentary in the Light of the Fathers* (Mount Athos: Cell of St. John the Theologian, 2009), 26. "[A]ccording to St. Dionysius the Aeropagite and the entire Patristic Tradition, at least up until St. Nicholas Cabasilas, the Eucharist alone gives meaning to every ecclesiastical and liturgical action precisely because *it is a synaxis of the entire Church* . . ." (Zizioulas, "Holy Baptism and Divine Liturgy," 23).

534. St. John Chrysostom, *Homily before his Exile*, 2, PG 52.429.

535. "Without the *synaxis* [of the Eucharist] no liturgical action of any kind can have any meaning whatsoever, nor even the entire Christian life, I would say, including asceticism, the virtues, etc." (Zizioulas, "Holy Baptism and Divine Liturgy," 23).

13

BAPTISM AND THE UNITY OF THE FAITH

Foremost among the diversions from the Orthodox, patristic ecclesiology that we've observed, the most egregious is the disconnection of Baptism from the unity of the faith.

As we stated at the outset of our analysis of the new ecclesiology, Latin theologians differentiate between the basis of communio, in Baptism, and its summit, in the Eucharist. They allow, that is, for a two-tiered Church life—one for those who have only received Baptism, another for those who have advanced on to communion in the Eucharist. Those "ecclesiastical communities" that have not maintained apostolic succession and a "valid" Eucharist are admitted, as it were, into the antechamber of the Church. Those "churches" that are recognized as having maintained apostolic succession and thus the genuine and complete substance of the Eucharistic mystery[536] have passed through the vestibule and entered into the nave of the Church. If these last lack in anything it is not on the vertical plane, in their communion with God, but on the horizontal plane, in their communion with the Roman Catholic Church. They may have Christ in the Eucharist, but they are nonetheless "wounded" because they lack His Vicar on earth, the Supreme Pontiff.[537]

536. See UR 22.
537. See chapters 11 ("The Twofold Unity of, and Membership in,

In the context of this new vision of the Church, then, let us examine Baptism and its connection to the unity of faith. We can see how the two are connected or disconnected in the following statements in the conciliar text.

First, in UR 3a dogmatic divergences from the confession of faith of the Church are not seen as obstacles to incorporation into the Church and the establishment of an incomplete communion:

> The differences that exist in varying degrees between [the separated brethren] and the Catholic Church—whether in doctrine and sometimes in discipline, or concerning the structure of the Church—do indeed create many obstacles, sometimes serious ones, to full ecclesiastical communion. The ecumenical movement is striving to overcome these obstacles. But even in spite of them it remains true that all who have been justified by faith in Baptism are members of Christ's body[538] and have a right to be called Christian, and so are correctly accepted as brothers by the children of the Catholic Church.[539]

Once considered necessary for any communion with the Church, doctrinal agreement is now necessary only for "full communion." In spite of doctrinal error and of not holding the faith confessed by the Roman Church, non–Roman Catholics

the Body of Christ") and 12 ("*Dominus Iesus*: Full Realization of the Church Requires Communion with the Pope") for an analysis of this idea that one can be in full communion with Christ but incomplete communion with the members of Christ on account of not being subjected to the Roman Pontiff.

538. Conc. Florentinum, Sess. VIII (1439), Decretum Exultate Deo: Mansi 31, 1055 A.

539. Cf. St. Augustine, In Ps. 32, Enarr. II, 29, PL 36, 299.

are seen to be "justified by faith" in Baptism. This is the first sign that a distinction is to be made between the faith confessed by the Church and the faith that justifies and initiates the believer at Baptism.

Second, the merits of that Baptism performed outside the Roman communion among the "churches and ecclesiastical communities" of the West are referred to in UR 22 in this way: "Whenever the Sacrament of Baptism is duly administered as Our Lord instituted it, and is received with the right dispositions, a person is truly incorporated into the crucified and glorified Christ, and reborn to a sharing of the divine life, as the Apostle says: 'You were buried together with Him in Baptism, and in Him also rose again through faith in the working of God, who raised Him from the dead.'"[540]

Here "the decree recognizes on principle the validity and effectiveness for grace ('fruitfulness') of the Baptism carried out in the Reformation Churches. Under the conditions mentioned . . . it has the saving effects mentioned in the text, incorporation into Christ (or into the Body of Christ, which is the Church) and rebirth into divine life."[541] This is the first level of communion in the Church, which brings one into an "incomplete communion." On this level, in Baptism, "a sacramental bond of unity" is established "which links all who have been reborn by it."[542] This regeneration in Christ is, however, sufficient neither

540. See UR 22a.

541. Johannes Feiner, "Commentary on the Decree," in *Commentary on the Documents of Vatican II*, vol. 2 (London: Burns and Oates Limited, 1968), 151.

542. UR 22b. The original "Ecumenical Directory" published by the Secretariat for Unity expands this, saying, "It follows from this that Baptism is the sacramental bond of unity, and indeed the basis of communion among all Christians" (Article 11).

to establish one in full communion with the Church nor to fully initiate him into the life in Christ.

UR 22b states: "Of itself Baptism is only a beginning, an inauguration wholly directed toward the Fullness of life in Christ. Baptism, therefore, envisages a complete profession of faith, complete incorporation in the system of salvation such as Christ willed it to be, and finally complete ingrafting in Eucharistic communion."[543]

Here we see that the Baptism that is envisioned as sufficient to incorporate the believer into Christ and make him a sharer of divine life (UR 22a) is not necessarily accompanied by a "complete" profession of faith, nor a "complete" incorporation into the "system of salvation" willed by Christ, nor a "complete" participation in the Eucharistic communion. There are, then, two kinds of initiation and two different results from the "one Baptism," initiating believers into different levels of communion depending on their ecclesiastical context. For those outside the Roman communion, then, the "complete" faith of the Church is not connected to Baptism.

The conciliar text goes on to explain more fully what is lacking in those without the "complete Eucharistic mystery": "the ecclesial Communities which are separated from us lack the Fullness of unity with us flowing from Baptism, and . . . we believe they have not retained the proper reality of the Eucharistic mystery in its Fullness, especially because of the absence of the sacrament of Orders . . ." (UR 22c).

Baptism normally should bring the baptized into full unity with the Church. For one baptized into the Roman communion this is the case because, among other things, there is full unity of faith. Baptism in the case of the "separated brethren," how-

543. Ibid.

ever, does not do this because they lack, among other things, "a complete profession of faith" (UR 22b)—the one faith of the Church. There is no oneness and unity of faith—and yet they are nonetheless baptized into Christ.

It is important to point out here that the conciliar text is not referring to the believer's personal faith or level of trust in Christ, which, in any case, varies and is ultimately indeterminable. The faith referred to is that which is "professed" by the Church, "the faith which was once delivered unto the saints" (Jude 1:3). It is this faith, a reflection of the entire experience of the Church, which the "separated brethren" do not confess, and for this reason, too, their communion with the Church and life in Christ remains "incomplete" (UR 22b).

Is it possible, however, to separate Baptism from the faith of the Church? Is it possible for one to be baptized into Christ without adopting and professing the faith of the Church? It would seem, at first, that according to one of *Unitatis Redintegratio*'s greatest proponents, Cardinal Kasper, it is not: "The sacramental basis of communio is the communio in the one Baptism. For through the one Baptism we have all been baptized into the one Body of Christ. . . . Baptism is the sacrament of faith. So, communio through Baptism *presupposes and implies communio in the common faith of the Church*, that is, communion in the Gospel. Both communion in faith and Baptism are the foundations of communio."[544]

If, then, communion in Baptism presupposes communion in the faith, how is it that the "separated brethren," who do

544. Walter Kasper, "Communio: The Guiding Concept of Catholic Ecumenical Theology," in *That They May All Be One: The Call to Unity Today* (London/New York: Burns and Oates, 2004), 54 (emphasis added).

not, in fact, hold to the faith of the Roman Church, are truly baptized? How is it that they are in a "real, but incomplete communion" (UR 3a)?

There appears to be only one way to reconcile what Cardinal Kasper and *Unitatis Redintegratio* are saying about the "sacramental basis" of communio. "Real communion" must refer to a communion "in the Gospel" and "incomplete" communion must refer to their lacking "a complete profession of faith." In other words, there are two kinds of confession of faith—incomplete and complete, "in the Gospel" and "a complete profession." What Cardinal Kasper is interpreting as the "common faith of the Church" is actually not the full confession of faith of the Roman Church but rather "communion in the Gospel." The "complete" confession is reserved only for those in "full communion" in the Eucharist. This seems to be the only viable answer if Baptism and faith are supposed to be inseparable, as Cardinal Kasper accepts.

The following passage from *Lumen Gentium* supports this interpretation: "The Church recognizes that in many ways she is linked with those who, being baptized, are honored with the name of Christian, though they do not profess the faith in its entirety. . . ."[545]

545. LG 15. Kevin McNamara in his commentary on LG agrees with Kasper and confirms our reading of the text: "Where [the bonds of Baptism, adherence to the Scriptures and loving faith in God] are present, we may interpret it as saying, the things that divide Christians, weighty and fraught with difficulty though they may be, are by comparison of secondary importance. Because of the profound unity of the gospel it may indeed be said that these basic principles implicitly include the entire Christian revelation, even if in good faith certain elements of it are explicitly rejected." *Vatican II: The Constitution on the Church: A Theological and Pastoral Commentary* (London: Geoffrey Chapman, 1968), 150.

The effects of the sacramental minimalism that began with Blessed Augustine can be seen here bearing ripened fruit. For the Orthodox observer, this distinction of faiths and double-level initiation means nothing less than a sign of ecclesiastical disintegration and sacramental minimalism in the new ecclesiology. The phrase "communion in the Gospel" does not hearken back to the ancient Church's Symbol of Faith, but rather to a Protestant "sola scriptura"–based invisible unity, a "unity of faith" that, allowing for a variety of interpretations based on a variety of experiences, leaves men disunited.

The conciliar texts and the interpretations of them by Latin scholars confirm that what the Fathers call heresy Vatican II calls "Christian" and "of the church." For, to "not profess the faith in its entirety" (LG 15) is another name for heresy. Heresy, like Truth, is not a matter of quantity. There are no greater or lesser heresies, serious or trivial diversions from Church teaching. Orthodox faith, worship, and ethics are one whole that cannot be divided.[546]

Although a sect may amass more of them over time, each heresy is equally divisive and destructive because each heresy separates those holding it from the Church. The passage of time, the good dispositions of those holding heresy or the amount of "elements" in their possession cannot change the reality and consequences of holding "worthless currency." As St. John Chrysostom remarks, echoing the entire patristic understanding: "As he who but partially pares away the image on a royal coin renders the whole spurious, so he who swerves ever

546. Πρωτ. Βασιλείου Α. Γεωργοπούλου, "Τὸ Μυστήριο τῆς Ἐκκλησίας καὶ τὸ Φαινόμενο τῶν Αἱρέσεων" [The Mystery of the Church and the Phenomenon of the Heresies], Ἐρώ 8 (Οκτ.–Δεκ. 2011), 77.

so little from the pure faith, soon proceeds from this to graver errors, and becomes entirely corrupted." [547]

As we've already noted in our examination of Blessed Augustine's departure from the patristic consensus (chap. 4), retainment of external elements such as pronouncing the Divine Names cannot make up for lacking the right faith of the Church. Perhaps the greatest witness to this truth from among the Fathers is St. Athanasius, who was present at the First Ecumenical Council and who spent nearly his entire life fighting against the Arian heresy. The great Saint, far from limiting himself to a consideration of the externals alone, of the form of Baptism among the heretics, makes it clear that orthodox faith is sine quo non for the performance of an authentic and salvific Mystery:

> [N]ot he who simply says, "O Lord," gives Baptism; but he who with the Name has also the right faith. On this account therefore our Savior also did not simply command to baptize, but first says, "Teach"; then thus: "Baptize into the Name of Father, and Son, and Holy Ghost"; that the right faith might follow upon learning and together with faith might come the consecration of Baptism. There are many other heresies too, which use the words only, but not in a right sense, as I have said, nor with sound faith, and in consequence the water which they administer is unprofitable, as deficient in piety, so that he who is sprinkled by them is rather polluted by irreligion than redeemed."[548]

547. PG 61.622: "Καθάπερ γὰρ ἐν τοῖς βασιλικοῖς νομίσμασιν ὁ μικρὸν τοῦ χαρακτῆρος περικόψας, ὅλον τὸ νόμισμα κίβδηλον εἰργάσατο· οὕτω καὶ ὁ τῆς ὑγιοῦς πίστεως καὶ τὸ βραχύτατον ἀνατρέψας, τῷ παντὶ λυμαίνεται, ἐπὶ τὰ χείρονα προϊὼν ἀπὸ τῆς ἀρχῆς."

548. St. Athanasius the Great, *Patrologia Græca*, Vol. XXVI, col. 237B

That the Church saw the fact of division, and not the degree of distance from dogmatic teaching, as of preeminent importance is clear from the controversy surrounding Baptism in the third century, but also from the following very characteristic case in ecclesiastical history.

During the first session of the Seventh Ecumenical Council the assembled fathers argued at length about how to receive the bishops of the iconoclasts. Some wanted to transfer the discussion to the dogmatic plane and posed the question: "Is the heresy that has now been manifested more grievous or less grievous than those that preceded? The holy Patriarch Tarasios, echoing the words of the Apostle James, "whosoever shall keep the whole law, and yet offend in one point, he is guilty of all" (James 2:10), replied: "Evil is evil, especially in matters of the Church, as far as dogmas are concerned, it is all the same to err to a small degree or to a great degree, because in one case or the other the law of God is broken." [549]

(*Second Discourse Against the Arians*, §§ 42–43): "Διὰ τοῦτο γοῦν καὶ ὁ Σωτὴρ οὐκ ἁπλῶς ἐντείλατο βαπτίζειν, ἀλλὰ πρῶτόν φησι, Μαθητεύσατε· εἶθ᾽ οὕτω· Βαπτίζετε εἰς ὄνομα Πατρός, καὶ Υἱοῦ, καί ἁγίου Πνεύματος· ἵν ἐκ τῆς μαθήσεως ἡ πίστις ὀρθή γένηται, καὶ μετά πίστεως ἡ τοῦ βαπτίσματος τελείωσις προστεθῇ. Πολλαὶ γοῦν καὶ ἄλλα αἱρέσεις λέγουσαι τὰ ὀνόματα μόνον, μὴ φρονοῦσαι δὲ ὀρθῶς, ὡς εἴρηται, μηδὲ τὴν πίστιν ὑγιαίνουσαν ἔχουσαι, ἀλυσιτελὲς ἔχουσι καὶ τὸ παρ᾽ αὐτῶν διδόμενον ὕδωρ, λειπόμενον εὐσεβεία· ὥστε καὶ τὸν ῥαντιζόμενον παρ᾽ αὐτῶν ῥυπαίνεσθαι μᾶλλον ἐν ἀσεβεία ἤ λυτροῦσθαι."

549. Mansi 12:1030: Κανόνες τῆς Ζ Οἰκουμενικῆς Συνόδου, Κανὼν 1 [Acts of the Seventh Ecumenical Council, Act I], 1031–1034: "Τὸ κακόν ἤδη κακόν ἐστι, καὶ μάλιστα ἐκκλησιαστικῶν πραγμάτων. Τὸ γὰρ ἐπὶ δόγμασιν εἴτε μικροῖς εἴτε μεγάλοις ἁμαρτάνειν ταυτόν ἐστιν. Ἐξ᾽ ἀμφοτέρων γὰρ ὁ νόμος τοῦ Θεοῦ ἀθετεῖται." This was said during the discussion of the problem of heretical ordination. See also New Hieromartyr Hilarion (Troitsky), Archbishop of Verey, *The Unity of the Church* (Montreal: Monastery Press, 1975), 51.

The Apostle Paul says the same when he speaks of an "ἕτερον εὐαγγέλιον" ("another gospel," Gal. 1:6) which those warring against him from among the Jewish Christians were preaching. It is quite characteristic that they had not overturned the entire Gospel of Christ but only certain minor points, such as observing the Jewish customs of the Sabbath and circumcision. This could have been an opportunity for the Apostle to seek, in the spirit of Vatican II, to maintain a "communion in the Gospel" and an "incomplete communion" with his fellow Jews who, in fact, held the "basic faith" of the Church. Not only did the Apostle not do this, he taught that anyone preaching anything different than the Gospel that he had preached brings about the total overturning of the Gospel. If any man (including himself) or any angel from heaven would do this, "ἀνάθεμα ἔστω" ("let him be anathema," Gal. 1:9).

The boldness of the Apostle is characteristic of true faith based on true experience. As Fr. Georges Florovsky has written, at the base of the "daring definitiveness with which the Apostle Paul anathematized those who would not teach what he had proclaimed" is the "direct fullness and self-verified experienced knowledge of God. . . . Faith is experience, and therefore with daring we confirm—'this is the true faith.'"[550] Dogmatic apodictism is essentially characteristic of faith, "for the Son of God, Jesus Christ, was not 'yes' and 'no' but in him was 'yes' (2 Cor. 1:19), as the Apostle has said."[551]

Observing a part of the Gospel's teachings does not establish a man in unity with the Church. Rather, just the opposite. As St. John Chrysostom notes, the Apostle teaches to shun such a

---

550. From the troparion (hymn) sung at the end of the Divine Liturgy of St. John Chrysostom: "We have seen the true light. . . ."

551. Georges Florovsky, "The House of the Father," in *Ecumenism I: A Doctrinal Approach, Collected Works,* 1:74.

man for much less than subverting the entire Gospel: "And he says not, if they preach a contrary Gospel or subvert the whole of the true one, let them be anathema; but, if they even slightly vary, or incidentally disturb, my doctrine."[552]

In this way the Apostle taught us how it is that the Gospel works to unite us, to remain a Gospel of unity. This is possible only when it is preserved whole and untarnished.[553] As Fr. George Metallinos has written: "The Gospel creates unity when it is 'orthodox'; when it is passed on as it has been received, in its fullness and entirety. Every alteration of the Gospel, even in the slightest, changes the Gospel into one of the many 'gospels' of the world, which not only don't save—they bring ruin."[554]

It is only in striving for an exact fulfillment of the commands of the Savior that the unity of the Gospel is made manifest. Indeed, the unity and harmony of the Gospel teachings and the unity of the catholic Faith and communion of the Holy Spirit can only be made manifest by such commitment to the ἀκρίβεια (exactitude) of the faith. Unity holds together only when all are committed to the precise observance of the commandments, only when there is general striving to observe ἀκρίβεια in everything.

Saint Basil the Great stresses this need of viewing each separate aspect as an indivisible part of the whole. St. Basil does not simplify and narrow down the requirements set forth by

---

552. PG 61.624: "Καὶ οὐκ εἶπεν, Ἐὰν ἐναντία καταγγέλλωσιν, ἢ ἀνατρέπωσι τὸ πᾶν, ἀλλά, Κἂν μικρόν τι εὐαγγελίζωνται παρ' ὃ εὐηγγελισάμεθα, κἂν τὸ τυχὸν παρακινήσωσιν, ἀνάθεμα ἔστωσαν." See also Blessed Theophylact of Bulgaria, PG 124.959.

553. Μεταλληνός, πρωτ. Γεώργιος, Κηρύγματα στὰ Ἀποστολικὰ Ἀναγνώσματα [Sermons on the Epistle Readings] (Thessaloniki: Orthodox Kypseli, 2010), 214.

554. Ibid.

the Lord, restricting himself to explicit references to Baptism. Just as Christ assumed the whole of humanity in taking flesh of the Virgin and in the fulfillment of all the law and the prophets, so too must the whole law of Christ be observed and implemented in order that the whole man may be redeemed and saved: "With regard to all these requirements, one rule obtains: that if one is neglected, all are equally imperiled. If the Lord says: 'one jot or tittle shall not pass of the law, till all are fulfilled,' how much more will this be true of the Gospel, in as much as the Lord Himself says: 'Heaven and earth shall pass, but my words shall not pass.' Wherefore the Apostle James makes bold to say: 'Whosoever shall keep the whole law but offend in one point, is become guilty of all.'"[555]

By disdaining some aspect or another of the teaching of our Lord Jesus Christ heretics and schismatics have fallen from the entire inheritance of the sons of God and become, according to St. Basil, "enemies of the faith."[556] According to the words of the Prophet, "Cursed be he that confirmeth not all the words of this law to do them" (Deut. 27:26); and the Lord Himself says, "He that rejecteth me, and receiveth not my words, hath one that judgeth him: the word that I have spoken, the same shall judge him in the last day" (John 12:48), and "except your righteousness shall exceed the righteousness of the scribes and Pharisees, ye shall in no case enter into the kingdom of heav-

555. PG 31, 1529A: "Καθ' ὧν δὴ ἡ ἀπόφασις μία, δηλονότι ἴσος καὶ ὁ κίνδυνος τοῖς πᾶσιν, ἑνὸς ἐλλειφθέντος. Εἰ γὰρ λέγει ὁ Κύριος, 'ἰῶτα ἓν ἢ μία κεραία οὐ μὴ παρέλθη ἀπὸ τοῦ νόμου, ἕως ἂν πάντα γένηται·' πόσῳ μᾶλλον ἀπὸ τοῦ Εὐαγγελίου, αὐτοῦ τοῦ Κυρίου λέγοντος· 'ὁ οὐρανὸς καὶ ἡ γῆ παρελεύσεται, οἱ δὲ λόγοι μου οὐ μὴ παρέλθωσιν'; Ὅθεν τεθαρσηκὼς Ἰάκωβος ὁ ἀπόστολος ἀπεφήνατο εἰπών· "Ὃς ἂν ποιήσῃ ὅλον τὸν νόμον, πταίσῃ δὲ ἐν ἑνί, ἔσται πάντων ἔνοχος.'"

556. PG 32, 556C, and PG 32, 996A.

en" (Matt. 5:20). Saint Basil likewise says as much, with the utmost force, in answer to the question "Whether we ought to associate with transgressors or have any part in the unfruitful works of darkness, when such persons or works are not under our charge": "An outlaw, indeed, is every man who does not keep the whole law or who violates even one commandment. For, by omission of only a small part, the whole is imperiled. That which is almost accomplished is yet not accomplished." [557]

While the extent to which heretics or schismatics have distanced themselves from the fullness that is Christ and His Church may either assist or hinder their return, it does not change the fact of their apostasy. This has been borne out in the history of the Church, and from the earliest times was confirmed by Saint Cyprian when he famously said that, even if those in schism "were slain in confession of the Name, that stain is not even washed away by blood: the inexpiable and grave fault of discord is not even purged by suffering. He cannot be a martyr who is not in the Church." [558]

St. John Chrysostom, showing that he both read and agreed

---

557. PG 31, 1612B: "Παράνομος μέν ἐστιν πᾶς ὁ μὴ ὁλόκληρον τὸν νόμον φυλάξας, ἢ καὶ ὁ μίαν ἐντολὴν παραβάς. Ἐν γὰρ τῇ ἐλλείψει καὶ τοῦ μικροῦ τὸ πᾶν κινδυνεύει. Τὸ γὰρ παρ' ὀλίγον γεγονὸς οὐ γέγονεν."

558. St. Cyprian, Treatise *On the Unity of the Church*, paragraph 14. Having set aside the view that non–Roman Catholics who hold heretical views or are in schism are responsible for their status, UR departed from this age-old position of the Saints, stating the opposite of St. Cyprian: "Catholics must gladly acknowledge and esteem the truly Christian endowments from our common heritage which are to be found among our separated brethren. It is right and salutary to recognize the riches of Christ and virtuous works in the lives of others who are bearing witness to Christ, sometimes even to the shedding of their blood. For God is always wonderful in His works and worthy of all praise" (UR 4h).

with St. Cyprian, quoted him in his eleventh homily on the Apostle Paul's Epistle to the Ephesians, saying: "Now a certain holy man said what might seem to be a bold thing; yet, nevertheless, he spoke it out. What then is this? He said, that not even the blood of martyrdom can wash out this sin. For tell me for what dost thou suffer as a martyr? Is it not for the glory of Christ? Thou then that yieldest up thy life for Christ's sake, how dost thou lay waste the Church, for whose sake Christ yielded up His life?"[559]

Far from seeing a graduated communion or "communion in the Gospel" or recognizing in schismatics the "common faith of the Church," St. John draws a clear line between those in the Church and those in apostasy from the Church—whether they be heretics or schismatics: "Shall it be said, 'Their faith is the same, they are orthodox as well as we'? If so, why then are they not with us? There is 'one Lord, one faith, one Baptism.' If their cause is right, then is ours wrong; if ours is right, then is theirs wrong."[560]

Clearly, the words of St. John cannot be reconciled with the idea put forward in *Unitatis Redintegratio* that there exists an "incomplete faith" that puts one in "incomplete communion" with the Church. For St. John Chrysostom, as with Ss. Cyprian, Firmilian, Basil, and the entire choir of Holy Fathers, there is

559. PG 62.85.38: "Ἀνὴρ δέ τις ἅγιος εἶπέ τι δοκοῦν εἶναι τολμηρὸν, πλὴν ἀλλ᾽ ὅμως ἐφθέγξατο. Τί δὴ τοῦτό ἐστιν; Οὐδὲ μαρτυρίου αἷμα ταύτην δύνασθαι ἐξαλείφειν τὴν ἁμαρτίαν ἔφησεν. Εἰπὲ γάρ μοι, τίνος ἕνεκεν μαρτυρεῖς; οὐ διὰ τὴν δόξαν τοῦ Χριστοῦ; Ὁ τοίνυν τὴν ψυχὴν προέμενος ὑπὲρ τοῦ Χριστοῦ, πῶς τὴν Ἐκκλησίαν πορθεῖς, ὑπὲρ ἧς τὴν ψυχὴν προήκατο ὁ Χριστός. . . ."

560. PG 62, 86A: "Τί λέγεις; ἡ αὐτὴ πίστις ἐστὶν, ὀρθόδοξοί εἰσι κἀκεῖνοι. Τίνος οὖν ἕνεκεν οὐκ εἰσὶ μεθ᾽ ἡμῶν· Εἷς Κύριος, μία πίστις, ἓν βάπτισμα. Εἰ τὰ ἐκείνων καλῶς γίνεται, τὰ ἡμέτερα κακῶς· εἰδὲ τὰ ἡμέτερα καλῶς, τὰ ἐκείνων κακῶς."

"one body, and one Spirit, even as ye are called in one hope of your calling; One Lord, one faith, one baptism, One God and Father of all, who is above all, and through all, and in you all" (Eph. 4:4–6). Differences in doctrine preclude unity in faith and unity of faith is a precondition for unity in the mysteries.

As St. John Chrysostom says elsewhere in his commentary on the above quoted words of the Apostle Paul: "For this is unity of faith: that we are all one, when we all understand the bond [of faith] in the same way."[561] All things are held in common in the Church—our faith, our hope, our love: "And all that believed were together, and had all things common" (Acts 2:44). As St. Maximus the Confessor has written, the Church is a type and image of God. Just as God holds all creation together in unity, the Church brings together all of the faithful into one unity in accordance with the one grace and calling of faith.[562]

Unity of faith is not expressed in a vague communion in the Gospel but in the manifest unity of the mysteries. The fact that the Orthodox Church does not allow the uninitiated and heterodox to partake of the food of incorruption, because he will "eat eternal condemnation as punishment,"[563] testifies that the unity of the faithful in the one faith is fashioned in the unity of the mysteries: "This bond uniting the faithful is engendered by Baptism, sanctified by Chrismation, and nourished and made to grow by Holy Communion. This is why only those who

561. On Ephesians, 11.3, PG 62.83.10: "Τοῦτο γάρ ἐστιν ἑνότης πί-στεως, ὅταν πάντες ἓν ὦμεν, ὅταν πάντες ὁμοίως τὸν σύνδεσμον [τῆς πίστεως] ἐπιγινώσκωμεν."

562. Cf. *Mystagogy*, 24, PG 91.705B. See also Hieromonk Gregorios, *The Divine Liturgy: A Commentary in the Light of the Fathers* (Mount Athos: Cell of St. John the Theologian. 2009), 260.

563. *Apostolic Constitutions*, 7.25, PG 1.1017B.

belong to the unity of the faith can take their places at the Mystical Supper. . . . Those who do not participate in the Truth cannot participate in the Life. Those who do not participate in the unity of the faith cannot enter into the communion of the Holy Spirit: 'Our faith is in accordance with the Eucharist, and the Eucharist confirms our faith.'[564] The common Cup presupposes a common faith."[565]

In the same vein, we must also say that just as a common faith is presupposed for the common cup, a common faith is also presupposed for a common Baptism.

It is within this context and this understanding of the one faith that unites that we ought to read these words of Saint Gregory Palamas: "Those who are of Christ's Church, are of the truth; those who are found to be not of the truth, neither are they of Christ's church."[566] This is so because "the Truth is no less than the whole Person of Christ the Theanthropos."[567] Therefore, to be "of the Truth" is not to hold true teachings or confess aspects of the true faith alone. To be "of the Truth" is to be a member of the Truth, the Body of Christ, to be in communion in the mysteries with the Truth, Who is Christ Himself. Truth is a Person with Whom we are in communion in the Church. No amount of true ideas can be held that would suffice

564. St. Irenaeus, *Against Heresies*, 4.18.5.

565. Hieromonk Gregorios, *The Divine Liturgy: A Commentary in the Light of the Fathers*, 260.

566. Ἀναίρεσις γράμματος Ἰγνατίου, 3, στή σειρά Π. Χρήστου, Γρηγορίου τοῦ Παλαμᾶ συγγράματα, τομ. Γ΄, Θεσσαλονίκη, 1983, 608: "Καί γάρ οἱ τῆς τοῦ Χριστοῦ ἐκκλησίας τῆς ἀληθείας εἰσί· καί οἱ μή τῆς ἀληθείας ὄντες οὐδὲ τῆς τοῦ Χριστοῦ ἐκκλησίας εἰσί."

567. Archimandrite Justin Popovich, *The Orthodox Church and Ecumenism*, trans. Benjamin Emmanuel Stanley (Birmingham: Lazarica Press, 2000), 28.

to put one in this communion. One must not simply believe in Christ, he must acquire Him, or, rather, be made one of His own members.

The criterion of the Truth, of the Faith, is not one or another aspect of the Holy Tradition, but the unity of Tradition. As Fr. Alexander Schmemann has written, Tradition includes the whole teaching and whole life of the Church, such that:

> The true sign and condition of the unity of all the [local] Churches, that is of the whole Catholic Church, is the unity of Tradition, which is that adequate interpretation of the Church's eschatological fullness *which alone permits us to comprehend and manifest our unity, not merely to believe in it but to possess it.* This is the unity in Truth, in real and objective Truth, not merely in a pale, relative and "historical" expression of it. (The whole Church says "we have the mind of Christ" and "not I, but Christ liveth in me.") And for this reason its Tradition, its faith and its Truth, received and witnessed by the Holy Spirit, are the true expression of its unity. *Our unity in Christ cannot be otherwise manifested by us than in this "unity of faith and love"* and it is thus that St. Ignatius of Antioch defines the Church. The eschatological unity of the Church, its identity in time and space, *is manifested in the actual historical and visible unity of faith;* and the criterion of this faith is, again, the historical tradition of the Church."[568]

There is no other "unity in faith" possible, no other "communion in the Gospel," except that manifested in the actu-

---

568. Fr. Alexander Schmemann, "Unity, Division, Reunion in the Light of Orthodox Ecclesiology," address given at the Annual Conference of the Fellowship of St. Alban and St. Sergius at Abingdon, England, in August 1950 (Θεολογία, ΚΒ), 243–54 (emphasis added).

al historical and visible unity of Faith. This unity of faith is manifested in "the full Catholic agreement of all the Churches; through this agreement each Church knows the others as it does itself, and in the others it knows the One Catholic Church" (ibid.). Only when there is total agreement in faith can one Church recognize the mysteries of another Church as its own and as those of the Church universal. Hence, the faith is always universal and complete, the faith of the Apostles, of the Fathers, and unity is always visible, the unity of the One Catholic Church throughout the earth (ibid.).

Without dogmatic agreement as the criterion of ecclesiality, of recognizing another church as the same Church, the One Church, the external unity of the Church does not express her ontological unity. For this reason, the Orthodox Church could never develop, as did Vatican II, a positive re-evaluation of heresy and schism. Recognition of unity can only come by way of dogmatic unity, "not a certain artificially defined dogmatic minimum, but an integration of the 'historical fullness' of Tradition—that very fullness and genuine catholicity of the Church's experience which both Fathers and Councils were able to express" (ibid.).

This fullness is precisely what every heresy and schism lacks, making the establishment of unity on any level impossible. This fullness cannot be simply acquired; it must also be received, for it is a given fullness, a revealed fullness. One can only be united to this already existing fullness when he sheds doctrinal inconsistencies that block his road to dogmatic unity. "Dogmatic unity is impossible without a measure of doctrinal unity. Dogmatic unity is the beginning of an endless growth into the fullness of unity . . ." (ibid.). This means that dogmatic unity is the criterion, the demarcation line, determining the presence of unity. Without it, no unity is possible. Outside dogmatic unity there can be many instances of doctrinal convergence without there being any true unity in faith and love, in the Holy Spirit, in the Church. This stands in contrast to the heart of the new ecclesiology of Vatican II that claims an "incomplete communion" can be established in Christ with those outside the fullness of unity in the faith. "Neither apostolic succession, nor the episcopate, nor the sacraments can in themselves be recognized as the foundation of unity, but only that faith of the Church manifested in tradition" (ibid.).

The Orthodox Faith, which has "established the universe,"[569] is the faith that is presupposed for Baptism to be the one Baptism. The faith of the Church is an expression of the life of the Church, and this life cannot be lived in division, cannot be experienced incompletely, for it is a personal experience of that unity of the faith once delivered to the saints.

Main Characteristics of Two Ecclesiologies

Vatican II	Orthodox
Communio	Eucharistic
Baptism basis of *communio*	Eucharist alone basis
Outside of Eucharistic Synaxis the Church *exists*	Outside of the Eucharistic Synaxis there is *no Church*
Full/Partial communion	Full, no partial communion
Whole-parts/Universal	Whole-Whole/Eucharist-local
Unity expressed in degrees	Unity expressed as Identity
Elements realized in separation	Elements not ecclesiastical in separation
Truth an idea had by measure	Truth as a Person indivisible
Baptism=initiation, no return	Repentance and return

569. Συνοδικὸν τῆς Ὀρθοδοξίας §15.

14

RESSOURCEMENT OR RENOVATION?

Vatican II and the ecclesiology it put forward in *Lumen Gentium* and *Unitatis Redintegratio* are widely held to be the fruit of a return to the sources (*ressourcement*) by twentieth-century Latin theologians.[570] This claim, as it pertains to ecclesiology, is shown to be vacuous. If the council actually effected a return to the sources in some other ways, it consciously avoided doing so in areas that were pivotal for the new ecumenical opening inaugurated at Vatican II.

As we have learned, a return to the patristic consensus regarding the mysteries of schismatics and heretics, or even to the unique views of Blessed Augustine, did not occur. Rather, the opposite took place: the Augustianian ecclesial exclusivity, a point he shared with the entire Tradition of the Church, was overturned. Following Congar and Bea, the council chose to build its new ecclesiology on the basis of a common Baptism— a view of the Baptism of non–Roman Catholics that was itself based upon the Thomistic idea of "baptismal character," which was in turn a distortion of Augustine's meaning of the term. In *Unitatis Redintegratio*, the Baptism of non–Roman Catholics is not simply "valid," it is also efficacious; that is, the Holy Spirit is understood to be present and active in it, uniting the baptized with the Body of Christ. Upon this efficaciousness of

570. See, for example, John W. O'Malley, *What Happened at Vatican II* (Cambridge, MA: Harvard University Press, 2008), 301.

schismatic or heretical baptism, seen as a work of the Holy Spirit, the entire edifice of the new ecclesiology was built—a view of the Church that would be unrecognizable to the Fathers of the Church.

A remarkable example of the failure to implement *ressourcement* at Vatican II was the council's acceptance of a slightly altered sixteenth-century theory from one of the leaders of the Reformation as one of the cornerstones of its new ecclesiology. As we have shown, the crucial idea of "ecclesiological elements" being present outside the Church, and thus making the Church fruitfully present among the schismatics and heretics, has its origins in a creative development on the part of Yves Congar of John Calvin's *vestigia ecclesiae*.[571] Such an idea was unknown to the early Church, for even Blessed Augustine, who allowed for "validity" and external marks of the Church to exist among the heterodox, nevertheless categorically denied spiritual profit from these unless and until there was a return to unity in the Church. Once again, on this crucial point, Vatican II was not a return to the patristic vision of the Church, but rather a further step away from it.

Since the aim of the council was to create an ecclesiology that would be inclusive, it likewise avoided a return to the "narrow" confines of the Pauline and patristic meaning of "members" of the Body. As Cardinal Ratzinger wrote rather frankly, the reason was quite simply to broaden the meaning of belonging to the Church.[572] If, however, as Ratzinger and Kasper maintain,

---

571. See John Calvin, *Institutes of the Christian Religion* 4 (1559 ed.), chap. 2, nos. 11–12; and Yves M.-J. Congar, *Divided Christendom, A Catholic Study of the Problem of Reunion,* trans. M. A. Bousfield (London: Geoffrey Bles: The Centenary Press, 1939), 224–48.

572. Cardinal Joseph Ratzinger, "The Ecclesiology of Vatican II," a talk given at the Pastoral Congress of the Diocese of Aversa, Italy, September 15, 2001.

ressourcement was truly one of the driving forces of the council, why would the very scriptural and Pauline meaning of "member" be abandoned? Why would the council fathers prefer the non-scriptural, non-patristic idea of "elements" or "multiple internal ties" to the scriptural and patristic vision of unity as based not only on a common Baptism, but in the Eucharist and in the unity of faith manifested in full catholic agreement of all the Churches? From the Orthodox patristic perspective, a true reclaiming of the Pauline ecclesiology of the Body of Christ, even if meant as a corrective to certain distortions introduced "on the road" of history or as a response to the ecumenical challenge, could not take the form of a redefinition of membership—even if this referred only to the "separated brethren." The Body of Christ, and membership within it, is "the same yesterday, and today and forever" (Heb. 13:8).

The option of changing or broadening the meaning of belonging to the Church is not open to the contemporary Church, for the Orthodox Church of today is the one and same Church of the Holy Fathers. All that is needed to confront and understand contemporary heterodoxy has been provided in the New Testament and writings of the Church Fathers, who provided us with the criteria and with God-pleasing examples. No new situation could precipitate an abandoning or superceding of the Holy Fathers' criteria, for "there is no new thing under the sun" (Ecc. 1:9).

Among the theologians that shaped Vatican II, however, a different view prevailed—a view of the diachronicity of the Church's Tradition that undermines a return to the sources. Shortly after the council, Fr. Ratzinger wrote: "The ecumenical movement grew out of a situation unknown to the New Testament and for which the New Testament can therefore offer no guidelines."[573] And, in his book *The Open Circle: The Meaning of Christian Brotherhood*, published shortly after the council, Ratzinger wrote that because neither the Fathers nor the New Testament provide guidance on how to conceive the relationship of Protestant "churches" to the Catholic Church, fresh thinking is needed "in the spirit of the New Testament."[574]

Ressourcement, apparently, has its limits, ending at the boundary where ecumenical suitability begins. The ease with which Ratzinger felt free to blaze new ecclesiological trails was also apparent in our chapter 7, dedicated to comparing Yves Congar's approach to that of Blessed Augustine. It may be that the idea of a "development of doctrine" is also connected to this particularly unpatristic view that exempts contemporary theologians from being "followers of the Holy Fathers" (ἑπόμενοι τοῖς ἁγίοις Πατράσιν).[575]

If the thinking of this man who was later to become Pope is accepted as representative of the approach of the council fathers as a whole, there appears to be a convergence of opinion with certain Russian Orthodox émigré theologians who were said to recognize the ecumenical movement as "an ontologically new phenomenon in Christian history requiring a deep rethinking and re-evaluation of Orthodox ecclesiology as shaped during the 'non-ecumenical' era."[576] There is, indeed, evidence

573. Cardinal Joseph Ratzinger, *Theological Highlights of Vatican II* (New York: Paulist Press, 2009), 112.

574. Cardinal Joseph Ratzinger, *The Open Circle: The Meaning of Christian Brotherhood*, trans. W. A. Glen-Doeple (New York: Sheed and Ward, 1966), 125.

575. *Concilium universale Chalcedonense anno 451* 2,1,2.129.23.

576. This is how Fr. Alexander Schmemann described the approach of certain Russian theologians to the phenomenon of the ecumenical movement and to the nature of Orthodox participation in it. Father

that certain key theologians of the council were significantly influenced by these theologians. Bishop Christopher Butler cites the views of P. Evdokimov, and in particular the following passage, as being a true expression of the council's ecclesiological stance: "We know where the Church is; it is not for us to . . . say where the Church is not."[577] This sort of apophatic, almost

Schmemann included as representatives of the above mentioned view such Russian émigré theologians as Sergius Bulgakov, Leo Zander, Nicholas Zernov, and Pavel Evdokimov. See Alexander Schmemann, *Russian Theology, 1920–1965* (Richmond: Union Theological Seminary in Virginia, 1969), 190–91, as quoted by Andrew Blane in *Georges Florovsky, Russian Intellectual and Orthodox Churchman* (New York: St. Vladimir's Seminary Press, 1993), 125. See also *Divine Ascent, A Journal of Orthodox Faith*, 1:2 (1997) (Monastery of St. John of Shanghai and San Francisco, Pt. Reyes, CA.), 43ff. Interestingly, Yves Congar's assessment of these theologians' views (Congar cites Zander and Nicholas Berdiaev in particular) is very similar to that of Fr. Schmemann. In his work *Divided Christendom, A Catholic Study of the Problem of Reunion*, trans. M. A. Bousfield (London: Geoffrey Bles: The Centenary Press, 1939), Fr. Congar writes that they see the new ecumenical reality justifying new activities that are open to the Holy Spirit and "not reducible to ecclesiastical categories hitherto prevailing" (138).

577. P. Evdokimov, *L'Orthodoxie* (Neuchatel: Delachaux et Niestlé, 1959), 343, as quoted in Christopher Butler, *The Theology of Vatican II* (London: Darton, Longman and Todd, 1967; rev. ed. 1981). Evdokimov also states, as cited by Butler, that "the non-Orthodox, considered from the point of view of their denominational allegiance, are no longer in the Orthodox Church; but for all their separation, the Church continues to be present and to act in presence of their faith and their correct intention of salvation" (as quoted in Christopher Butler, *The Idea of the Church* [Baltimore: Helicon Press, 1962]). Evdokimov was an official observer at Vatican II and had personal contact with those theologians who shaped the new ecclesiology. Bishop Kallistos Ware echoes these words of Evdokimov in his book *The Orthodox Church*: "Many people may be members of the Church who are not visibly so; invisible bonds may exist despite outward separation. The Spirit of God blows where

agnostic, approach to ecclesiology was especially appealing to Roman Catholics, many of whom felt confined by the one-dimensional juridical view of the Church and were eager for ecumenical elbow room for their labors.[578]

Yves Congar, the council's preeminent ecclesiologist, was also greatly influenced by Russian émigré theologians. His views on ecumenicity, catholicity, and fullness—much of which passed directly into the texts of Vatican II—were decisively influenced by, if not wholly taken from, Nicholas Berdiaev. Berdiaev "distinguished an ecumenical Church—that would have the fullness of the truth—from the Orthodox Church as a denomination, bearing necessarily the marks of human limitation. From this perspective," in Berdiaev's view, "the Orthodox Church is truer than the others, but its truth will remain incomplete until the fullness of the ecumenical Church is accomplished in and beyond it—beyond its present narrow denominational limits."[579] This is very similar to the reasoning that

it will, and, as Irenaeus said, where the Spirit is, there is the Church. We know where the Church is but we cannot be sure where it is not; and so we must refrain from passing judgment. . . ." Timothy Ware [Bishop Kallistos of Diokleia], *The Orthodox Church* (London: Penguin, 1997), 308.

578. It is possible that the influence was reciprocal for some, for no less notable a theologian than Vladimir Lossky also maintained a position in some ways identical to that expressed in LG and UR. In the introduction to an article on the Church by the Patriarch Sergius of Moscow, Lossky wrote that, "there is only one true Church, the sole bestower of sacramental grace; but there are several ways of being separated from that one true Church, and *varying degrees of diminishing ecclesial reality outside* its visible limits." Vladimir Lossky, introductory note to the article of Patriarch Sergius of Moscow, "L'Église du Christ et les communautés dissidentes," *Messager de l'Exarchat du Patriarche Russe en Europe Occidentale* 21 (Paris, 1955), 9–10 (emphasis added).

579. Joseph Famerée, "Orthodox Influence on the Roman Catholic

Congar went on to apply to the Roman Catholic Church and that passed into the conciliar decrees. As Joseph Famarée summarized Congar's view, "this is the very Church, it is catholic, but it is not yet fully or perfectly catholic."[580] *Unitatis Redintegratio* states the same idea in a slightly different way: "the divisions among Christians prevent the Church from attaining the fullness of catholicity proper to her, in those of her sons who, though attached to her by Baptism, are yet separated from full communion with her" (UR 4J).

It is ironic and tragic that precisely when the dead end of Scholasticism and Tridentine Catholicism came into sight and a beginning of a return to the Fathers was being made, those Orthodox who were sought out for counsel did not guide them to the *consensus patrum* but were, in part, a source for further innovation.

Theologian Yves Congar, O.P.," *St. Vladimir's Theological Quarterly* 39 (1995), 412–13. Congar cites Berdiaev's work *Esprit et liberté, Essai de philosophie chrétienne* (Paris, Ed. Je sers, 1933) as the source for this view.

580. Famerée, 413.

III

A Summary and Conclusion

SUMMARY
OF AN ORTHODOX EXAMINATION

I n sum, we have seen that the roots of the Latin development of the doctrine of Baptism and the Church reach
back into the first centuries of the Church, in particular to
the third century when controversy arose between Pope Stephen and St. Cyprian of Carthage concerning heretical Baptism. Pope Stephen held the minority view, which supposed a
mystery of the Church, Baptism, could be possessed—if only
partially—outside the unity of the Faith and Church. This
fundamental divergence from the patristic consensus—which
refused to recognize any mystery not of the Church to be of
Christ—was to remain a cornerstone of Latin ecclesiology until
and after Vatican II. And, yet, the consequences of Rome's view
were deferred as long as it maintained, together with the entire Church, that the Holy Spirit (as purifying and sanctifying
energy) was not at work among the schismatics and heretics.

Blessed Augustine can be said to be the father of Latin sacramental theology and in particular the peculiar divorce of the
theology of the sacraments from the theology of the Church.
The North African bishop's penchant for reducing the mystery
to a consideration of "validity" was to become the foundation
for a general sacramental minimalism during the centuries following the Great Schism. And, yet, in spite of his peculiar innovations, Augustine, like Pope Stephen, held that, even though
schismatics and heretics could possess the external signs of
the Church, they did not possess the Holy Spirit as long as

they remained outside the unity of the Church. On this particularly important point for ecclesiology—a point Augustine shared with the entire Church Tradition—Rome officially broke ranks in its seventeenth-century condemnation of Jansenism, thus taking one giant step away from the *consensus patrum* and toward the new ecclesiology.

It would, therefore, be a flagrant error to suppose (as one leading Orthodox ecumenical officer has done) that with *Unitatis Redintegratio* Rome returned to its roots in Blessed Augustine. Although Augustine's views on grace, freedom, and a whole host of other issues dominated Western theology for centuries, it was not until after the Great Schism that his innovative views on the sacraments and the Church came to dominate theological thought in the West—only to be selectively rejected, as in the case of the Jansenist condemnation.

Yet, in one respect directly bearing on our examination of Baptism—the meaning he attributed to "baptismal character"—Augustine's innovative views were distorted by Thomas Aquinas and the subsequent Scholastic tradition. This Thomistic redefinition proved crucial in the formation of Rome's view of membership in the Church.

Long before that, however, important diversions from the *consensus patrum* took place during the centuries immediately following the Great Schism—changes that combined to shape the Latin view of Baptism. The teaching that even an unbeliever, in case of need, could baptize was given institutional weight at the Lateran and Florence councils. The abandonment of immersion as the normal form of Baptism and its replacement by affusion likewise received weighty theological support from Thomas Aquinas during this same period. During the centuries following the schism, in the West the unity of the mysteries was shattered in practice such that an infant was baptized but neither chrismated nor communed until years later. From the Middle Ages until our own day, the West has experienced initiation into the life of the Church as Baptism (or, rather, affusion) alone. All of these innovations combined to set the stage for viewing Baptism in a legalistic, minimalistic light, as an autonomous, almost magical, rite of initiation separate from the unity of faith.

This state of things, lasting for many centuries, led to the most critical stage in the history of the development of the view of Baptism presented in *Unitatis Redintegratio:* the seventeenth to nineteenth centuries. This was a period when the Thomistic idea of "baptismal character" was elevated as determinative for Church membership. A string of misinterpretations of what constituted membership in the Church would lead finally to Canon 87 of the 1917 Code of Canon Law. This canon is based upon a brief of Pope Benedict XIV, who drew in turn from the Jesuit theologian Francisco Suárez, who likewise drew from Augustine's treatise on Baptism. The process of disintegration we have described with regard to the rites of initiation is fully apparent in the theology of initiation and membership expressed in this canon. For Augustine, membership was located within the threefold unity of faith, Baptism, and "Catholic peace" or Church unity. For Suárez, who refers back to Augustine but misunderstands him, it was faith, righteousness, and baptismal character. For Benedict XIV, referring back to Suárez, the criterion for Church membership had been reduced to baptismal character, depending only upon "the proper form and matter" (validity). This minimalistic and legalistic idea of Church membership came to serve as a basis for the views of the twentieth-century theologians behind *Unitatis Redintegratio*, including most notably Yves Congar and Cardinal Bea.

If, however, Augustine's total understanding of sacrament and character is held in view, Congar, and Vatican II after him, not only ignored Augustine's teaching—they inverted it. In *Unitatis Redintegratio,* one who is manifestly separated from the unity of the Church can, by way of an external sign, gain an internal, spiritual reality that unites him to the Church internally, invisibly, though not externally. For Augustine it was possible outside the unity of the Church to gain an external sign of belonging to the Church without there being any internal, spiritual reality accompanying this sign, and therefore without the spiritual reality of unity. On this most crucial point, Vatican II clearly chose not to return to the patristic sources, or even to Augustine, but to remain with and further develop ecclesiologically the idea of membership connected with Aquinas' understanding of "baptismal character."

Thus, on the eve of the council, a majority of Latin theologians had arrived at a new consensus that, on the strength of certain elements, first of all which was Baptism, non–Roman Catholics participated, on different levels, in the life of the Church. During the assembly this consensus favoring a graduated participation in the life of the Church became the basis for the setting forth of a full-fledged, new ecclesiology in the final texts of the council. Changes were made to key aspects of Rome's self-understanding and consideration of the dissidents as well—changes whose roots may be traced back to the long disintegration of the rites of initiation and theology of Baptism.

As part of the ecumenical overture and the drive to be inclusive of the heterodox in the mystery of the Church, Vatican II accepted the idea that the Roman Church is not the entirety of the Body of Christ, but only a part of it. This is evident in the abandonment of the simple identification of the Roman Church with the Church of Christ and the introduction of the famous phrase "The One Church of Christ . . . subsists in the Catholic Church." It is also apparent, however, in the distinction between "full" and "incomplete" communion and the recognition of "ecclesial elements" outside the Church—ideas fundamental to the new ecclesiology. This idea that, on the strength of ecclesial elements held in common, the "separated brethren" are not only in partial communion with the Roman Church, but, in fact, form a part of the universal Church, even if somehow in a degraded fashion, is largely based upon the acceptance of a "common Baptism."

The image of the Church that emerges in *Unitatis Redintegratio* and *Lumen Gentium* is a peculiar two-tiered Church, with two kinds of Baptism, or two results from the one Baptism. According to *Unitatis Redintegratio*, those who possess Baptism alone, without the reality of the Eucharist (which would mean most Protestants), are "truly incorporated" into the Body of Christ in Baptism without, however, sharing in the Blood of Christ in the Eucharist. For those who are considered to possess a "valid" Eucharist because they possess apostolic succession, which includes the Orthodox, even though they are truly partakers of the Body and Blood of Christ they are still "wounded," lacking not the fullness of Christ but the fullness of communion with His Vicar, the Supreme Pontiff.

This image of the Church, however, and in particular, such an idea of Baptism with such results, is unthinkable for the Holy Fathers and the Orthodox Church. Those who are initiated into Christ are intiated into His Fullness, which is His Body. Can a Baptism not consummated in the Eucharist rightly be called Holy Baptism? And can those who participate in the Eucharist, which is the perfection of communion with Christ and among the Faithful, as Rome grants that the Orthodox do, be said to lack anything?

The state of incomplete communion described in *Unitatis Redintegratio*—a communion based on "elements" and outside the unity of Faith—has no precedent or place in the Church. It stands in direct contradiction of the letter and spirit of Holy Scripture and the mind of Christ as clearly presented by the Apostle Paul. Communion in Christ means to hold Him, or be held by Him, in common: "we, being many, are one body in Christ, and every one members one of another" (Rom. 12:5). Unity in Christ means to be in the same "space" with Him, that is, to be in Him, as members of His Body. As the proponents of the new ecclesiology themselves admitted when avoiding the term "member" as inconvenient, there can be no "incomplete members" of Christ, "from whom the whole body fitly joined together and compacted by that which every joint supplieth, according to the effectual working in the measure of every part, maketh increase of the body unto the edifying of itself in love" (Eph. 4:16). There is no incomplete union or communion in the Church because the Church is fullness, the Church is "his body, the fulness of him that filleth all in all" (Eph. 1:23).

There cannot be two different realms of ecclesial possibilities, or two different classes of the baptized, for "in one Spirit are we all baptized into one body" (1 Cor. 12:13). There cannot be two different kinds of communion or unity in Christ—one full and another incomplete, for we "are all one in Christ Jesus" (Gal. 3:28). There are not two different kinds of churches or bodies of Christians within the One Church—one that is by the will of God and another that is not the express will of Christ, for the entire "church is subject unto Christ" (Eph. 5:24), Who sanctifies and cleanses "that he might present it to himself a glorious church, not having spot, or wrinkle, or any such thing; but that it should be holy and without blemish" (Eph. 5:27).

The Church is one, and her unity is both vertical and horizontal, with God and among men, with the Holy Fathers of the past and the Christians of the last time. This unity encompasses only those who are communicants of the life-giving energy of the Holy Trinity. As St. Nicholas Cabasilas has written, this unity is made manifest in the mysteries—each one separately and all of them together. The unity of the mysteries and of the mystical life in Christ means that participation in the Holy Trinity's life-giving and salvific energy is not given once and for all by Baptism. For not only is initiation into this life-giving energy not by Baptism alone, but our continued sojourning in the Body as Spirit-bearers requires the continual forming of Christ within, through communion in the immaculate mysteries of the Eucharist.

From all that this study has striven to present, we believe it should be clear that the theory of baptismal unity presented in *Unitatis Redintegratio* is incompatible with the ecclesiology of the Holy Fathers. This conclusion has been borne out in the many examples we've cited both from *Unitatis Redintegratio* and commentary on it by leading Latin theologians and from the patristic witness of both the early and the contemporary Church.

Pillars of the New Ecclesiology

- ❧ Holy Spirit given and sanctifies in schismatical/heretical bodies

- ❧ Schism-heresy no longer applicable

- ❧ Schismatical/heretical bodies recognized as churches and ecclesiastical communities

- ❧ Church now includes all "baptized," who participate by degrees

- ❧ Distinction of full communion and incomplete communion

- ❧ Confession of orthodox faith no longer necessary in order to belong to the Church

CONCLUSION

THE ORTHODOX RESPONSE TO THE
THEOLOGICAL CHALLENGE BEFORE US

In undertaking this examinination of the new approach to schismatic and heretical baptism taken by Vatican II's Decree on Ecumenism and its importance for the formation of the council's new ecclesiology, we have sought to understand not only what the conciliar document intended to say but how and why the council arrived at such a vision of Baptism and the Church. We have shown that the new ecclesiology embraced by this council is not at all a return to the patristic vision of the Church, but rather an innovation and further departure from it. In particular, one of the main pillars of the new ecclesiology—the recognition, on the basis of a valid and efficacious baptism, of the "ecclesiality" of confessions traditionally labelled schisms or heresies—has been shown to be incompatible not only with the patristic ecclesiology of the early Church (Ss. Ignatius, Irenaeus, Cyprian, et al.) but also with the recently expounded "eucharistic ecclesiology."

It is a fundamental presupposition of the Holy Fathers that the unity of the Church is unity in the Eucharist, never apart from it. All unity "in Christ," whether between men or between local churches, is unity in the Eucharist. All mysteries, including, first of all, Holy Baptism, exist and are experienced and made effective within the mystery of the Church, within the Eucharistic Synaxis. The mystery of the Incarnation, the mystery of the Church, the mystery of the Eucharist, and all of the

holy mysteries are, in the final analysis, inseparable, as expressing the One Mystery of Christ. Consequently, there can be no
"differentiated participation" in the Church as proposed by the
theologians of the Vatican Council, for all participation takes
place within the context of the Eucharist. Participation in the
life of the Church presupposes unity, and unity presupposes
identity, that of Christ, since ecclesiastical unity is "in Christ."

In the Nicene-Constantinople Symbol of Faith, proclaimed
at every Divine Liturgy, Orthodox Christians confess their faith
"in One, Holy, Catholic and Apostolic Church." This confession
of faith in the Church follows confession of faith in the Holy
Trinity and precedes confession of one Baptism. In this context,
the Doctrine of the Church as the Body of Christ, the human
nature which man "puts on" in Baptism, is understood to be
no mere metaphor, but the very foundation of the Orthodox
concept of salvation.

It follows, then, that by introducing a new ecclesiology in
the conciliar documents *Lumen Gentium* and *Unitatis Redintegratio*, an ecclesiology at variance with the Orthodox confession
of Faith, the Second Vatican Council has not simply added another peculiar teaching of secondary importance, but, indeed, a
new dogma, or rather heresy. For, every new dogmatic teaching, including a new teaching as to the nature of the Church,
the Body of Christ—a teaching not in agreement with the two-
thousand-year-old experience and Tradition of the Church—
necessarily constitutes heresy, a belief that is totally alien to the
Faith.

It is our conviction that, seen in its proper historical and
theological context, the new image of the Church revealed in
the ecclesiological texts of Vatican II is the last in a long line
of steps away from the patristic consensus, if not, indeed, a
"second Reformation" of the Roman Church, this time serving

to bring Rome closer to Protestantism. Yet, the consequences of the new ecclesiology are not limited to the theological mileu of Catholicism and Protestantism. In this age of ecumenism, Orthodox theology has also clearly been affected.

Indeed, the implications of the new ecclesiology are immense for Orthodox participation in the ecumenical movement and the international theological dialogue with Roman Catholicism. That the Orthodox participants in the Joint International Commission for Theological Dialogue Between the Catholic Church and the Orthodox Church have not only seen no need to examine, let alone address, this new departure from the Faith, but have rather reduced the ecclesiological question to one of primacy, reveals the dire state of our witness in this regard.

It is in fact remarkable that, although fifty years have passed since the conciliar texts were promulgated, the bibliography of Orthodox critical examinations spans less than half a page. Not only have Orthodox theologians and bishops failed to provide a critique of the new ecclesiology from the Orthodox perspective (with very few exceptions), but highly placed representatives of the Church have adopted and expressed aspects of it as if it were in harmony with Orthodox dogma. Noted Orthodox theologians and hierarchs have written and spoken of the Church and Her Baptism in terms nearly identical to those used in the texts of Vatican II and contemporary Roman Catholic theology.

The joint agreement reached at Balamand, the various "common baptism" agreements signed by representatives in America, Germany, and Australia that recognize the baptisms of the heterodox per se, and increased discussion of a "divided church," understood to include both the Orthodox Church and Roman Catholicism, are all examples of the slow adoption among some Orthodox of the essentials of the new ecclesiology.

The new ecclesiological convergence centers in the acceptance of a Church divided in time. It might be characterized as ecclesiological Nestorianism, in which the Church is divided into two separate beings: on the one hand the Church in heaven, outside of time, alone true and whole; on the other, the Church, or rather "churches," on earth, in time, deficient and relative, lost in history's shadows, seeking to draw near to one another and to that transcendent perfection, as much as is possible given the weakness of the impermanent human will.

In this ecclesiology, the tumultuous and injurious divisions of human history have overcome the Church "in time." The human nature of the Church, being divided and rent asunder, has been separated from the Theanthropic Head. This is a Church on earth deprived of its ontological nature and not "one and holy," no longer possessing all the truth through its hypostatic union with the divine nature of the Logos.

"Baptismal theology" and the new ecclesiology are examples of succumbing to the temptation to lower the high bar of Church unity to a minimum of the least common elements and to forge an ecclesiology of inclusiveness that embraces falsehood.

We espouse the views of Fr. Georges Florovsky, although written decades before the Second Vatican Council, for they are applicable not only to theology of Reform Protestantism but also to the new ecclesiology of Papal Protestantism. Hidden behind the new image of the Church presented in *Unitatis Redintegratio* and *Lumen Gentium* is:

> a unique church-historic Docetism, an insensitivity toward reality and the *fullness* of Divine Revelation in the world, an insensitivity to the mystery of the Church, a misunderstanding of its profound natural nature. Indeed, not only mystically, but also historically, division in

faith always appeared through schism and falling away, through separation from the Church. The single path of their redefinition is the path of *re*unification or return, and *not union*. One might say that the discordant "creeds" in general are not unified, for each is a self-enclosed whole. *In the Church a mosaic of different parts is impossible.* There stand opposite each other not "creeds" with equal rights, but the Church and the schism, united in spirit of opposition. It can be whole only through elimination, through a return to the Church. *There is no and can be no "partial" Christianity*—"can it be Christ was divided?"(1 Cor. 1:13). There is only One, Holy, Catholic, Apostolic Church—a single Father's House; and the believers, as St. Cyprian of Carthage said, "do not have any other home than the one Church."[581]

Whether one sees in it ecclesiological Nestorianism or church-historic Docetism, the new ecclesiology is, without doubt, at total odds with the Orthodox confession of faith in One, Holy, Catholic and Apostolic Church.

In conclusion, we return once again to the important examination of the ecclesiology of St. Ignatius of Antioch by Fr. John Romanides, which well describes the diachronic self-understanding of the Orthodox Church regarding all ecclesiastical unity as passing through the Eucharist:

> In sharp contrast to his spiritualistic adversaries, Ignatius presents a mysticism completely Christocentric and indeed Sarkocentric—only the flesh and blood of the res-

581. St. Cyprian, *De Catholicae Ecclesiae Unitate*, chap. 6, PL 4.502. Fr. Georges Florovsky, "The House of the Father," in *Ecumenism I: A Doctrinal Approach, Collected Works*, 1379 (emphasis added).

urrected God-man are the source of life and resurrection
of all men of all ages. (Ign. Eph. 1, 7, 19, 20; Mag. 6, 8;
Smyr. 1, 3; Pol. 3; Mag. 9; Phil. 5, 9.) The human nature
of God is none other than salvation itself—namely (1)
the restoration of immortality to those who partake cor-
porately in selfless love, (2) the justification of man by
the destruction of death and man's accuser and captor,
the devil, and (3) the granting of the power to defeat the
devil by struggling to attain to selfless love for God and
neighbor through the flesh of Christ. The Christocentric
and flesh-centered mysticism of Ignatius is not a simple
luxury of the more enthusiastically inclined, but on the
contrary *an absolute necessity for salvation, and constitutes
the very basis of his ecclesiology, which is indeed that of the
New Testament and ancient Church.*[582]

St. Ignatius is unequivocal that outside the Eucharist there
can be no unity in Christ. Pleading with his fellow Christians
some nineteen hundred years ago to hasten to unity of the
faith and unity in the Eucharist, outside of which there can be
no unity, he wrote: "Hasten, then, to come together frequently
for [the Eucharistic] thanksgiving to God and glorification. For
when you come together frequently, Satan's powers are de-
molished and his destructiveness is dissolved by your unity of
faith."[583] "Let no one deceive himself. If one is not within the
place of sacrifice (θυσιαστήριον) he is deprived of the bread of
God. . . . Therefore, he who does not assemble *epi to auto* [in
the eucharistic synaxis] is in pride and has already condemned
himself."[584]

582. John S. Romanides, "The Ecclesiology of St. Ignatius," *The Greek
Orthodox Theological Review* 7:1 and 2 (1961–62) (emphasis added).
583. St. Ignatius of Antioch, *Epistle to the Ephesians*, 13.
584. Ibid., 5.

The Church of Christ, as the Apostle Paul supremely defined it, is His body, the fullness of him that filleth all in all (ἐστὶν τὸ σῶμα αὐτοῦ, τὸ πλήρωμα τοῦ τὰ πάντα ἐν πᾶσιν πληρουμένου). The fullness of Christ is identified with the Body of Christ, which is, as Christ Himself when He walked on earth in time, as Theanthropos, visible and indivisible, being marked by divine-human characteristics.

As Vladimir Lossky has written, "all that can be asserted or denied about Christ can equally well be applied to the Church, inasmuch as it is a theandric organism."[585] It follows, then, that just as we could never assert that Christ is divided or that one could be His partially, incompletely, neither could we countenance the Church ever being divided (cf. 1 Cor 1:13) or participation in the Church being piecemeal. If some Orthodox were to accept the division of the Church, they would be accepting the nullification of the Incarnation and the salvation of the world. If such a departure from Orthodox faith and teaching is passively accepted by the pleroma of the Church, one can only expect the most dire consequences, not only for an Orthodox witness to the heterodox, but even for Orthodox unity. If contemporary Orthodox theology is to be consistent with the identity and self-understanding of the Orthodox Church as the One, Holy, Catholic and Apostolic Church, a reorientation and redirection of Orthodox engagement with the heterodox is absolutely necessary.

In particular:

1. A thorough examination of the so-called "baptismal theology" or "baptismal ecclesiology" espoused within Roman Catholicism, the World Council of Churches, and

585. Lossky, Vladimir, *The Mystical Theology of the Easter Church* (Crestwood, New York: St. Vladimir's Seminary Press, 1976), 187.

even by some Orthodox theologians is necessary on the basis of the centrality of the Eucharist to the unity of the Church.

2. It is necessary to further illuminate the historical path and theological evolution of the new ecclesiology, in order to clearly locate its theological origins in the post-schism West.

3. Likewise, further research is needed to clarify the nature and degree of departure of St. Augustine's ecclesiology from the patristic consensus before him, and also, the nature and degree of departure of Aquinas from St. Augustine's ecclesiology, especially as it pertains to the baptism of schismatics and heretics.

The new ecclesiology expressed in *Unitatis Redintegratio* is a spiritual and theological challenge of our day to which every Orthodox Christian remains indifferent to his own peril, for it carries with it soteriological consequences. In the face of a terribly divisive and deceptive heresy, we are all called to confess Christ today, as did our ancient forebears in the days of Arianism. Our confession of faith, however, is not only in His Person in the Incarnation, but His Person in the continuation of the Incarnation, the Church. To confess the faith today is to confess and declare the unity of His divine and human natures in His Body, the one and only Orthodox Church—"unmixed, unchanged, undivided and inseparable." [586]

---

586. From the Oros of the Fourth Ecumenical Council: "ἀσυγχύτως, ἀτρέπτως, ἀδιαιρέτως, ἀχωρίστως."

BIBLIOGRAPHY

Abbot, Walter M., S.J., general editor. *The Documents of Vatican II*. New York/Cleveland: Corpus Books, 1966.

Acta Synodalia Sacrosancti Concilii Oecumenici Vaticani II. Vatican City: Typis Polyglottis Vaticanis, 1962–1965.

Adam, Karl. *The Spirit of Catholicism*. New York: Macmillan, 1943; Crossroad, 1997.

Αγαπίου, Ιερομονάχου, και Μοναχού Νικοδήμου [Agapiou, Hiero-monk, and Monk Nikodemos]. Πηδάλιον [*Pedalion*]. Αθήνα: Κωνσταντίνου Γκαρπολά, 1841.

Amerio, Romano. *Iota Unum: A Study of Changes in the Catholic Church in the XXth Century*. Kansas City, MO: Sarto House, 1996.

The Apostolic Fathers. I Clement. II Clement. Ignatius. Polycarp. Didache. Barnabas (Greek text edition). Edited by Kirsopp Lake. Loeb Classical Library. New York: Macmillan, 1913; repr. 1997. Online at Christian Classics Ethereal Library: http://www.ccel.org/ccel/lake/fathers2.html.

Aquinas, Thomas. *Summa Theologica*. Part III. Second and Revised Edition. London/New York: Burns, Oates and Washburne, 1920.

Arenas, Sandra. "Merely Quantifiable Realities? The 'Vestigia Ecclesiae' in the Thought of John Calvin and Its Twentieth-Century Reception." Pp. 69–89 in *John Calvin's Ecclesiology: Ecumenical Perspectives*. Edited by Gerard Mannion and Eduardus Van der Borght. London: T & T Clark, 2011.

Αργέντη, Ευστράτιου [Argenti, Eustratios]. Εγχειρίδιον περί Βαπτίσματος καλούμενον χειραγωγία πλανωμένων [A Manual of Baptism, named a Guide to those in error]. Constantinople, 1756.

Arseniev, N. "The Second Vatican Council's 'Constitutio de Ecclesia'." *St. Vladimir's Theological Quarterly* 9 (1965), 21.

Athanasius the Great, Saint. *Second Discourse Against the Arians*. In *Nicene and Post-Nicene Fathers. Second Series*. Volume 4. Also in J. Migne, *Patrologia Graeca*. Volume 26.

Augustine. *Contra epistolam Parmeniani*, PL 43: 33-108.

Augustine. *De Correctione Donatistarum*, Online at Christian Classics Ethereal Library: http://www.ccel.org/ccel/schaff/npnf104.v.vi.i.html

Augustine. *On Baptism* [*De Baptismo*]. *Nicene and Post-Nicene Fathers. First Series*. Volume 4. Edited by Philip Schaff. Buffalo, NY: Christian Literature Publishing Co., 1887.

Augustine. *Tractates on the Gospel of John*. In *Nicene and Post-Nicene Fathers. First Series*. Volume 7. Online at: http://www.ccel.org/ccel/schaff/npnf107.toc.html.

"Australian Churches Covenanting Together." "Covenanting Document" of the National Council of Churches of Australia (2004). Online at: http://www.ncca.org.au/files/Departments/Faith_and_Unity/ Covenanting/2010_July_Australian_Churches_Covenanting_Together.pdf.

Bailey, Charles-James N. "Validity and Authenticity: The Difference between Western and Orthodox Views on Orders." *St. Vladimir's Theological Quarterly* 8 (1964).

Baptism, Eucharist and Ministry (Faith and Order Paper no. 111), 15 January 1982, Online at World Council of Churches: http://www.oikoumene.org/en/resources/documents/commissions/faith-and-order/i-unity-the-church-and-its-mission/baptism-eucharist-and-ministry-faith-and-order-paper-no-111-the-lima--text

Baptism and Sacramental Economy, An Agreed Statement of The North American Orthodox–Catholic Theological Consultation. St. Vladimir's Orthodox Seminary, Crestwood, New York, June 3, 1999.

Baum, Gregory, O.S.A. "The Ecclesial Reality of the Other Churches." In *The Church and Ecumenism* (New York: Paulist Press, 1965).

Bea, Augustin, Cardinal. *The Unity of Christians*. New York: Herder and Herder, 1961.

Becker, Karl. "The Teaching of Vatican II on Baptism: A Stimulus for Theology." In René Latourelle, editor, *Vatican II: Assessment and Perspectives, Twenty-five Years After (1962-1987)*. Volume 2. New York: Paulist Press, 1989.

Benedict XVI, Pope. *Joseph Ratzinger in Communio: Volume 1, The Unity of the Church: Ressourcement, Retrieval and Renewal in Catholic Thought*. Grand Rapids, MI: Eerdmans, 2010.

Benedict XVI, Pope. *See also* Ratzinger, Joseph.

Benson, E. W. *Cyprian, His Life, His Times, His Work*. London: Macmillan, 1897.

Best, Thomas. "Baptism Today: Showing Forth Our Unity in Christ." In *Baptism Today: Understanding, Practice, Ecumenical Implications*. Collegeville: WCC Publications, 2008.

Best, Thomas F., and Dagmar Heller, editors. *Becoming a Christian: The Ecumenical Implications of Our Common Baptism*. Faith and Order Paper 184. Geneva: WCC Publications, 1999.

Blane, Andrew. *Georges Florovsky: Russian Intellectual and Orthodox Churchman*. Crestwood, NY: Saint Vladimir's Seminary Press, 1997.

Bulman, Raymond F. "Introduction: The Historical Context." In *From Trent to Vatican II: Historical and Theological Investigations*. Edited by Raymond Bulman and Frederick J. Parrella. Oxford, UK: Oxford University Press, 2006.

Bulman, Raymond F. "Vatican Council II (1962–1965)." In *Encyclopedia of the Vatican and Papacy*. Edited by Frank J. Coppa. Westport, CT: Greenwood Press, 1999.

Butler, Christopher. *The Idea of the Church*. Baltimore: Helicon Press, 1962.

Butler, Christopher. *The Theology of Vatican II*. London: Darton, Longman and Todd, 1967; revised edition 1981.

Cabasilas, Nicholas, Saint. *A Commentary on the Divine Liturgy*, 38; PG 150.

Cabasilas, Nicholas, Saint. *The Life in Christ*. Crestwood, NY: St. Vladimir's Seminary Press, 1974.

Calvin, John. *Institutes of the Christian Religion* 4 (1559 edition). Peabody, MA: Hendrickson, 2007. Online at Christian Classics Ethereal Library: http://www.ccel.org/ccel/calvin/institutes.html.

Cary, Philip. *Outward Signs: The Powerlessness of External Things in Augustine's Thought*. Oxford, UK: Oxford University Press, 2008.

Cassidy, Edward Idris, Cardinal. *Ecumenism and Interreligious Dialogue: Unitatis Redintegratio, Nostra Aetate*. New York: Paulist Press, 2005.

Catechism of the Catholic Church. New York: Doubleday, 1997.

Catechism of the Council of Trent. Translated into English by Rev. J. Donovan. Baltimore: Lucas Brothers, 1829; CreateSpace Independent Publishing Platform, 2013.

Clement XI, Pope. *Unigenitus*. Encyclical *In Condemnation of the Errors of Paschasius Quesnel*. September 8, 1713.

Clendenin, Daniel. *Eastern Orthodox Theology*. Grand Rapids: Baker Academic, 2003.

Cohen, Will. "Sacraments and the Visible Unity of the Church." *Ecclesiology* 4:1 (2007).

Commentary on the Documents of Vatican II. Volume I2. London: Burns and Oates Limited, 1968.

Congar, Yves M.-J. *Dialogue between Christians: Catholic Contributions to Ecumenism*. Translated by Philip Loretz. London: Geoffrey Chapman, 1966.

Congar, Yves M.-J. *Divided Christendom, A Catholic Study of the Problem of Reunion* [Chrétiens désunis: principes d'un oecuménisme catholique]. Translated by M. A. Bousfield. Geoffrey Bles: The Centenary Press: London, 1939 [Paris: Cerf, 1937].

Congar, Yves M.-J. *A History of Theology*. Edited and translated by Hunter Guthrie. New York: Doubleday, 1968.

Congar, Yves M.-J. *Die Kirche als Volk Gottes*. Conc (D) 1 (1965): 5–16.

Congar, Yves M.-J. "A Last Look at the Council." Pp. 337–58 in *Vatican II by Those Who Were There*. Edited by Alberic Stacpoole. London: Geoffrey Chapman, 1986.

Congar, Yves M.-J. "My Path-findings in Theology of Laity and Ministries." *Jurist* 32 (1972).

Congar, Yves M.-J. "What Belonging to the Church Has Come to Mean." Translated by Francis M. Chew. *Communio* 4 (1977).

"Council of Arles." In C. Munier, *Concilia Galliae* A.314–A.506. Turnhout: Brepols, 1963.

Cowdrey, H. E. J. "The Dissemination of Blessed Augustine's Doctrine of Holy Orders during the Later Patristic Age." *Journal of Theological Studies*, n.s., 10:2 (October 1969).

Damascene, Hieromonk. *Fr. Seraphim Rose: His Life and Works*. Platina, CA: St. Herman Brotherhood, 2003.

Δαμασκηνού, Αγίου Ιωάννη [Damascene, Saint John]. Έκδοσις Ακριβής της Ορθοδόξου Πίστεως [Exact Exposition of the Orthodox Faith]. Θεσσαλονίκη: εκδ. Πουρναράς, 1983.

The Declaration of the Seventh Plenary Session of the Joint International Commission for Theological Dialogue Between the Catholic Church and the Orthodox Church. "Uniatism, Method of Union of the Past, and the Present Search for Full Communion." Balamand, Lebanon, 1993.

Denzinger, Henry. *The Sources of Catholic Dogma*. Fitzwilliam, NH: Loreto, 2007. English translation of the thirtieth edition of Fr. Heinrich Denzinger's *Enchiridion Symbolorum*, revised by Karl Rahner, S.J., published in 1954 by Herder and Co., Freiburg.

Διαδόχου Φωτικής [Diadohos Fotikis]. "Λόγος ἀσκητικὸς χωρισμένος σὲ 100 πρακτικὰ κεφάλαια πνευματικῆς γνώσεως καὶ διακρίσεως" [Ascetic homily divided into 100 practical chapters of spiritual knowledge and discernment]. Φιλοκαλία τῶν ἱερῶν Νηπτικῶν, τ. Α΄, (Ἀθήνα: Ἐκδόσεις Ἀστήρ, 1982), 258, § ος΄.

Didache, or The Teaching of the Twelve Apostles. See The Apostolic Fathers. Several English translations available online.

Directory for the Application of Principles and Norms on Ecumenism. Online at: www.vatican.va/roman_curia/pontifical_councils/ chrstuni/generaldocs/rc_pc_chrstuni_doc_19930325_directory_ en.html.

Divine Ascent: A Journal of Orthodox Faith. Monastery of St. John of Shanghai and San Francisco. Manton, California.

Dix, Dom Gregory. *The Shape of the Liturgy*. [Westminster] London: Dacre Press, 1945.

Dominus Iesus: On the Unicity and Salvific Universality of Jesus Christ and the Church. Boston: Pauline Books and Media, 2000. Online at: http://www.vatican.va/roman_curia/congregations/cfaith/documents/rc_con_cfaith_doc_20000806_dominus-iesus_en.html.

Doyle, Dennis M. "Journet, Congar, and the Roots of Communion Ecclesiology." *Theological Studies* 58 (1997).

Dragas, George Dion. "The Church in St. Maximus' Mystagogy: The Problem and the Orthodox Perspective." *Theology* 1 (1995).

Dragas, George Dion. "The Manner of Reception of Roman Catholic Converts into the Orthodox Church." A paper prepared for the Orthodox–Roman Catholic Dialogue in the U.S.A. in 1998. Online at: http://www.myriobiblos.gr/texts/english/Dragas_RomanCatholic.html.

Dulles, Avery, S.J. "The Church, The Churches, The Catholic Church." *Theological Studies* 33:2 (1972), 199–234.

Dulles, Avery, S.J. "Ecumenism Without Illusions: A Catholic Perspective." *First Things* (June/July 1990).

Dulles, Avery, S.J. "Yves Congar: In Appreciation." *America* 173, July 15, 1995.

Dumont, C. "Unité de l'Église et unité chrétienne." In *Les Voies de l'unité chrétienne. Doctrine et spiritualité.* Paris, 1954.

"Ecclesiological and Ecumenical Implications of a Common Baptism, A Joint Working Group Study." *Information Service of the Pontifical Council for Promoting Christian Unity.* No. 117. Vatican City: 2004/IV.

Ench. Vat., Volume 1, *Documenti del Concilio Vaticano II.* Bologna, 1981. Online at: http://www.vatican.va/roman_curia/pontifical_councils/chrstuni/card-kasper-docs/rc_pc_chrstuni_doc_20031110_unitatis-redintegratio_en.html.

Encyclical of the Eastern Patriarchs: A Reply to the Epistle of Pope Pius IX, "To the Easterns." 1848. Online at: http://ecommons.library.cornell.edu/handle/1813/671.

Epiphanius of Salamis. *The Panarion of Epiphanius of Salamis, Books II and III. De Fide.* Translated by Frank Williams. Boston: Brill, 2013; second revised edition.

Evdokimov, Paul. *L'Orthodoxie*. Neuchatel: Delachaux et Niestlé, 1959. [Later published in Greek as Ἡ Ὀρθοδοξία. Αθήνα: Εκδόσεις Βασ. Ρηγόπουλου. 1972.]

Famerée, Joseph. "Orthodox Influence on the Roman Catholic Theologian Yves Congar, O.P." *St. Vladimir's Theological Quarterly* 39:4 (1995).

Fanning, William. "Baptism." *The Catholic Encyclopedia*. Volume 2. New York: Robert Appleton Company, 1907.

Feiner, Johannes. "Commentary on the Decree." In *Commentary on the Documents of Vatican II*. Volume 2. London: Burns and Oates Limited, 1968.

Ferguson, Everett. *Baptism in the Early Church: History, Theology, and Liturgy in the First Five Centuries*. Grand Rapids, MI: Eerdmans, 2009.

Fisher, J. D. C. *Baptism in the Medieval West: A Study in the Disintegration of the Primitive Rite of Initiation*. London: S.P.C.K., 1965. Chicago: Hillenbrand Books, 2007: retitled *Christian Initiation: Baptism in the Medieval West*.

Florovsky, Georges. "The Church: Her Nature and Task." In *Collected Works* (q.v.), Volume 1: *Bible, Church, Tradition*. 1972. [Originally published in French as "L'Église, sa nature et sa tache." In *L'Église universelle dans le Dessein de Dieu*. Neuchatel-Paris, 1949.]

Florovsky, Georges. *Collected Works*. Volumes 1–5: Belmont, MA: Nordland, 1972–1979. Volumes 6–14: Vaduz, Europa: Büchervertriebsanstalt, 1987–1989.

Florovsky, Georges. *Creation and Redemption. See Collected Works*, Volume 3. 1976.

Florovsky, Georges. *Ecumenism I: A Doctrinal Approach. See Collected Works*, Volume 13. 1989.

Florovsky, Georges. "The House of the Father." In *Collected Works*, Volume 13: *Ecumenism I: A Doctrinal Approach*. 1989. [Published in Greek as "Ὁ Οἶκος τοῦ Πατρός." εἰς τὸ ἔργον: Ἀνατομία Προβλημάτων τῆς Πίστεως. ἐκδόσεις "Ἱερᾶς Μητροπόλεως Νικοπόλεως," Πρέβεζα, 2006.]

Florovsky, Georges. "Terms of Communion in the Undivided Church." In *Intercommunion. The Report of the Theological Commission Appointed by the Continuation Committee of the World Conference on Faith and Order together with a Selection from the Material Presented to the Commission*. Edited by D. Baillie and John Marsh. London, 1952.

Flynn, Gabriel. *Yves Congar's Vision of the Church in a World of Unbelief*. Burlington, VT: Ashgate Publishing, 2004.

Fries, H. "Der ekklesiologische Status der evangelischen Kirche in katholischer Sicht." In *Aspekte der Kirche*. Stuttgart, 1963.

Γαλίτης, Γ. [Galitis, G.]. Το Πρόβλημα της μυστηριακής κοινωνίας μετά των ετεροδόξων, εξ' επόψεως Ορθοδόξου: Βιβλική και Εκκλησιολογική Μελέτη [The problem of intercommunion with the heterodox from an Orthodox point of view: A biblical and ecclesiological study]. Αθήνα, 1966.

Γιέφτιτς, Αθανασίου Μ., Ιερομονάχου [Yevtich, Athanasius M., Hieromonk]. Ἡ ἐκκλησιολογία τοῦ ἀποστόλου Παύλου κατὰ τὸν ἱερὸ Χρυσόστομο [The Ecclesiology of the Apostle Paul according to Blessed Chrysostom]. Αθήνα: Εκδ. Γρηγόρη, 1984.

Γιέβτιτς, Αθανασίου Μ., Ιερομονάχου [Yevtich, Athanasius M., Hieromonk]. Επισκόπου πρ. Ζαχουμίου και Ερζεγοβίνης, "Ο π. Γεώργιος Φλωρόφσκυ περί των ορίων της Εκκλήσίας" [Fr. George Florovsky on the boundaries of the Church]. Θεολογία 81:4 (Οκτ.-Δεκ. 2010), 137–58.

Γεωργιάδης, Δημήτριος αρχιμ [Georgiadis, Demetrios, Archimandrite]. "Το βάπτισμα των αιρετικών" [The baptism of heretics]. Νέα Σιών 19 (1924), 73–83, 97–112, 165–81, 253–60.

Γεωργοπούλου, Πρωτ. Βασιλείου Α. [Georgopoulou, Protopresbyter Basil]. "Το Μυστήριο της Εκκλησίας και το Φαινόμενο των Αιρέσεων" [The mystery of the Church and the phenomenon of heresy]. περιοδικό 'ΕΡΩ', τ. 8 (Οκτ.-Δεκ. 2011).

Γρηγορίου, Ιερομονάχου [Gregorios, Hieromonk]. Το Άγιον Βάπτισμα [Holy Baptism]. Άγιον Όρος: Κελλίον Άγιος Ιωάννης Θεολόγος, 1992.

Gregorios, Hieromonk. *The Divine Liturgy: A Commentary in the Light of the Fathers*. Mount Athos: Cell of St. John the Theologian, 2009. [Originally published in Greek as Ἡ Θεία Λειτουργία: Σχόλια. Ἅγιον Ὄρος: Ἰ. Κουτλουμουσιανόν Κελλίον Ἅγιος Ἰωάννης Θεολόγος, 2000.]

Gribomont, J. "Du sacrament de l'Église et de ses realizations imparfaits." *Irenikon* 22 (1949).

Guardini, Romano. *Vom Sinn der Kirche*. Mainz: Mathias Grünewald Verlag, 1922.

Hebblethwaite, Peter. *Pope John XXIII*. Garden City, NY: Doubleday, 1985.

Hefele, K. J., *History of the Councils of the Church* (vol. 1). Online at Christian Classics Ethereal Library: http://www.ccel.org/ccel/schaff/hcc2.v.vii.xvi.html

Heim, Maximilian Heinrich. *Joseph Ratzinger: Life in the Church and Living Theology: Fundamentals of Ecclesiology with Reference to Lumen Gentium*. Translated by Michael J. Miller. San Francisco: Ignatius Press, 2007.

Heith-Stade, David. "Receiving the Non-Orthodox: A Historical Study of Greek Orthodox Canon Law." *Studia canonica* 44 (2010).

Hertling, Ludwig, S.J. *Communio: Church and Papacy in Early Christianity*. Translated by Jared Wicks, S.J. Chicago: Loyola University, 1972.

Holeton. David. "The Communion of Infants and Young Children: A Sacrament of Community." In *And Do Not Hinder Them: An Ecumenical Plea for the Admission of Children to the Eucharist*. Edited by Geiko Müller-Fahrenholz. Faith and Order Paper 109. Geneva: WCC, 1982.

Hugh of St. Victor. *De Sacramentis christianae fidei*. Patrologia Latina. Available in English as *Hugh of Saint Victor on the Sacraments of the Christian Faith: De Sacramentis*. Eugene, OR: Wipf and Stock, 2007.

Huillier, Peter, Archbishop. "Believing in One Church: An Insight into Patristic Tradition." *St. Vladimir's Theological Quarterly* 48:1 (2004), 21.

Huillier, Peter, Archbishop. *The Church of the Ancient Councils*. Crestwood, NY: St. Vladimir's Seminary Press, 1996.

Informations Catholiques Internationales. No. 336, May 15, 1969.

John Paul II. *Ut Unum Sint*. 1995.05.25. Online at: http://www.vatican.va/ holy_father/john_paul_ii/encyclicals/documents/hf_jpii_enc_25051995_ut-unum-sint_en.

Johnson, Maxwell E. *The Rites of Christian Initiation: Their Evolution and Interpretation*. Collegeville, MN: Liturgical Press, 1999.

Joint Working Group of the World Council of Churches and the Roman Catholic Church, "Ecclesiological and Ecumenical Implications of a Common Baptism." Information Service of the Pontifical Council for Promoting Christian Unity. No. 117. Vatican City: 2004/IV.

Jordan, Mark. *Ordering Wisdom: The Hierarchy of Philosophical Discourses in Aquinas*. Notre Dame: University of Notre Dame Press, 1996.

Jossua, Jean-Pierre. "Le Père Congar: La théologie au service du peuple de Dieu." *Chrétiens de Tous les Temps* 20. Paris: Cerf, 1967.

Journet, Charles. *The Church of the Word Incarnate: An Essay in Speculative Theology*. Sheed and Ward, 1955. Available online at www.ewtn.com/library/THEOLOGY/CHWORDIN.htm. [Originally published in French as *L'Église du Verbe incarné*. Volume 2. Paris: Desclée de Brouwer, 1951.]

Kallistos, Bishop of Diokleia. *See* Ware, Timothy.

Καρμίρης, Ιωάννης [Karmiris, Ioannis]. Ἡ Ἐκκλησιολογία τῶν Τριῶν Ἱεραρχῶν [The ecclesiology of the Three Hierarchs]. Ἀθῆναι, 1962.

Καρμίρη, Ιωαννου [Karmiris, Ioannis]. Το Δογματικόν Σύνταγμα "Περί Ἐκκλησίας," τῆς Β' Βατικάνειου Συνόδου [The dogmatic constitution "On the Church" of the Second Vatican Council]. Ἀθῆναι, 1969.

Kasper, Walter, Cardinal. "Communio: The Guiding Concept of Catholic Ecumenical Theology." In *That They May All Be One: The Call to Unity Today*. London/New York: Burns and Oates, 2004.

Kasper, Walter. "The Decree on Ecumenism—Read Anew After Forty Years." Pontifical Council for Promoting Christian Unity. Conference on the 40th Anniversary of the Promulgation of the Conciliar Decree "Unitatis Redintegratio." Rocca di Papa, Mondo Migliore, November 11, 12 and 13, 2004.

Kasper, Walter. "Ecclesiological and Ecumenical Implications of Baptism." *The Ecumenical Review*. Geneva: WCC, 2000.

Kasper, Walter, Cardinal. "The Fortieth Anniversary of the Vatican Council II Decree *Unitatis Redintegratio*." *Information Service of the Pontifical Council for Promoting Unity*. No. 115. Vatican City: 2004.

Kasper, Walter, Cardinal. "Reflections on the Nature and Purpose of Ecumenical Dialogue." Online at: http://www.vatican.va/roman_curia/ pontifical_councils/chrstuni/sub-index/index_card-kasper.htm.

Kasper, Walter, Cardinal. *That They May All Be One: The Call to Unity Today*. London/New York: Burns and Oates, 2004.

Kavanagh, Aidan. *The Shape of Baptism: The Rite of Christian Initiation—Studies in the Reform Rites of the Catholic Church*. Volume 1. Collegeville, MN: Liturgical Press, 1974/1991.

Kokkinakis, Athenagoras. *The Thyateira Confession*. London: The Faith Press, 1975.

Koskela, Douglas M. *Ecclesiality and Ecumenism: Yves Congar and the Road to Unity*. Milwaukee: Marquette University Press, 2008.

Kung, Hans, ed. *The Church and Ecumenism*. Volume 4. New York: Paulist Press, 1965.

Lakeland, Paul. *Yves Congar: Essential Writings*. Maryknoll, NY: Orbis, 2010.

Lampe, G. W. H. *The Seal of the Spirit*. London: S.P.C.K., 1967.

Lane, Emmanuel. "A Catholic Perspective." In *The Unity of the Church as Koinonia. Ecumenical Perspectives on the 1991 Canberra Statement on Unity*. Edited by G. Gabmann and J. Radano. Faith and Order Paper 163. Geneva: WCC, 1991.

Lanterius. "The Dogma of Ecumenism." Translated by Fr. Du Chalard. In *Si Si, No No* 27:6 (June 2005). Kansas City, MO: Angelus Press.

La Rocque, Abbé Patrick de. "Le présuppose oecumenique de Lumen Gentium." In *Penser Vatican II quarante ans apres: Actes du VI Congres Theologique de si si no no*. Rome: Publications Courier de Rome, 2004.

Latourelle, René, Editor. *Vatican II: Assessment and Perspectives, Twenty-five Years After (1962-1987)*. Three volumes. New York: Paulist Press, 1989.

Leeming, Bernard, S.J. *Principles of Sacramental Theology*. Westminster, MD: Newman Press, 1960.

Lossky, Vladimir. Introductory Note to an article of Patriarch Sergius of Moscow, "L'Église du Christ et les communautés dissidentes." *Messager de l'Exarchat du Patriarche Russe en Europe Occidentale* 21. Paris, 1955.

Lossky, Vladimir. The Mystical Theology of the Easter Church. Crestwood, New York: St. Vladimir's Seminary Press, 1976.

McNamara, Kevin. *Vatican II: The Constitution on the Church: A Theological and Pastoral Commentary*. London: Geoffrey Chapman, 1968.

Mahieu, Éric, and Bernard Dupuy. *Yves Congar: Mon journal du Concile, coffret de 2 livres*. Paris: Cerf, 2002. [My Journal of the Council. In English at: http://www.book-info.com/isbn/0-8146-8029-1.htm.]

Mansi, Giovan Domenico. *Sacrorum Conciliorum nova et amplissima collectio*. Graz: J. D. Mansi, 1960–61. Original Latin text digitized by Google and Gallica.

Martina, Giacomo. "The Historical Context in Which the Idea of a New Ecumenical Council Was Born." In *Vatican II: Assessment and Perspectives*. Edited by René Latourelle. New York: Paulist Press, 1988–1989.

May, George. *Die Okumenismusfalle* [The ecumenism trap]. Stuttgart: Sarto Verlag, 2004.

Μεταλληνού, π. Γ. Δ. [Metallinos, George]. Δοκίμια Ορθόδοξης Μαρτυρίας [Essays giving an Orthodox witness]. Αθήνα: Εκδόσεις Άθως, 2001.

Metallinos, George. *I Confess One Baptism: Interpretation and Application of Canon VII of the Second Ecumenical Council by the Kollyvades and Constantine Oikonomos*. Mt. Athos, Greece: St. Paul's Monastery, 1994.

Μεταλληνός, πρ.ωτ. Γεώργιος [Metallinos, George]. Κηρύγματα στα Αποστολικά Αναγνώσματα [Sermons for readings of the Epistles]. Θεσσαλονίκη: Ορθόδοξος Κυψέλη, 2010.

Mettepenningen, Jürgen. *Nouvelle Théologie–New Theology: Inheritor of Modernism, Precusor of Vatican II*. New York/Bloomsbury: T & T Clark International, 2010.

Meyendorff, John. *Byzantine Theology: Historical Trends and Doctrinal Themes*. New York, Fordham University Press, 1970.

Meyendorff, John, "Μία Κάμπη εἰς τὸν Οἰκουμενισμὸν τῆς Ρωμαϊκῆς Ἐκκλησίας" [A turning-point in the ecumenism of the Roman Church]. στο τόμο Ὀρθόδοξος Θεώρησις τῆς Β' Συνόδου τοῦ Βατικανοῦ, ἐπιμέλεια Μαρίας Δ. Σπυροπούλου. Αθήναι, 1967.

Morerod, Charles, O.P. "A Roman Catholic Point of View about the Limits of the Church." *Greek Orthodox Theological Review* 42: 3-4 (1997).

Munier, C. *Concilia Galliae*. Turnhout: Brepols, 1963.

Murphy, Francesca Aran. "De Lubac, Ratzinger and von Balthasar: A Communal Adventure in Ecclesiology." In *Ecumenism Today: The Universal Church in the Twenty-first Century*. Edited by Francesca Aran Murphy and Chris Asprey. Hampshire, UK: Ashgate, 2008.

Newman, J. H. "Heretical and Schismatical Bodies No Prejudice to Catholicity of the Church." In *Certain Difficulties Felt by Anglicans in Catholic Teaching Considered*. New York: Norton/Ulan, 2012 (first published 1908).

Nichols, Aidan. *Yves Congar*. London: Morehouse-Barlow, 1989.

Ocáriz, Fernando. "Christ's Church Subsists in the Catholic Church." *L'Osservatore Romano*. Weekly Edition in English. December 21, 2005.

O'Malley, John W. *What Happened at Vatican II*. Cambridge, MA: Harvard University Press, 2008.

Ὀρθόδοξος Θεώρησις τῆς Β´ Συνόδου τοῦ Βατικανοῦ [Orthodox consideration of the Second Vatican Council]. ἐπιμέλεια Μαρίας Δ. Σπυροπούλου. Αθήναι, 1967.

Outlet, Albert. *Methodist Observer at Vatican II*. Westminster, MD: Newman Press, 1967.

Παλαμᾶ, Αγ. Γρηγορίου [Palamas, St. Gregory]. Ἀναίρεσις γράμματος Ἰγνατίου, 3, στή σειρά Π. Χρήστου, Γρηγορίου τοῦ Παλαμᾶ συγγράματα, τομ. Γ´ [Refutation of the epistle of Ignatius, 3, in the series by P. Christou, The Words of St. Gregory Palamas, vol. 3]. Θεσσαλονίκη, 1983.

Παπαθανασίου, Χρήστου [Papathanasiou, Christos]. Το "Κατ' Ακρίβειαν" Βάπτισμα και Οι Εξ Αυτού Παρεκκλίσεις" [The "Kat'Akrivian" baptism and diversions from it]. Αθήνα: Γρηγόρη, 2001.

Pelikan, Jaroslav. *The Christian Tradition: A History of the Development of Doctrine. Volume 1: The Emergence of the Catholic Tradition* (100–600). Chicago: University of Chicago Press, 1973.

Pentecostarion, Orthodox. Holy Transfiguration Monastery. Brookline, MA: 2014.

Phidas, Vlassios. "The Limits of the Church in an Orthodox Perspective." *The Greek Orthodox Theological Review* 43:1-4 (1998).

Pius XI, Pope. *Mortalium Animos*. Encyclical *On Religious Unity*. January 7, 1928.

Pius XII, Pope. *Humani Generis*. Encyclical *Concerning Some False Opinions Threatening to Undermine the Foundations of Catholic Doctrine* (sections 29, 30, 32, and 34). August 12, 1950.

Pius XII, Pope. Mediator Dei. Encyclical On the Sacred Liturgy. November 20, 1947.

Pius XII, Pope. *Mystici Corporis Christi*. Encyclical *On the Mystical Body of Christ*. June 29, 1943.

Πόποβιτς, [ἅγιος] Αρχιμανδρίτης Ιουστίνος [Popovich, (St.) Archimandrite Justin]. Ερμηνεία της Επιστολής του Αποστόλου Παύλου προς Εφεσίους [Interpretation of the Epistle of the Apostle Paul to the Ephesians]. Θεσσαλονίκη, εκδ. Β. Ρηγοπούλου, 1989.

Popovich, Justin, Archimandrite (Saint). *The Orthodox Church and Ecumenism.* Translated by Benjamin Emmanuel Stanley. Birmingham: Lazarica Press, 2000.

Portalié, Eugène. "Teaching of Blessed Augustine of Hippo." *The Catholic Encyclopedia.* Volume 2. New York: Robert Appleton Company, 1907.

Rahner, Karl. The New Image of the Church. Translated by David Bourke. London: Darton, Longman and Todd, 1973.

Rahner, Karl, and Herbert Vorgrimler. *Concise Theological Dictionary.* London: Burns and Oates, 1965.

Ratzinger, Joseph. *Church, Ecumenism, and Politics, New Endeavors in Ecclesiology.* San Francisco: Ignatius Press, 2008.

Ratzinger, Joseph. "The Ecclesiology of Vatican II." A talk given at the Pastoral Congress of the Diocese of Aversa, Italy, September 15, 2001. Online at: http://www.ewtn.com/library/CURIA/CDFECCV2.HTM.

Ratzinger, Joseph. *Joseph Ratzinger in Communio: Volume I—The Unity of the Church. See* Benedict XVI, Pope.

Ratzinger, Joseph. *The Open Circle: The Meaning of Christian Brotherhood.* Translated by W. A. Glen Doeple. New York: Sheed and Ward, 1966.

Ratzinger, Joseph. *Pilgrim Fellowship of Faith: The Church as Communion.* Translated and edited by Henry Taylor, Stephan Otto Horn, and Vinzenz Pfnur. San Francisco: Ignatius Press, 2005 (German 2002).

Ratzinger, Joseph. "Protestantismus: III. Beurteilung vom Standpunkt des Katholizismus," [Protestantism: III. Evaluation from the Catholic viewpoint.], στο έργο *Religion in Geschichte und Gegenwart*, 3rd edition. Volume 5 (1961).

Ratzinger, Joseph, Cardinal. *Theological Highlights of Vatican II.* New York: Paulist Press, 2009.

Roman Catholic Church, Synod of Bishops. "The Final Report." *Origins* 15:27. December 19, 1985.

Romanides, John S. *The Ancestral Sin*. Ridgewood, NJ: Zephyr, 2002.

Romanides, John S. "The Ecclesiology of St. Ignatius of Antioch." *The Greek Orthodox Theological Review* 7:1 and 2 (1961–62).

Romanides, John S. "Life in Christ." [Originally published as "La vie dans Christ." In ΣΥΝΑΞΙΣ 21:26–28) and 22:23–26.]. Available online in English at: www.johnsanidopoulos.com/2010/03/life-in-chirist-by-fr-john-romanides.html.

Romanides, John S. "Orthodox Ecclesiology According to Alexis Khomiakov." *The Greek Orthodox Theological Review* 2:1 (1956).

Romanides, John S. *An Outline of Orthodox Patristic Dogmatics* [Επίτομος Ορθόδοξος Πατερική Δογματική]. Rollinsford, NH: Orthodox Research Institute, 2004.

Romanides, John S. *Patristic Theology*. Thessaloniki, Greece: Uncut Mountain Press, 2008.

Root, Michael, and Risto Saarinen. Editors. *Baptism and the Unity of the Church*. Grand Rapids and Geneva: Eerdmans and WCC Publications, 1998.

The Rudder or *Pedalion*. The English version: Comp. Agapius a Hieromonk and Nicodemus a Monk. First printed and published A.D. 1800. Trans. D. Cummings, from the 5th edition published by John Nicolaides (Kesisoglou the Caesarian) in Athens, Greece, in 1908. Chicago: The Orthodox Christian Educational Society, 1957; Repr., New York, N.Y.: Luna Printing Co., 1983.

Scampini, Jorge A., O.P. "We acknowledge one Baptism for the forgiveness of sins." Address given at the Faith and Order Plenary Commission in Kuala, Malaysia, July 28– August 6, 2004. PDF available online.

Schmemann, Alexander. *Of Water and the Spirit*. Crestwood, New York: St. Vladimir's Seminary Press, 1974.

Schmemann, Alexander. *Russian Theology, 1920–1965*. Richmond: Union Theological Seminary in Virginia, 1969.

Schmemann, Alexander. "Unity, Division, Reunion in the Light of Orthodox Ecclesiology." Address given at the Annual Conference of the Fellowship of St. Alban and St Sergius at Abingdon, England, in August 1950. Θεολογία, ΚΒ, 243–54.

Σπιτέρης, I. [Spiteris, I.] "Η Καθολική Εκκλησία και οι άλλες χριστιανικές Εκκλησίες" Θ. Κοντίδης (επιμ.) [The Catholic Church and the other Christian Churches]. Ο Καθολικισμος: Αθήνα, 2000.

Staniloae, Dimitru. Για έναν Ορθόδοξο Οικουμενισμό [Toward an Orthodox ecumenism]. Πειραιεύς: Άθως, 1976.

Stauffer, S. Anita. "Baptism and Communio." *The Ecumenical Review* (April 2000). Geneva: WCC Publications.

Sullivan, Francis A., S.J. *The Church We Believe In*. Dublin: Gill and Macmillan, 1988.

Sullivan, Francis A., S.J. *Salvation Outside the Church? Tracing the History of the Catholic Response*. New York: Paulist Press, 1992; Eugene, OR: Wipf and Stock, 2002.

Sullivan, Francis A., S.J. "The Significance of the Vatican II Declaration that the Church of Christ 'Subsists in' the Roman Catholic Church." In René Latourelle, editor, *Vatican II: Assessment and Perspectives, Twenty-five Years After (1962-1987)*. Volume 2. New York: Paulist Press, 1989.

Supreme Sacred Congregation of the Holy Office, Letter of August 8, 1949, to the Archbishop of Boston, Richard J. Cushing, published by the Archdiocese of Boston on September 4, 1952, as Protocol *Suprema haec sacra* in *AER* 127:4 (Oct. 1952).

Swidler, Leonard. "The Context: Breaking Reform by Breaking Theologians and Religious." In *The Church in Anguish: Has the Vatican Betrayed Vatican II?* Edited by Hans Kung and Leonard Swidler. San Francisco: Harper and Row, 1987.

Τρεμπέλας, Π. [Trembelas, P.]. Δογματική τῆς Ὀρθοδόξου Καθολικῆς Ἐκκλησίας [Dogmatics of the Orthodox Catholic Church]. Τόμ. Γ´ Αθήνα, 1961.

Τρεμπέλας, Π. [Trembelas, P.]. Τάξις Χειροθεσιών και Χειροτονιών [The Typikon (or The Order) of the laying on of hands and of Ordination]. Αθήνα, 1949.

Troitsky, Hilarion, Archbishop of Verey, New Hieromartyr. "Holy Scripture and the Church." *The Orthodox Word* 45: 1–2 (Jan.–

Apr. 2009), 264–65. Translated by Igor Radev. Platina, CA: St. Herman Press, 2009.

Troitsky, Hilarion, Archbishop of Verey, New Hieromartyr. *The Unity of the Church*. Montreal: Monastery Press, 1975. [English translation from the Russian, originally written in 1917.]

Τσελεγγίδης Δημ. [Tselingides, Demetrios]. Ἡ λειτουργία τῆς ἑνότητας τῆς Ἐκκλησίας καὶ οἱ ἐσφαλμένες θεολογικὲς προϋποθέσεις τοῦ Παπικοῦ πρωτείου, Εἰσήγηση στην Ημερίδα της Μητροπόλεως Πειραιώς με θέμα: "Πρωτεῖον," Συνοδικότης καὶ Ἑνότης τῆς Ἐκκλησίας [The function of the unity of the Church and the fallicious theological presuppositions of papal primacy, lecture at the Conference of the Metropolis of Peireus "Primacy, Conciliarity and the Unity of the Church"]. Available online in English at: www.impantokratoros.gr/unity-church.en.aspx.

Τσομπανίδης, Στυλιανός X. [Tsombanidis, Stylianos X.]. Η Διακήρυξη "Dominus Iesus" και η Οικουμενική Σημασία της [The declaration "Dominus Iesus" and its ecumenical meaning]. Πουρναρά: Θεσσαλονίκη, 2003.

Turner, C. H. "Apostolic Succession." In *Essays on the Early History of the Church and the Ministry*. Edited by H. B. Swete. London: Macmillan, 1918.

Vatican II: Assessment and Perspectives, Twenty-five Years After (1962-1987). Volume 2. Edited by René Latourelle, et al. New York: Paulist Press, 1989.

Vereb, Jerome-Michael. *"Because He Was a German": Cardinal Bea and the Origins of Roman Catholic Engagement in the Ecumenical Movement*. Grand Rapids, MI: Eerdmans, 2006.

Voulgaris, Christos Sp. *The Church, the Body of Christ*. Online at: http://www.myriobiblos.gr/texts/english/voulgaris_churchbody.html.

Vries, Wilhelm de, S.J. "Communicatio in Sacris." *The Church and Ecumenism*. Volume 4. New York: Paulist Press, 1965.

Walsh, Michael J. "The History of the Council." In *Modern Catholi-*

cism: Vatican II and After. Edited by Adrian Hastings. New York: Oxford University Press, 1991.

Ware, Timothy [Bishop Kallistos of Diokleia]. *Communion and Intercommunion: A Study of Communion and Intercommunion Based on the Theology and Practice of the Eastern Church.* Minneapolis: Light and Life, 1980.

Ware, Timothy [Bishop Kallistos of Diokleia]. "Decree on the Eastern Catholic Churches." *Eastern Churches Review* 1:1 (1966).

Ware, Timothy [Bishop Kallistos of Diokleia]. *Eustratios Argenti, A Study of the Greek Church under Turkish Rule.* Oxford: Clarendon Press, 1964.

Ware, Timothy [Bishop Kallistos of Diokleia]. "Intercommunion: The Decisions of Vatican II and the Orthodox Standpoint." *Sobornost*, Series 5, no. 4 (1966).

Ware, Timothy [Bishop Kallistos of Diokleia]. *The Orthodox Church.* London: Penguin, 1997.

Ware, Timothy [Bishop Kallistos of Diokleia]. "The Rebaptism of Heretics in the Orthodox Canonical Tradition." In *Heresy and the Making of European Culture: Medieval and Modern Perspectives.* Edited by James R. Simpson and Andrew P. Roach. London and Burlington: Ashgate, 2013.

Weinandy, Thomas, et al. Editor. *Aquinas on Doctrine: A Critical Introduction.* London: T & T Clark, 2004.

Willebrands, Johannes, Cardinal. "Vatican II's Ecclesiology of Communion." *Origins* 17 (1987).

Willis, Geoffrey Grimshaw. *Saint Augustine and the Donatist Controversy.* Eugene OR: Wipf and Stock, 2005; reprint of London: S.P.C.K., 1950.

Wittstadt, Klaus. "On the Eve of the Second Vatican Council (July 1–October 10, 1962)." In *History of Vatican II.* Edited by Giuseppe Alberigo. English version edited by Joseph A. Komonchak. Five volumes. Maryknoll: Orbis; Louvain: Peeters, 1995.

Χαρκιανάκι, Στυλιανού, Αρχιμ. [Harkianaki, Stylianos, Archimandrite.]. Το Περί Εκκλησίας Σύνταγμα της Β΄ Βατικανής

Συνόδου [The Constitution on the Church of the Second Vatican Council]. Θεσσαλονίκη, 1969.

Yazigi, I. (Hani), Ἱεροδ. [Yazigi, I, Hierodeacon]. Ἡ τελετή τοῦ ἁγίου βαπτίσματος (Ἱστορική, θεολογική καί τελετουργική θεώρησις) [The service of holy Baptism: Historic, theological and liturgical consideration]. Doctoral thesis. Thessaloniki, 1982.

Yocum, John P. "Sacraments in Aquinas." In *Aquinas on Doctrine: A Critical Introduction.* Edited by Thomas G. Weinandy et al. London: T & T Clark, 2004.

Zizioulas, John (Metropolitan of Pergamon). *Being As Communion: Studies in Personhood and the Church.* Crestwood, NY: St. Vladimir's Seminary Press, 1993.

Zizioulas, John (Metropolitan of Pergamon). "Holy Baptism and Divine Liturgy." In *Holy Baptism: Our Incorporation into the Church of Christ* [In Greek: "Ἅγιον Βάπτισμα καὶ Θεία Λειτουργία" στο Τό Ἅγιο Βάπτισμα: Ἡ ἔνταξή μας στήν Ἐκκλησία τοῦ Χριστοῦ]. Athens: Apostoliki Diakonia: 2002.

Zizioulas, John (Metropolitan of Pergamon). "Orthodox Ecclesiology and the Ecumenical Movement." *Sourozh Diocesan Magazine* (UK) 21 (August 1985).

Zizioulas, J. D. "The Pneumatological Dimension of the Church." *International Catholic Review* 2: 2 (1973).

Zizioulas, John (Metropolitan of Pergamon). "Unitatis Redintegratio: An Orthodox Reflection." In *Searching for Christian Unity.* New York: New City Press, 2007.

Ζηζιούλα, Ιωάννου, Μητροπολίτου Περγάμου [Zizioulas, John, Metropolitan of Pergamon]. Ἡ ἑνότης τῆς Ἐκκλησίας ἐν τῇ Θείᾳ Εὐχαριστίᾳ καί τῷ Ἐπισκόπῳ κατά τούς τρεῖς πρώτους αἰώνας [The unity of the Church in the Divine Eucharist and the Bishop during the first three centuries]. Α΄ ἐκδ. 1965, Β΄ ἐκδ. Ἐκδόσεις Γρηγόρη: Ἀθήνα, 1990.

SCRIPTURAL INDEX

INDEX